DOUG BROWN   **TIRATH VIRDEE**

T0206467

DATA ALCHEMY

THE **GENESIS** OF **BUSINESS VALUE**

Published by
LID Publishing
An imprint of LID Business Media Ltd.
The Record Hall, Studio 304,
16-16a Baldwins Gardens,
London EC1N 7RJ, UK

info@lidpublishing.com
www.lidpublishing.com

A member of:

businesspublishersroundtable.com

Printed by Gutenberg Press, Malta

ISBN: 978-1-912555-83-3
ISBN: 978-1-911671-21-3 (ebook)

Cover and page design: Caroline Li

DOUG BROWN   TIRATH VIRDEE

DATA ALCHEMY

THE GENESIS OF BUSINESS VALUE

MADRID | MEXICO CITY | LONDON
NEW YORK | BUENOS AIRES
BOGOTA | SHANGHAI | NEW DELHI

To data: I am but a bunch of neurons;
without you, I would be useless.
With true love, I dedicate this work to you.
And to Ajit.

Tirath Virdee

With deepest love and gratitude to my parents, who provided the freedom to express creative ideas and the confidence to act on them, together with Maureen, Hannah and Emily for their eternal encouragement, laughter and inspiration.

Doug Brown

CONTENTS

ACKNOWLEDGEMENTS

We would like to express our sincere gratitude to our superb team within Capita plc, with whom we have had some engaging and enlightening conversations in writing this book. These people include Dr Oli Freestone, Dr Sarah Gates, Dr Scott Stainton, Dr Shaun Barney, Michelle Prance and Peter Rogers. We also thank Dr Hira Virdee of Lumi Space and Dr Mann Virdee of the RAND Europe for their incisive observations and advice.

We would also like to thank Professor Stephen Roberts, Dr Davide Zilli and numerous others at the Mind Foundry, University of Oxford; Professor Deeph Chana of Imperial College London; and Professor Ashok Jashapara, Chair of Innovation Studies at Royal Holloway, University of London.

CHAPTER 1

ALCHEMY AND DATA INTELLIGENCE

It is time to take a philosophical and business view of the value of data and the role of artificial intelligence (AI) in amplifying human and natural brilliance. The story of humans, data and AI is one that invites us to consider a world where our intelligence is not the only one and the possibilities for intelligence are more than human.[1] Businesses' adoption and application of AI are accelerating the creation of new sources of value for consumers and citizens. The process of data alchemy, or the fusion and exchange of data, intelligence and experience, has profound seismic implications for our understanding and engagement with the world and each other. As businesses continue to explore the technological and ethical boundaries of recreating human intelligence using machines, the intimacy of our personal and professional lives is raising complex questions regarding truth, ownership, governance and value. In a world where the 'natural order' is being challenged daily, it is the process of creating value and the role of businesses in defining our future that data alchemy seeks to address.

Our fascination with technology and our historical desire to advance science, expand intelligence and extend life lead us to explore the relationships between fundamental elements of the natural and artificial world and the transformative processes required to create value. The desire to create and combine elements to produce innovation has been a constant feature in the relentless search throughout the ages for intellectual attainment, individual reward and societal benefit.

Various civilizations and religious traditions, from Arabic mathematics to the science of the Enlightenment and Shintoism, have sought to understand transformative value processes. This interest has been expressed in many forms, from magic to popular culture and scientific enterprise. However, this ancient desire has evolved into our modern ability to seek to codify rational thought and decode the brain's ability to create intelligence. This has taken the form of understanding the brain's decision-making processes and developing neural networks whereby computer programs self-improve over time. This self-teachable technology, combined with the ability to access and use sensory data, allows us to create new types of value and experiences via the process of data alchemy. It is the endless evolution of our world, defined by data and enabled by AI and machine learning (ML), that allows us to challenge the concept of what is natural and how we want to shape our lives and environment, whether in the physical world or the virtual world, both of which we now inhabit as humans.

The accelerated pace at which the boundaries between technology and human life become fused leads us to explore ethical questions relating to data governance, privacy, freedom, truth and accountability. Data and AI are applied everywhere in our everyday experiences, yet they are difficult to see and comprehend. Data is enabling the development of AI and the endeavour to understand and recreate human intelligence using machines to extend the frontiers of intelligence and value in every part of our existence. It is this process of data alchemy that we will explore in the following pages to discover approaches to creating value for businesses, consumers and citizens in an increasingly complex and uncertain digital world.

WHAT IS ALCHEMY?

Over time, the practice of alchemy has developed from achieving metallic transmutation to understanding the process of transformation, creation or combination of elements to create value. The development of alchemy has its origins in the rise of alchemical doctrines codified in the early Hellenistic period by Bolos, by the Greek alchemists of Alexandri and in the Greek philosophers' consideration of substances (monism) – for example, Democritus studied atoms, Aristotle looked at prime matter and Thales considered water.[2] However, after the fall of the Latin Empire, alchemy was practically forgotten in Western Europe and even in Byzantium. In contrast, in the Islamic, Arabian–Persian world, alchemy was rediscovered and developed in close relation to metallurgy and medicine.[3] It returned to Western Europe between the 10th and 12th centuries, and by the end of the Middle Ages it was considered a mature and established subject, studied in royal courts by scholars and practitioners alike. The union of these doctrines, and the artisanal application of the practice and principles of transformative processes to base elements, led to the development of alchemy's central goals: achieving metallic transmutation, producing better medicines, improving and using natural substances, and understanding material change.

When considering alchemy, especially in relation to data and AI, it is important to state what it is *not* in addition to what it is perceived to be. For example, to be considered or classified as alchemy, a process should be transformative. Alchemy, like other scientific pursuits, is more than a collection of specific recipes or approaches. For a process to be alchemical, it must be part of an intellectual framework that underpins the practical transformative approach. Throughout history, alchemy has been about much more than making copies of precious substances; rather, it has provided clear intellectual pathways of relevant discovery to advance its practice and application. Examples of this replication (rather than a transformative approach) can be found in the Leyden and Stockholm Papyri, 3rd-century Greek texts that describe the process of imitating specific substances (e.g. gold, silver, textile dyes and precious metals).[4]

The Enlightenment contributed both to alchemy's development and to its ultimate demise as a credible science in 18th-century Europe. The rise of critical thought and philosophy, the challenge to the 'dark arts', and superstitious beliefs in magic and witchcraft gave way to the development of modern chemistry as a science. However, even once the world became characterized as binary with the advancement of reason-based discoveries in the age of Galileo (1564–1642), René Descartes (1596–1650) and Isaac Newton (1643–1727), the polarizing rhetoric of the 18th century made it appear impossible for science to coexist with alchemy.[5]

Nevertheless, alchemy as a concept persisted as a way to understand the means of experimental change and transmutation, and it has continued to this day.

Alchemy has been described as a 'noble art', engendering images of dark arts where alchemists, surrounded by the paraphernalia of science and discovery, seek to experiment with base substances to create a valuable asset or material. It has been used both as a term of abuse and as a herald of success, spanning such mediums as popular culture, music, science, psychology and medicine. Indeed, many people will have encountered the concept of alchemy without being aware of its meaning. Literature is full of references to it, from modern examples such as J. K. Rowling's *Harry Potter and the Philosopher's Stone*, Paulo Coelho's *The Alchemist* and Ian McEwan's *Machines Like Me* to older texts such as Dante's *Divine Comedy*. These authors are part of a long line of poets and playwrights who have explored the key aspect of the alchemical tradition in the arts using the transformative nature of the scientific process to reflect human behavioural traits, intelligence and relationships.[6]

UNVEILING THE SECRETS: THE PROCESS OF ALCHEMY AND VALUE CREATION

Given the extensive and diverse use of codes, misdirection techniques and technical language to describe the process of alchemy over the past 1,500 years, it is little wonder that there has not been any agreement on how the transmutation process of turning base materials into noble metals can be achieved. One of the most famous ancient alchemists was Zosimos of Panopolis, a Greco-Egyptian alchemist active around AD 300.[7] He employed encrypted (secret) code, a common method of alchemists, to protect his transformative insights, and this alchemical use of cover names later gained the term 'Decknamen'. While obscuring the literal meaning of a text by substituting one word for another, these allegorical words often referred to related meanings to facilitate communication and decipher elicit knowledge.

The early alchemists' use of cryptic and symbolic language obscures our ability to trace their mutual influences and relationships, and it fuels our interest in discovering hidden meaning and secrets. It also acts as a barrier to the process of verification, stymies attempts to find evidence of the value created by the application of such processes and perpetuates mistrust of the techniques employed. These features apply to the understanding of AI today just as they did to alchemical processes of the past. Each new wave of technological advancement has its advocates and poster children. Equally, such waves are often characterized by a high degree of hype and manifestation of false prophets, and AI is no exception.

One of the most notable advocates of alchemy and chemistry was Basil Valentine, a 15th-century native of the Upper Rhineland who purported to be a Benedictine monk. His first book, *Of the Great Stone of the Ancients*, provides general principles and cryptic advice about the Philosopher's Stone and then relates details of 12 'keys', in the form of 12 short allegorical chapters complemented by allegorical woodcut images. Each coded key reveals a part of the alchemical process used to create the Philosopher's Stone. If the reader could decipher the secret language correctly, they would presumably learn the whole procedure. Valentine's development of the 12 keys, while encrypted, did, according to his Principle (method), succeed in volatizing gold. However, there are some discernible commonalities that relate to the combining of two or more materials or substances to produce the Philosopher's Stone, as shown in *Figure 1*.

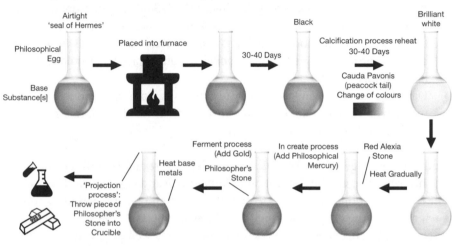

FIGURE 1: The process of alchemy: creating the Philosopher's Stone

The alchemical process of creating the Philosopher's Stone has parallels with the modern-day design and application of AI algorithms. It also provides insights into how value can be created from data assets and analytical processes:

- Alchemy is a process obscured by history and practice. The process of how AI algorithms are created is also obscure and is often referred to as a 'black box'. This is because although the answer can be verified and tested, the process is shrouded in the myriad calculations, languages and models that create the outcome.
- The freshly completed Philosopher's Stone is said to be capable of transmuting about ten times its weight in base metal, but the process of multiplication can substantially augment that multiple. Similarly, the use of individual data cohorts can, when combined (speech, textual, behavioural and transactional), create multiple assets that can be used for a variety of purposes.
- Alchemists usually conceal their knowledge, revealing it only to the most talented and worthiest readers. Data scientists display similar traits when seeking to explain and demonstrate the evidence of their data-driven decisions. This is partly due to how AI is applied and the fact that it is generally a complex and unfamiliar practice to business practitioners.

- The extensive use of allegorical language and imagery to convey specific discernible meanings acts as a barrier to understanding and comprehension in both alchemy and AI.
- Like alchemy, AI requires the work of artisan specialists with scarce skills to undertake transformation processes to produce rare outputs.
- Both processes require a combination of separate disciplines to be effective – namely chemistry, medicine, theology and philosophy for alchemy and mathematics, statistics and computer science for AI.
- It is suggested that redissolving the Philosopher's Stone in philosophical mercury and recycling it would result in a tenfold increase in its potency. The use of an ensemble model, which combines several base models in order to produce one optimal predictive AI model, to solve a problem would arguably have a similar effect.
- Data, like natural elements, is by nature impure. Both data and natural elements require significant effort to transform their raw form into a state that can be used to create value.

In the modern age, advancements are considered to result from the creations of the human mind via the application of intelligence and experience. The resultant transformations of either base materials or emotions are viewed by some, such as Carl Jung (1875–1961) and Israel Regardie (1907–1985), as occurring in an altered state of consciousness where alchemy is seen primarily as a means of psychic development.[8] However, the critical difference between the value of human intelligence and that of AI lies in the understanding and interpretation of real-world knowledge via experience and data. To be efficient and learn, AI algorithms require vast amounts of experiential training data. Simulations are not yet enough to generate effective real-world applications of AI. The current situation, where algorithms have a limited ability to undertake multichain reasoning and humans are able to swiftly recognize sequential patterns from small amounts of data via transfer learning, means that the genesis of business value emanates from a combination of experience and data where AI augments human decision-making.

While alchemy is still considered to be the noble art, data science is where art meets science to produce value.[9] We have witnessed how the new scientific discoveries of the 19th and 20th centuries marked a revival of the interest in alchemy. One example is the discovery in 1896 of radiation, radioactivity, the elemental decay of radioactive elements and the bombardment of lighter elements with radiation. When the element radium was discovered two years later, it was hailed as a modern Philosopher's Stone because its radiations could transform one element into another.[10] Alchemists conceptualized metals as compounds whereas we now know them to be elements. Alchemy was not limited to physical products but also aimed to produce knowledge about the processes of the natural world.

Similarly to the development of alchemy, the advancement of AI has extended the boundaries of consciousness and intelligence. Since around 2010, there has been exponential growth in the parallel development of the computing power and cloud technology necessary to apply the mathematical models and approaches that underpin AI and ML. This has resulted in material changes in the quality and diversity of the insights and value derived from data. As Ray Kurzweil observes, "we're going to continue to enhance ourselves through technology, and so the best way to ensure the safety of AI is to attend to how we govern ourselves as humans."[11]

However, we require a new approach to understand, codify and apply AI in such a way as to ensure that data is a force for societal good. This is embodied in our approach to data alchemy and our AI Periodic Table, which provides a framework that defines relationships between key data elements with the aim of fostering innovation and advancing intelligence via the application of data and experience to create value.

Although considered a pseudoscience, the idea of alchemy has the benefit of helping us to conceptualize a process of transmutation that is analogous to the process of transforming data into information, information into knowledge and knowledge into actionable insight (see *Figure 2*).

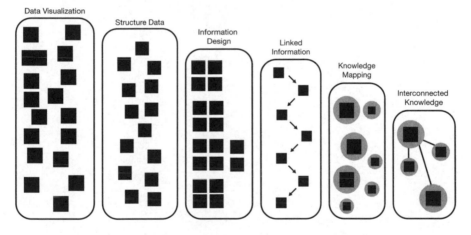

Figure 2: Data transformation
Source: Based on a data classification in David McCandless's *Knowledge is Beautiful*[12]

These transformations focus on data as a base element that is captured, collated and combined so it can be used to create actionable insight. The fact that natural language can be understood by AI through the use of artificial neural networks (explored in *Chapters 5* and *6*), based on our understanding of fractional dimensions of space and behaviours of quantum states in nature, implies a universally scalable vision of data as an alchemical substance. It is via this alchemical process that we can understand and experience the value of data in the digital world. This process often begins with value exchange.

CHAPTER 2

DATA INTELLIGENCE AND VALUE EXCHANGE

When considering value, Oscar Wilde observed that a cynic is one "who knows the price of everything and the value of nothing."[13] This is equally as applicable to businesses as it is to their customers. The ability to know, target, sell and service different customers differently has been a long-held objective for businesses. This has manifested itself in the search for the 'golden source' – a continuously updated and unified customer profile that can enable businesses to proactively engage with customers by understanding their buying preferences and purchasing patterns. It has driven businesses to create vast data lakes dedicated to the pursuit of customer insight and intimacy, often via personalized experiences. Personalized omnichannel experiences are not possible without data exchange.

However, with the advent of data regulations such as the General Data Protection Regulation (GDPR), which since May 2018 has given consumers in the European Union and the United Kingdom more control over how their data is shared and used, and with the increasing proliferation of cross-channel offers, the permission-based interaction between brands and consumers has dissipated. There has been an erosion of the reliance on cookies, credit scores and click trails to reflect online personas or to use as a past view on which to base future outcomes. In our increasingly digital world, data plays a critical role in connecting businesses with digital consumers and defines the value of that interaction. Welcome to the value exchange economy. Welcome to the data passport era, where personal ownership is governing how marketers collect the data they use to power their campaigns and craft personalized behavioural interventions, and where the use of consumers' own data is becoming the key source of value, redefining the relationship between brands and consumers.

WHAT IS DATA INTELLIGENCE VALUE EXCHANGE?

'Value' is a subjective term that has been used and misused in reference to both its generation and its destruction. It has often been confused with associated terms (such as 'wealth,' 'productivity,' 'money,' 'price' and 'social utility') to the extent that the term itself has become devalued. However, in the information age, with its exponential increase in the application of artificial narrow intelligence (defined in *Chapter 3*),[14] the use of this frontier intelligence requires us to redefine the term 'value' and its meaning in an omnichannel digital world.

In *The Value of Everything*, Mariana Mazzucato captures the essence of value when she states:

> By 'value creation' I mean the ways in which different types of resources (human, physical and intangible) are established and interact to produce new goods and services. By 'value extraction' I mean activities focused on

moving around existing resources and outputs and gaining disproportionately from the ensuing trade.[15]

Indeed, when considering the process of value or wealth creation, Mazzucato contends that it is a flow:

This flow of course results in actual things, whether tangible (a loaf of bread) or intangible (new knowledge). Wealth instead is regarded as a cumulative stock of the value already created.[16]

It is the process of wealth creation, the focus on value exchange and the forces of data creation that we collectively call data alchemy.

A BRIEF HISTORY OF VALUE EXCHANGE

The concept of value exchange has a long historical lineage beginning with bartering and trading. The mechanisms and processes of value creation have continually changed, from the price-driven, income-led definition of value to the more recent reclassification of the term in the sense of maximizing or destroying shareholder value (as exemplified by the Wall Street Crash of 1929, the 2008 financial crisis and the economic downturn associated with the ramifications of COVID-19). Relatedly, the measurement of value exchange has often been considered a driver of adverse human behaviour, such as the focus on short-termism associated with maximizing shareholder returns. Adam Smith (1723–1790) makes this point in *The Wealth of Nations* (1776), stating that how humans define 'productive' and 'unproductive' activities is the arbiter of value. In the 19th century, Karl Marx (1818–1883) developed his theory of surplus value (i.e. the value created by workers in excess of their own labour cost), which is appropriated by capitalists as profit when products are sold.

Does the fact that chief executives earn ten times as much as the average wage of their salaried employees alter the value of the exchange? Do we need to verify that a transaction has occurred before we can agree that value has been generated (which would exclude black-market transactions and social care provisions, for example)? If we consider the wealth management industry, maybe it's not the involvement of a product or service that provides the basis of value. This can be seen in what Hyman Minsky refers to as 'money manager capitalism' or 'casino capitalism,' the rise of financial institutions making money simply from money.[17] These examples illustrate the range of types of value generated and the difficulty of being able to quantify and measure it on a collective basis, never mind when it is created by individual interactions. Value derived from data and intelligence themselves and their application is not exempt from the challenge of tangible measurement, but it does raise the more labyrinthine problem of evaluating intangible measures of value.

DATA VALUE EXCHANGE

What is the worth of the data created about or by you? Currently, insurance renewal data can be worth around £40 and a retail sales lead might cost £4.[18] Presently, about 2 megabytes of data is being created for each person on the planet every second. With the exponential growth of the Internet of Things (IoT) and the take-up of 5G technology, many objects (e.g. radio frequency identification, field sensors, wearable gadgets, self-driving vehicles, robotic devices, grid-edge and cloud-edge devices, and the components of smart cities) contribute even greater amounts of data than humans can.

This great clamour for information has enabled several prime movers (notably Amazon, Facebook and Google) to freely collect and exploit data, becoming some of the most valuable companies on the face of the earth. It seems extraordinary to be talking about calculating the value of data just as we would gold or oil. Perhaps, just like these and other commodities, the price of data is determined by supply and demand? At one level, the analogy of data being new oil is not such a bad one. Crude data, like crude oil, is not of much use until it has been refined to make specific components. The only fallacy in this argument is that crude oil has a limited number of constituents. Data is a far richer proposition, and some types of data can only be extracted from very specific sources. Every individual is a source of unique and valuable data, which is used by various agencies to create trillions of datasets.

While commentators are promoting data as 'the new oil,' in effect it is more like plutonium in that it is difficult to handle and store and can be toxic to both people and the environment. Therefore, if oil is not a good metaphor, what are other useful ways of thinking about data and its various types? Can different types of data be compared with different elements and other commodities (e.g. silver, iron, gold, dysprosium, wheat or coffee)? Even if different types of data are like different elements, consider carbon, one of the most abundant elements on earth and the building block of life. Carbon can be both as cheap as coal (pennies per kilogram) and as expensive as diamond (£50,000 per gram). We might even consider the rare earth elements (a group of 17 elements that are found in low concentrations and have extensive uses in military and civilian applications such as magnets, lasers and electronics) as good metaphors for data that is difficult to mine and is unique. This type of data is of strategic and national importance. We feel that the periodic table of elements is a reasonable starting point for considering the types of data and their different values and uses (from the perspectives of mining, ownership, trading, monopolies, etc.).

The Economic Value of Data, a discussion paper published by HM Treasury in 2018, states:

> Data-driven innovation holds the keys to addressing some of the most significant challenges confronting modern Britain, whether that is tackling

congestion and improving air quality in our cities, developing ground-breaking diagnosis systems to support our NHS, or making our businesses more productive. The UK's strengths in cutting-edge research and the intangible economy make it well-placed to be a world leader, and estimates suggest that data-driven technologies will contribute over £60 billion per year to the UK economy by 2020.

What is interesting is that the discussion paper also says:

Alongside maintaining a secure, trusted data environment, the government has an important role to play in laying the foundations for a flourishing data-driven economy. This means pursuing policies that improve the flow of data through our economy and ensure that those companies who want to innovate have appropriate access to high-quality and well-maintained data.[19]

In other words, businesses should be able to get (potentially cheap or free) access to a certain amount of high-quality critical data, perhaps even data with geospatial elements, to enable them to innovate and create value from that data.

The value of data depends, of course, on its usability by a business and means of exchange. When determining the value of data, consider whether it is akin to one of the rare earth elements or whether it is as common as coal. In 2016, Microsoft paid just over $26 billion for LinkedIn, which at the time had approximately 100 million active users per month. The question arises: was this a fair price? And how much of the fee was for the user data and how much of it was for the platform and the advertising revenue it could bring in? Following the deal, Moody's Investors Service carried out a credit rating and its primary focus was on the value of the LinkedIn data to Microsoft.[20]

It is hard to estimate a company's business value and future potential accurately. This is particularly the case if the company's top management does not have any idea of the worth of its data assets. However, data valuation is even more difficult because data is an asset not yet recognized by generally accepted accounting practices. The future potential of a business can be underestimated by the absence of a realistic valuation of its data assets. Therefore, the creation of a data operating model and the measurement of data value metrics, both internally and across the partner ecosystem, are crucial to unlocking the real value of business data.

However, there are models that purport to enable the measurement of information value and, critically, link the variable inputs of the formulas to market dynamics and business model performance. These include the equations shown in *Figure 3*.

Business Value of Information (BVI)

The BVI recognizes the relevance of the information to business activities, as well as the quality and timeliness of that information.

$$BVI = \sum_{p=1}^{n} R_p \times V \times C \times T$$

The formula for the Business Value of Information (BVI)

- Relevance (R)(p) – The potential usefulness (0 to 1) of the information to the business process
- Validity (V) –The percent of records with correct values
- Coverage (C) – The number of records in the dataset as a percentage of the total universe of potential records
- Timeliness (T) – The probability that at any time, the information is current (matches real-world facts). This is a more easily measured version of the time-log between real-world events and the appearance of those events in a dataset.

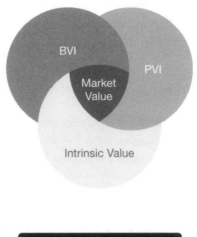

Performance Value of Information (PVI)

The PVI approach defines the value of information by its impact on improving some business performance driver, as measured by a Key Performance Indicator (KPI).

$$PVI = [(\frac{KPI_i}{KPI_c}) - 1] \times \frac{T}{t}$$

The formula for the Performance Value of Information (PVI)

- KPI (i) – The KPI for the business process with the information
- KPI (c) – The KPI for the business process without the information (control group)
- T – The usable life of any datum
- t – The time over which the KPI was measured

Intrinsic Value

$$Iv = f (v,c,s,\lambda)$$

FIGURE 3: Measure of information value: business value and performance value

Source: https://showmethedata.blog/how-to-measure-the-value-of-data and the book authors

While these equations are open to criticism[21] – for example, the BVI could be seen as a simplistic summation and perhaps hides the real complexity of the functional metric, whereas the PVI is a useful metric but relies on a posteriori tracking of realized value over time, which may be problematic – ultimately, they do provide an important signpost as to how data value (intangible and tangible) can be measured as part of an enterprise's balanced scorecard. The way in which data assets are measured and valued will become a critical business competency and market differentiator as businesses compete in both the virtual and the physical worlds, especially as data is increasingly being traded and exchanged for social value and better outcomes.

Within the current digital world, there are many examples of data exchanges that are primarily centred on the relationship between consumers and brands. It is estimated that each consumer has a digital shadow of 2.5 gigabytes of personally identifiable information (PII).[22] PII is information that, when used alone or with other relevant data, can identify an individual. It may contain direct identifiers (e.g. passport information) that can identify a person uniquely, or quasi-identifiers (e.g. race) that can be combined with other quasi-identifiers (e.g. date of birth) to successfully recognize an individual. Consumers commonly exchange their PII for access to products and services or an improved customer experience. For example:

- Accepting a customer agreement that allows a company to track the user's multi-device digital journeys via cookies (and thereby provide an integrated experience when the user moves between devices and channels)
- Sharing location information to gain access to specific services or apps (e.g. Deliveroo) based on geography
- Giving companies access to relevant personalized content (e.g. on Facebook) in order to improve the upsell and cross-sell of products and services based on individual need
- Using a loyalty card, which enables a company to track individuals' personal shopping and behavioural information and to send them personalized offers

However, these examples of exchanges raise ethical and governance questions, such as:

- Is the data collection essential to the transaction?
- Does the exchange provide value to the customer?
- Does the data-exchange transaction represent fair value for both parties?
- Is all data equal? If not, how does that affect the value of the data exchange?
- Who defines the value that accrues as part of or as the outcome of the exchange?
- How much choice is involved?
- Is the exchange conscious or unconscious (i.e. implicit or explicit)?

In practice, many consumers do not read or even review legal terms and conditions, and this has continued since the implementation of the GDPR. Nevertheless, the answers to the questions highlight the quality of the perceived relationship prior to the transaction, the experience of the transaction and the post-event data exchange; in turn, this exchange reflects the value of the brand and relationship, and forms a bridge to the next interaction. It is not merely permission to access personal data that defines the fairness of the exchange but also the type and quality of the experience. The outcome can engender mutual trust based on transparency and consumer choice.

For instance, the absence of friction in a personalized experience based on a brand's knowledge of you as a consumer facilitates a fair and sustainable exchange. It is an experience where consumers are willing and often expect to exchange their PII to receive this personalization across multiple channels. For a business, this process of data alchemy creates new and accurate data assets based on the exchange, which is a 'moment of truth' that enables the business to discover hidden ways it can add value (e.g. by identifying products that customers desire and understanding their motivation to purchase). This enables the use of predictive insight to upsell and use cross-initiatives designed to increase the mutual value created.

In recent times, we have seen the development of more permission-based approaches to the exchange of personal information, such as the Swiss railway system (ticketless purchases and access to trains), the Australian air border control system (personal recognition with no boarding passes required) and the New Zealand postal service's system (personal verification of government services via blockchain, a digital record of transactions). Each of these initiatives involves the use of blockchain technology to ensure that they are characterized not simply by a movement of data but also by an exchange based on consumers' encrypted permission to access their data, which forms the basis of the value created.

This approach has led to the creation of open-source solutions such as Sovrin (sovrin.org), which implements privacy by design on a global scale, including pairwise pseudonymous identifiers, peer-to-peer private agents and selective disclosure of personal data using cryptography based on zero-knowledge proof. It uses hyperledger blockchains (infrastructure and standards for developing blockchain systems and applications) to replace trust in humans with trust in mathematics. This is a form of data passporting: an exchange of data for a premium sensory experience. The democratization of data and AI, together with the rise of data passporting, will facilitate a situation where consumers can create and publicize their own data personas, which will include the types and nature of their data as well as details about its use and access conditions, in return for value (monetary or experience based). This is the data economy at work (*Figure 4*).

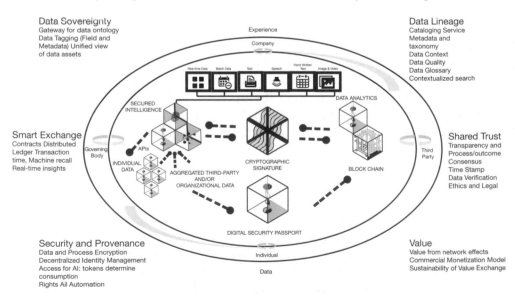

FIGURE 4: Data passporting and data value exchange

(API: application programming interface)

Value exchange between parties will come at a price. Companies need to invest in ways to conduct such data exchanges and deliver personalized experiences, often in near real time. Consumers will want to be engaged, entertained, educated and incentivized to opt in and make an exchange. They will no longer simply compare companies within a specific industry sector. Their comparisons will span the gamut of their collective data-exchange digital history, and their expectations will be formulated and forged based on their individual experiences. Due to the ongoing development in AI and the application of machine intelligence, the previously perceived technological obstacles and barriers to adoption may no longer be as salient or tricky to overcome, as digital technology will become the primary means of data exchange for consumers.

The fact remains that there is considerable variation across industries regarding businesses' maturity (especially within the UK market) in terms of their ability to engage with and exploit digital opportunities. Those businesses that avoid the mass extinction that COVID-19 threatens will win in the post-COVID-19 world because they understand data and how the process of data alchemy can help them to achieve a sustainable basis for value exchange. Digital maturity will also be an increasing feature of consumer engagement as businesses make progress in their technological sophistication and adoption, leading to the possibility of the mainstream use of advanced types of experience and convenience associated with augmented reality (AR) and virtual reality (VR).

There is also the question of the price of an exchange and the rights and consents upon which it is based. In a move reminiscent of George Orwell's novel *Nineteen Eighty-Four* (1949), China has introduced a social credit system that rewards and punishes citizens and corporations by using technology and data to record various measures of financial credit, personal behaviour and corporate misdeeds. In essence, this is the exploitation of personal data (expressed as personal trustworthiness points) to control and reinforce certain behavioural traits in return for social rewards and access to new experiences.

This begs the question: does this change the value of the data exchange? Clearly, from a Western perspective, it does. The value attributed to such an exchange must be lower as there is a degree of coercion that devalues the exchange. There is no choice or ownership for the citizen or corporation in terms of the use of their data for social good. However, is this any different from the actions of the four main technology companies (Amazon, Apple, Facebook and Google), which are almost nation-states in their own right, expounding their own foreign policies and governance regimes, which affect the day-to-day lives of citizens and consumers alike? Similarly, in the time of COVID-19, there is a trade-off in the exchange of personal location data for services such as track-and-trace apps, which are intended to benefit society as a whole and protect health services. The key difference between the China scenario and large-scale uses of data in the West is one of consumer or citizen choice about the uses of data and access to the type of value created.

It could be argued that for consumers, data exchange in advertising is having an adverse effect on the value created.[23] This assertion is based on the contention that consumers are essentially paying twice for a single exchange: first with their attention (a growing number of pop-ups, ad videos, etc. are taking over the online experience) and second with their data. Privacy intrusion is being added to interruption as a new consumer downside.

There has therefore been a seismic shift in the relationships between brands and consumers, enabled by AI and intelligent edge devices via the experience of interconnectivity and traffic translation between or at the different networks' boundaries. But do the above inferences drawn from the brand–consumer experience also apply to the employer–employee experience? With the advent of COVID-19, many employees began to effectively work from home but live at work, and one dimension of the future of work will involve considering this new social contract as well as the basis of the employee experience and the safeguarding of sensitive data.[24]

In 2020, Capita plc conducted a survey titled "Human to Hybrid" involving over 3,000 business leaders and HR business professionals. The results highlighted differences in people's data-sharing preferences between their personal and professional lives. While 63% of employees stated that they expected their employer to offer them a personalized experience based on data exchange, they were significantly more sceptical about the benefits of sharing non-work-related data.

The critical point of these examples is that data exchange is not just about the transaction or 'deal content' itself but also about the resultant quality of the relationship generated by the data alchemy process, which in turn is important in determining the value created.

SHARED TRUST AND SOCIAL CURRENCY

As Shoshana Zuboff observes in her book *The Age of Surveillance Capitalism*, "our private information has become the currency of a new surveillance economy and shared trust is the only real protection from uncertainty."[25] The process of using data alchemy to facilitate value exchange can also produce adverse repercussions for the relationships between businesses and consumers. Soon, as alluded to above, we may witness the creation of a data marketplace where individuals can aggregate their behavioural, demographic and lifestyle data and then specify the terms on which this data can be exchanged for value. In the permission-based economy, data has already become a form of currency. Is it time for consumers to own and monetize their data in a way that rewards them either tangibly or intangibly? This is about more than just being paid for the use of data. Intangible value may be generated from using someone's data for social good (e.g. contributing to our understanding of a treatment for cancer or measuring an individual's social impact on global sustainability by sharing data on a permission basis).

Data is the currency of connection. People are already moving away from the use of physical cash and are using alternative means to enable value exchange. This has taken the form of using phone credits and electricity units as tradeable commodities to elicit value. We have seen the emergence of digitally native companies whose sole rationale is to act as data brokers between brands and consumers.

However, while the means are available, there is significant ground to cover to persuade consumers to adopt this new approach to data exchange. In a 2018 study of over 7,000 consumers around the world, nearly half of the respondents thought companies should use their personal data to provide a better service and 70% agreed that it was important for companies to understand their current situation before sending them a marketing message.[26] The survey also sounded a note of caution in that only one in five consumers was willing to provide data to brands up front to improve their experience, with 40% of global respondents noting that they were "more annoyed" by companies in 2018 compared to five years ago. If a brand's request for data is deemed "too much," some consumers (nearly 30% in the survey) are willing to abandon the brand altogether. Moreover, brands are having to do more personalized marketing with less information as company data practices are top of mind for most consumers; 75% of the respondents expressed concern over the threat of a data breach and 88% reported concern that their data would be shared across companies without their consent. This raises the tricky question of how businesses can effectively manage the trust aspect of a data exchange.

Value exchange is by its very nature a two-way process. Trust is fragile. However, in entrusting valuable data to a business, it is not just the consumer who is taking a risk (in exchange for a personalized experience); the company also bears the risk of significant brand damage and financial penalty if there is a data breach. Examples of data breaches and misuse range from the Facebook–Cambridge Analytica scandal in 2018 to the loss of data due to cyberhacking incidents. Each of these instances highlights the corrosive and destructive impacts that data can have on businesses and consumers alike.

However, businesses have an advantage in addressing these challenges when they can deliver seamless experiences, the value of which may lead consumers to forgive a brand for its transgressions and reengage with it to establish renewed trust. It seems like a contradiction, but the more a brand knows about a consumer and can provide the products and services the consumer desires, the higher the level of brand forgiveness. Forgiveness is a virtue and a value as it pertains to brand engagement. In a survey conducted in 2017, four out of ten consumers said that their trust in a brand or company goes up when a breach is handled swiftly and correctly.[27] Moreover, eight in ten said that trust is a key driver of brand loyalty. This tells us that consumers will give the brands they like the benefit of the doubt when it comes to protecting their PII if it is used to enhance the customer experience. Arguably, it is better for businesses if consumers own their own data, in which case the process of verification and permission becomes the currency rather than the data itself. Businesses can effectively 'rent' the value associated with consumer data to extract value.

Value is a difficult concept to articulate as it is dependent on the parties involved in a transaction and their purposes of engaging in that transaction. The value of data is based on its rarity, frequency and volume, where these qualities increase the data's entropy (see *Chapter 4*). However, value is often thought of as relating to money, which by and large is the instrument by which we measure things. In a world where doing the right thing by taking a purpose-led approach is increasingly being seen as important for humanity, purely monetary transactions are not seen in the same light as they were in the past. Alan Macfarlane argues that 'money' (capitalistic relations, market values, trade and exchange) ushers in a world of moral disorder, primarily because money makes it impossible to discriminate between good and evil (where 'good and evil' is seen as a human value system for establishing societal order). This leads to a disruption of the moral as well as the economic world.[28] Money invites a complex differentiation and multiplication of the parts and qualities of being human. More broadly, money, markets and market capitalism eliminate absolute moralities.

Increasingly, the value of data alchemy will not be measured in dollars, euros or yuan. It will be measured in data-exchange mechanisms. Measurement will be undertaken using digital currencies that connect to specific value systems governed by a value exchange system that rules them all. That system will be distributed without nation-states and artificial temporary boundaries. This is because the value system will be based around the decentralized data of individuals, multinationals and international regulatory frameworks. However, historically, it has been only businesses or corporations that have been able to manage the complexity and governance that characterize data-exchange mechanisms. For these exchanges to acquire legitimacy and proliferate, they should be driven by values (morals and ethics). The development of data value is being driven by the rise of data democratization. This is where the value of data alchemy is much more than business value. It is value.

DATA DEMOCRATIZATION: DATA-EXCHANGE MARKETPLACES

Data democratization would eliminate gatekeepers, allowing everybody to access data. However, as the volume of data increases, given that the consumers of that data are intelligent systems, the need for automated data provenance expands. Not only that, organizations need to democratize data through decentralization and have an appropriate model for its monetary worth. These are issues that they need to solve at scale and speed. However, to achieve this, organizations need to consider how to address what we term the 'quaternion of issues' via their data-driven business strategy.

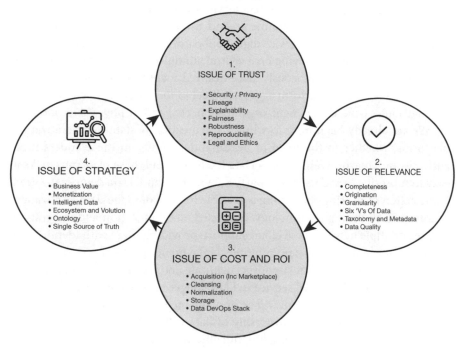

Figure 5: The genesis of intelligence: the quaternion of issues
(ROI: return on investment; for more on the six Vs, see *Figure 17*)

Figure 5 highlights the quaternion of issues around data in terms of quality, monetization, value, evolution and intelligence derived from it, and these issues together will be the next big play in the connected digital revolution. These issues are leading to every network being connected, linking users, applications and ecosystems across blockchain networks, and using multiple trust layers to facilitate interactions and value creation. However, for businesses undertaking this digital journey, there are significant data, technological and people challenges to address, especially if they are seeking to reinvent existing capabilities. Massive volumes of siloed data are clogging today's manufacturing, supply, distribution and user experience systems, which is exposing enterprises to operational risk, latency, high costs and low efficiency.

When it comes to connecting assets, there are two features that will accelerate the adoption and use of data democratization: decentralized identity management and individual monetization of data ownership. Centralized identity management is on the way out. Current approaches – such as Microsoft's Active Directory and authentication with a single cloud – are limiting and cumbersome as they assume a single organization or 'super-admin' that undertakes all duties.

Decentralized identity management is on the way in. It enables multiple individuals and organizations to identify, authenticate and authorize participants and organizations, allowing them to access services, data and systems across multiple networks, organizations, environments and use cases. It empowers users and enables a personalized, self-service digital onboarding system that allows users to self-authenticate without relying on a central administration function to process their information. Simultaneously, decentralized identity management ensures users are authorized to perform actions subject to the system's policies based on their attributes (role, department, organization, etc.) and/or physical location.

We are already beginning to witness the creation of data-democratization platforms, whether in the form of personal data 'pods' in the Flanders local authority or Amazon Web Services Data Exchange, and these platforms make it easy to subscribe to and use third-party data in the cloud. Data democratization is the action of making something accessible to everyone: the democratization of information through technology. Increased interconnection and integration will see multiple new forms of cloud support, providing users with identity and privacy management that spans multiple deployments, projects and clouds, and doing this in a manner that supports corporate and national governance policies. Access to products and services will no longer be restricted to a company's ability to sell and distribute but will be implemented via multiple data-exchange marketplaces.[29] Control and ownership of data will continue to be viewed as a currency and managed accordingly. Critically, individuals rather than corporate entities will be able to trade and rent their data in a manner commensurate with the value and purpose of its use. In this model of data exchange, the underlying platform could be a permissioned blockchain network based on connecting Hyperledger Fabric nodes (see www.hyperledger.org), enabling versioning and validation of a single source by using a suite of stable frameworks, tools and libraries for enterprise-grade blockchain deployments. This platform would record the data's origins and changes, and it would be securely shared among multiple parties or on an open registry (a multi-party solution helps to tackle the various challenges posed by siloed data and multi-tier supply chains).

THE EMERGENCE OF SHADOW INTELLIGENCE AND THE PHOENIX DOCTRINE

One of the key attributes of data is its innate ability to be combined with other datasets to replicate and create new sources of value. Each consumer interaction or experience creates data, which can be mined and provide the basis of new yet latent value. We create vaults to store data, we use lakes or lochs to extract it, and we police its use. This process of non-degradable value renewal is the basis of data alchemy. In his *Capitalism, Socialism and Democracy* (1942), the Austrian economist Joseph Schumpeter (1883–1950) developed the doctrine of creative destruction, in which capitalism is the destroyer of the old and the creator of the new. While there is merit in the argument that "value destruction is opening space for the new. New ideas and businesses; new industries as yet unimagined,"[30] the idea of the 'phoenix doctrine' – where, during the process of data alchemy, data can be renewed and increase in value each time it undergoes a transformation – may explain the enduring fascination with data and the desire to acquire it and find insights in it. We have long sought to multiply the value of data by combining it with other sources to create a new asset or intellectual property.

Could we reach a situation where we worship data (just like the 21st-century obsession with money), where the 0s and 1s of binary define the value of our social, emotional and sensory connections? Capitalism focuses on the equation where price is equated with value to generate income, but what if Marx's theory of surplus value and utility could be measured by the intangible currency of data? Zuboff's assertion that surveillance capitalism unilaterally claims human experience as free raw material for translation into behavioural data certainly has merit.[31] The reaction against this free exploitation of personal data is the essence of data alchemy, which changes the relationship and value exchange between parties regarding the use of data.

Data is just the beginning. Businesses are now hyper-focused on surfacing meaningful, timely and actionable insights from proprietary and third-party data. Technologies such as the cloud and AI are forming new partnerships between humans and machines. The barriers to entry have fallen. As AI becomes increasingly democratized, businesses are no longer only testing and experimenting with machine learning (ML). ML is now being deployed in key departments such as risk management, pre-trade analytics and customer analytics. However, there remains a significant range in the level of businesses' maturity in this area and their adoption of both business analytics and AI capabilities. This is partly due to capital constraints and the absence of skilled people but also to a paucity of knowledge about how to create a data-driven enterprise where value creation is a fundamental capability of the target operating model.

However, technology's role is to enable us to go beyond our human limitations. How we govern technology and data affects who shares in the benefits of its application. Progression toward a bio-symbiotic relationship between humans and machines will characterize the development of our species over the next 50 years. If we view our core process as programming our own development, then data is the fundamental DNA of artificial life. The creation of 'shadow intelligence' (which reflects and shapes us but is not us), where technology becomes our companion and is fused into our own intelligence cortex, will require us to rewrite the nature and definition of value. This will enable us to redistribute the wealth that data alchemy can engender to ensure equitable distribution of the value that it creates and avoid social inequality. This is less the dystopian world of the movies (where it is human versus machine) and more of an augmented one, where AI enables humans to live their best lives.

CHAPTER 3

UNDERSTANDING INTELLIGENCE AND INTELLIGENT SYSTEMS

This chapter explores the fundamentals of natural intelligence and its relationship with AI and ML, without delving into the depths of academia and metaphysics. We explain the emergence of natural intelligence and its various manifestations, the workings of the nervous system, the localization of various cognitive functions within it, the role of neurons, and the mechanisms for communicating and sending data between them. This kind of knowledge helps scientists to understand the similarities between natural and artificial intelligence and to develop AI in constructive ways that build on the progress of biology.

Our understanding of intelligence is not seamless. This chapter discusses some of the gaps and problems with this topic, such as how to explain the meanings and origins of consciousness, intentionality and intelligence. Acknowledging the missing mechanisms and abstractions enables us to apply AI in a more precise and productive way, as it highlights those areas of research within AI that will lead the next wave of transformation. This chapter also outlines how we propose intelligence should be understood, representing this symbolically through our concept of the AI Periodic Table and even more so through the groups within that table. We also cover aspects related to naturally and artificially intelligent systems' characteristics to articulate the stark differences and similarities between them.

INSPIRATION FROM NATURE

Natural evolution has solved many of the problems related to performing and functioning in the physical environment, and biological systems have guided human ingenuity. The motion of a horse and the flight of a bird inspired modern gear systems and aeroplanes, respectively. Other examples of natural phenomena inspiring human applications include the aerodynamics of the boxfish, the reduction of drag and noise on turbine blades by studying warty ridges on humpback whales, and adhesives based on the mechanisms used by geckos' feet.[32]

In every example, humans have been able to mimic nature and improve it beyond the products of natural evolution. Artificial horses (e.g. the Shanghai maglev train) can now travel at over 250 miles per hour and carry more than 500 people at once. Similarly, artificial birds (e.g. *Voyager 1*) have enabled us to explore space and wander into extra-terrestrial environments that previously no living entity from earth had been aware of. We study, we learn and, in this process, we try to advance nature. It was only a matter of time before discoveries would inspire humans working in the fields of neurobiology, neurophysiology, neuroscience, cognition, consciousness and intelligence. These discoveries, merged with digital data technologies, have given us profound clues and tools to enable us to invent artificially intelligent systems for applications in research, medicine, business and more. We are just at the beginning: the journey that we are embarking upon will change the very fabric of the universe.

It is difficult to comprehend how the first glimmers of intelligence came into being. The emergence of life (known as abiogenesis) from inorganic physical and chemical processes in cells, producing carbon-based creatures on earth, must be one of the foremost miracles in the universe. Over the course of evolution, primordial organisms were attracted to various energy sources to fulfil their functional needs. In this process, they learned to adapt to a wide range of physical environments in what could be described as the first step in the development of intellectual faculties. Following that epic jump from the inorganic to the organic, natural intelligence developed over billions of years into myriad life forms adapted to, and in harmony with, their environments.[33] As a result, natural intelligence is based on data from the environment (past and present and, in the case of humans, a synthesized perception of the future) and a process of natural selection that allows for change, propagation, adaptation and evolution. In many ways, we humans, with our perfectly sized brains for the scale of the natural environment we live in, represent the pinnacle of that achievement. We excel at the prime directives of life, such as reasoning, planning, problem-solving in complex and quasi-random environments, and using abstract thought to learn from experience and change. We have evolved to adapt and engage with our changing environment, and we have also created lifestyles, values and technologies that have changed the environment itself to suit us. As we have outdone our natural environments in some ways, we have started to believe that our collective creations will outdo us in the foreseeable future.

The effort to understand natural intelligence is a vast interdisciplinary research field in the natural sciences and includes neuroscience, anthropology, education and linguistics. Through these fields, we have built up narratives that enable us to communicate, record and progress in scientific and social contexts. We can reason from abstractions (epistemology, ontology, taxonomy and metaphysics) to their manifestations and connections to reality (teleology).[34]

Guided by human instincts and the need to plan for the future, scientists are deepening our understanding of natural systems and creating abstractions that enable us to build better solutions to our problems. This process may even enable us to build *better* systems than nature has given us through evolution and adaptation. The current vogue concerns building intelligent systems around the digitalized world. The primary motivation is to be able to improve business processes and the value they bring to societies. On this journey toward improved systems and processes, we can proceed without the need to wander into metaphysical questions or nebulous concepts of intelligence and consciousness. Rather, we need to wrestle with concepts around 'being good at a particular task' and the performance of a system to tackle a specific set of problems. To understand the creation of the next generation of digital intelligence, however, exploring these high-level topics is essential.

The topic of AI is so widely discussed that any unbounded search as to 'what is intelligence?' almost exclusively produces results about AI rather than topics related to natural biological intelligence. In his book, Sternberg[35] explains that the different underlying metaphors and assumptions about human intelligence in fields of study such as anthropology, computers and psychology lead us to different conclusions about the idea of intelligence. Therefore, most questions around intelligence are open, and almost all the answers are controversial and conversational. The narrative around intelligence tends to focus on "a certain property that is based around problem-solving performance."[36] In this sense, intelligence started with life itself.

THE EMERGENCE OF INTELLIGENCE

We assume that life on earth emerged through natural processes in the universe. Life is an entity that is composed of cells, undergoes metabolic processes, can adapt and grow in its environment, can respond to that environment, and can reproduce and evolve. Life largely involves inter-cellular interactions in the physical environment. The kingdoms of life include bacteria, protists, archaea, fungi, plants and animals. To survive, cells evolved methods to detect and respond to their environments. Those that failed to adapt to the specific demands of their environment died away. Those that could withstand the challenges they faced survived and over time evolved into multicellular organisms that could respond to their environment's signals in more sophisticated ways.[37] Nervous systems emerged through the cellular response of detection and signalling with foreign species, and in time the nervous system began coordinating all of an organism's activities.

Organisms (e.g. animals, plants and fungi) are defined as assemblies of molecules capable of reproduction, growth, development and maintenance. Perhaps surprisingly, all known organisms have their foundations in a set of 355 genes (our last universal common ancestor). In essence, any natural intelligence (as opposed to intelligence imparted on a short-term basis as memes) is embedded in a combination and manifestation of these genes. We can only speculate at present as to how many artificial genetic algorithms we may need in order to construct intelligence in a form that humans can relate to.

Locomotion is a fundamental way in which organisms interact with their environment. The original means of locomotion was swimming by flexing the body in a horizontal plane, and the travels of early organisms were largely governed by the tides, the seasons, and night and day. This was when the rhythms of the natural environment began to be embedded into life. This phenomenon is primordial and spans the whole of life on earth. We recognize this as musical intelligence (see the section 'Manifestations of intelligence' below). This and other forms of intelligence (i.e. detecting and responding) became more complex as creatures evolved beyond their humble beginnings. When species started to inhabit dry land, they started using legs in the vertical plane instead of their previous mode of swimming movement. Walking and running became the fundamental modes of motion for slow- and fast-moving vertebrates, respectively. There are currently around 70,000 species of vertebrates on earth, including us.[38]

All vertebrates are characterized by a complex nervous system that takes sensory data and coordinates actions in tandem with an endocrine system (a chemical messenger system that regulates physiology and behaviour – digestion, metabolism, sensory perception, sleep, mood, consumption, excretion, reproduction, etc.). The nervous system consists of a central nervous system (CNS) and a peripheral nervous system (PNS). The CNS is composed of the brain (shown in *Figure 6* and discussed below) and the spinal cord, whereas the PNS is composed of nerves that extend the influence of the CNS to every part of the body. The PNS is further subdivided into three separate subsystems: somatic (which controls voluntary movement), autonomic (which regulates the body during emergencies and when we are in a relaxed state) and enteric (which controls food consumption and regulation).[39]

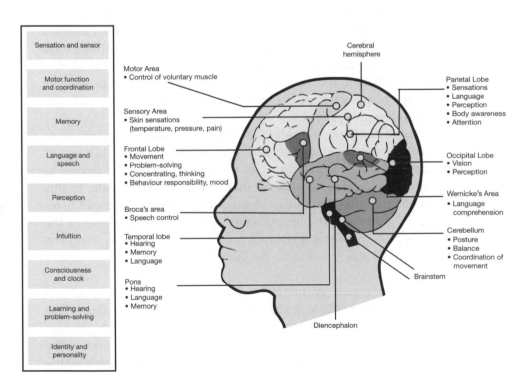

FIGURE 6: Functional areas of the human brain

The CNS's function is to send the results of analysis (data) from one cell to another and to receive feedback (more data). It is where data is received from the sensory neurons and stored and managed. It controls the inner processes in the body and coordinates the motor functions of the organism. Following are some of the CNS's key components found in the human brain:

- The **cerebrum** (also known as the telencephalon) is the largest component of the brain and is made up of the frontal lobe, temporal lobe, parietal lobe and occipital lobe, as shown in *Figure 6*. This part of the brain is responsible for abstract thinking processes. It is divided into two hemispheres, which are organized in a folded structure. These cerebral hemispheres are connected by one strong nerve cord and several small ones. Many neurons are located in the cerebral cortex (also just called the cortex), which is divided into multiple cortical fields, each having a specific task. The primary cortical fields are responsible for processing qualitative data, such as by managing perceptions (e.g. vision and audio are controlled by the visual and auditory cortexes, respectively). The associated cortical fields perform more abstract association and thinking processes, and they also appear to have functions relating to memory.
- The **cerebellum** controls and coordinates motor functions. It is located below the cerebrum and is closer to the spinal cord. It serves fewer abstract functions with higher priorities: here, large parts of motor coordination are overseen, including balance and control coordination. In the human brain, the cerebellum is considerably smaller than the cerebrum, but this is rather an exception among the vertebrate family, as in many vertebrates that ratio is less pronounced.
- The **diencephalon** (interbrain) is made up of the thalamus and hypothalamus, and it controls fundamental physiological processes. This part of the brain mediates between sensory and motor signals and the cerebrum. The thalamus filters the information that is sent to the cerebrum. In this process, the thalamus discards unimportant sensory data to avoid overloading the cerebrum. The hypothalamus plays a significant role in the regulation of hormones and the maintenance of body temperature. The diencephalon is also involved in the circadian rhythm ('internal clock') and pain sensation.
- The **brainstem** (made up of the midbrain, pons and medulla oblongata) connects the brain with the spinal cord and controls reflexes. The brainstem can be considered an extension of the spinal cord. It provides bridges (in the pons) between the brain and the body. This area of the brain is responsible for fundamental reflexes such as coughing, blinking and sneezing.

All parts of the nervous system are involved in data processing. This is accomplished by a large number of very similar neural cells, whose structure appears to be simple and that communicate continuously. Due to this continuous process, the body has a vast capacity to process information.

Not only do vertebrates have to survive on their own and with others like them, but they must also display behaviours that enable sensory data to be transmitted to and received from other species. These signals can be in the form of pheromones, sound, sight, touch or even more esoteric things such as electric shocks. While interspecies interaction is generally competitive, it can be mutualistic, such as the relationship between plants and pollinators. These relationships, embedded over time as part of evolution, result in intelligence manifested as inter- and intrapersonal intelligence, spatial intelligence, verbal intelligence, linguistic intelligence and so on. There is a whole spectrum of these characteristics in vertebrates. In systems theory, this complex adaptation toward intelligence is known as 'emergence.' Emergence occurs when a behaviour is observed among a collection of entities but that same behaviour is not significantly found when observing one of the entities on its own. So, one might argue that linguistic intelligence is an emergent property of a community, or that life is an emergent property of biochemistry. Emergence is an essential concept in terms of dissecting and demystifying intelligence and even consciousness.[40]

Having said the above, there are several additional facets that are worth including as they affect how we perceive the relationship between neurons and intelligence:

- **Neurons** – The human brain has about 86 billion neurons, while the spinal cord has around 14 million motor neurons and around 18 billion sensory neurons. The number of synapses just in the brain (number of connections between neurons) is around 125 trillion.[41] This means there are about 1,700 synapses per neuron. Recent studies[42] show that the integration of information (processing) may happen not only in the neurons but also in the synapses irrespective of their numbers. It is worth noting that there are creatures that have bigger brains than those of humans – the African elephant has the largest land mammalian brain (around 260 billion neurons), weighing in at around 4–5 kg, and the sperm whale has the largest brain of any creature (around 500 billion neurons), weighing in at 8 kg. What is key is that it is the number of neurons in the neocortex (where higher functions are performed) and their arrangement that seem to be the primary indicators of intelligence, where intelligence is measured using the ability of a creature to be proactive in a changing environment.[43] The human brain in comparison weighs about 1.5 kg, and on purely comparative measures there seems nothing extraordinary about it![44]

- **'Hacking' the brain** – When people talk about hacking the brain, they generally mean improving performance in one area of living. For example, there is an area of the brain that sets the circadian rhythm and sends signals about the intensity of blue colours. These signals are linked to a part of the thalamus that relates to pain. Avoiding blue light at night is thus useful for feeling calm and for sleep, and so one hack is to filter out blue light from electronics and bedrooms to improve sleep. There are techniques that can be used to alter people's view of reality. These include the use of disinformation and the 'illusory truth effect,'[45] various drugs, devices implanted in and connected to the brain, and the use of evolutionary vulnerabilities in basic human psychology related to reward centres (which control pleasure) and fear centres (which invoke emotion and attention).

- **Other facts about the brain** – The brain reaches full maturity at around the age of 25 years. Approximately 60% of the dry brain weight is fat. It takes around 20% of the blood being pumped by the heart and as little as 100 microseconds to generate an action. Human brains cannot multitask. There are more than 10,000 specific types of neurons (differing from one another functionally and genetically), and neuroimaging shows that we create around 70,000 thoughts per day (70% of which tend to be negative). This implies that one of the drivers of intelligence and consciousness is the ability to handle unexpected and unfavourable conditions. Human brains have evolved to be significantly smaller over the past 20,000 years.[46]

One aspect of interest relating to the future development of AI models is the structure of the cerebral cortex; it is the site of the most extensive neural integration and its structure is a marvel in terms of its complex folds, lobes, layers and columns. Its compactness, power supply, heat sinks, asymmetrical nature, and resilience in the face of damage and outages provide a masterclass in natural design and function. Different parts of the neural cortex work at different temporal dynamics; that is, different types of data are handled at different clock rates. Some are handled as slowly as 2 Hz and others are processed as quickly as a few kilohertz.[47]

A crucial point to take away from this brief review of brain science is that we have much to learn from nature. Computational neuroscientists are discovering that neuronal topologies have similarities with the topologies being suggested by specialists in artificial neural networks.[48]

NEURONS: THE BUILDING BLOCKS OF NATURAL INTELLIGENCE

Neurons are nerve cells (see *Figure 7*) that can send and receive data (signals and information). They have a lot in common with other body cells, but they are structurally and functionally unique.[49]

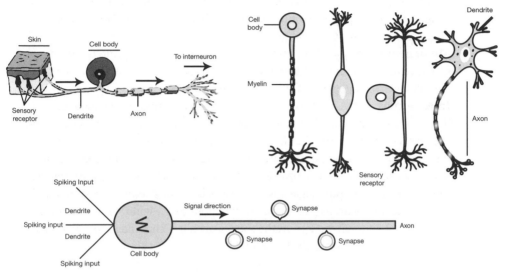

FIGURE 7: The nerve system

Neurons vary in shape, size and structure depending on where they are located and their function. Almost all neurons have three parts:

- The **cell body** (also known as a soma) is the neuron's core, from which other features extend. It regulates the genetic code and acts as a repository of energy, driving all activities. It is also responsible for maintaining the structure of the neuron. It contains a nucleus and other large organelles, each of which has a particular task to perform in the cellular structure. It is surrounded by a membrane, which protects it from intruders (such as viruses).
- The **axon** is a long, tail-like structure that connects with the cell body. An electrical signal is generated in the axon with the help of myelin, which is a fatty substance that covers the structure of the axon. There is one primary axon present in each neuron.
- **Dendrites** are fibrous materials that usually protrude from the cell's body. They process data received from the axons of other neurons. If neurons have more than one set of dendrites, these are known as 'dendritic trees.' The number of dendrites a neuron carries generally depends on its role. Dendritic trees are developed differently in different parts of the brain and can allow neurons to receive thousands of signals (data inputs).

TYPES OF NEURONS

Neurons vary in structure, function and genetic makeup.[50] There are thousands of types of neurons, but they fall into three broad classes:

- **Sensory neurons** enable us to taste, smell, hear, see and feel things. The physical and chemical inputs from our environment usually stimulate sensory neurons. Examples of physical inputs are sound, light and touch, and examples of chemical inputs are smell and taste.
- **Motor neurons** play a role in movement, including voluntary and involuntary movements. The brain and spinal cord communicate with other body parts and the muscles and glands through motor neurons.
- **Interneurons** are the most common type of neuron, found as intermediaries in the brain and spinal cord. They are responsible for exchanging information from the sensory neurons and other interneurons with the motor neurons and other interneurons. These neurons create complex circuits that govern our response to an external event. For instance, if our hand is in contact with a hot substance, sensory neurons in our fingertips send signals to interneurons in our spinal cord. Some interneurons pass on the instructions to the hand's motor neurons, making the hand pull away from the source of pain. Other interneurons send a signal to the pain centre in the brain, and we experience pain.

It is important to note that while neurons are largely similar, they do have important variations in shape, size, function, structure and genetic makeup. When we talk about AI, we generally see all neurons as having very similar functions, even if some may have a distinct relationship to other neurons (such as through memory or sequencing). We believe that a crucial aspect of the advancement of AI will be seen in big data enabling further refinement of the current basic models.

FUNCTION OF NEURONS

Neurons send signals using action potentials.[51] An action potential is a shift in a neuron's electric potential caused by the flow of ions in and out of the neural membrane. Chemical and electrical synapses can both be activated through action potentials:

- In a **chemical synapse**, a neuron releases neurotransmitter molecules into a space that is close to another neuron. Neurotransmitters can cause the neuron receiving the signal to be in a state of excitation, which makes the postsynaptic neuron generate an action potential of its own. In contrast, neurotransmitters can also impede the postsynaptic neuron, in which case it does not create an action potential.
- **Electrical synapses** can only excite. They are only possible when two neurons are linked via a gap junction. This gap is much smaller than a synapse and includes ion channels, which facilitate the direct transmission of a positive

electrical signal. As a result, electrical synapses are much faster at transmitting signals than chemical synapses are. However, electrical synapses' transmission capability is low as the signal weakens from one neuron to the next.

Chemical synapses depend on the release of neurotransmitter molecules (e.g. acetylcholine for muscle control and memory; serotonin for mood regulation, sleep and intestinal movements; dopamine for voluntary movement, reward pathways and cognition; norepinephrine for the fight-or-flight response, etc). There is an approximately one-millisecond delay between when the axon potential reaches the presynaptic terminal and when the neurotransmitter leads to the opening of the postsynaptic ion channels. In contrast, electrical synapses operate virtually instantaneously (essential reflexes require an instantaneous response), and a few electrical synapses proceed in both directions (i.e. they are bidirectional). Electrical synapses are more dependable as there is less possibility of them being blocked, and they are important for coordinating the electrical response of a cluster of neurons.

As action potentials are key features of neuron functions, this phenomenon is worth a closer look. An action potential is a sudden climb followed by a fall in membrane potential or voltage across a cellular structure. To activate an action potential, a significant amount of current is required to depolarize the membrane to the threshold level. Otherwise, a voltage response in the cellular structure will not be created. Examples include muscle cells and neurons, which are activated via action potentials.

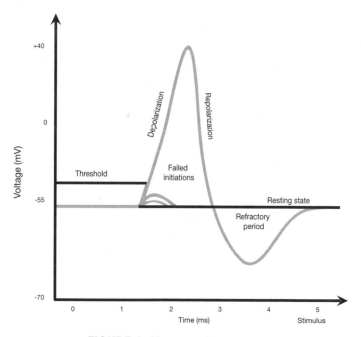

FIGURE 8: Neuron action potential

Figure 8 outlines how an action potential works:

- Once the stimulus is reached, there is an abrupt increase in the voltage across the cellular membrane. The stimulus starts the rapid change in voltage or action potential. A significant amount of current must be supplied to increase the voltage across the cellular structure to accelerate its depolarization process.
- Next, the potential increase because of depolarization causes a considerable influx of sodium ions across the membrane.
- Once the activation potential has been achieved, repolarization of the potassium ions begins. At this stage, the sodium channel is inactivated and a large influx of potassium ions starts.
- Hyperpolarization is a lowered membrane potential caused by the potassium ions' efflux and the closing of the potassium channel.
- Finally, the membrane attains the resting state where membrane potential is again equal to the resting voltage.

Signals can be received from dendrites and sent down the axon once enough signals have been received. These output signals can be used as inputs for other neurons, making this a cyclical process. Some signals are more important than others and can trigger some neurons to fire more easily. Connections between different neurons' dendrites can become stronger or weaker, and new connections can appear while others may cease to exist, giving the brain plasticity.

In terms of AI, we can mimic most of this process by coming up with a function that receives a list of weighted input signals and outputs some signal if the sum of these weighted inputs reaches a particular bias (offset). Simple classification tasks can easily be performed using this model, and this can serve as a basis of AI.

THE NEUROPHYSIOLOGY OF COGNITION

The emergence of many of the CNS's functions is a great marvel. The phenomenon of cognition and its manifestation in expressions and emotions arises naturally out of the electrical activity of large systems of neurons within the brain and the PNS. While our understanding is still in its infancy, modern blood-flow-sensing techniques reveal the localization of metabolic demand in the brain when it is subjected to various cognitive tasks. Suppose we could relate cognitive functions to areas of the brain. This would enable us to look at details of those areas of the brain further and understand attributes of cognition more objectively. Unfortunately, attempts at this localization have not yet provided the insights that we are after; many cognitive functions are not neatly localized to any one specific part of the brain.

More significant insights come from measuring individual neurons' electrical activity through the use of microelectrodes.[52] Increasingly, scientists understand that the impediments to understanding cognitive neuroscience are not conceptual but technical. As more technological advancements are being made, we are getting closer to reaching the ability to measure and localize cognitive functions both spatially and temporally. Models of interactions between cortical areas will become more spatially precise and will be measurable to the level of microseconds. With this progress, our cognitive models will undoubtedly reveal new insights – this precision, for example, will enable the relationship between specific neural structures and cognitive functions to be established.

The implications for society of advances in understanding the neurophysiology of cognition are immense. The use of information to design intelligent machines will become more fruitful. Data, as described in *Chapter 4*, will fundamentally affect how we understand ourselves and society. There are two aspects of this narrative – conscious experience and decision-making:

- **Consciousness** – Many researchers contend that consciousness can only be understood through the first-person experience. We believe that once an operational definition of conscious experience can be formulated, its scientific study and consequential implications for ML can be implemented. The fundamental aspect of how consciousness emerges from collections of neurons, action potentials and synapses perhaps need not be such an impenetrable mystery.[53]
- **Decision-making** – One of the keys to unlocking the decision-making process is to look at the link between perception and action: the relationship between input data and the invocation of motor neurons. These decision-making processes are informed by reward, expectation, and memory of experiences and sensory evidence. Central to decision-making in natural systems is adaptability and the ability to evolve in response to the changing environment. If the decision-making process were to be deterministically rooted in pure logic, we would end up with systems based on the same critical modes of failure, and we would make repeated mistakes. Finding the balance between physical determinism and adaptability (which can seem akin to personal freedom) is an essential step in understanding human value and the experiences of cognitive depth.[54] Consequently, memes and social contracts' role in influencing personal beliefs and behaviour is also crucial in decision-making.

SMARTER PEOPLE HAVE BIGGER AND FASTER NEURONS

Our brain is composed of billions of neurons that store, process and transmit information to other parts of our body via electrical signals. However, not much is known about the variation of these cells from person to person. To date, scientists have not established robust relationships that deterministically explain the link between neurons and intelligence.

The Human Brain Project is a flagship initiative started in 2013 to look at experimental studies and develop models and theories related to the brain's underlying information processing, from cellular signalling to larger-scale networks. Its researchers study the brain's complexity by looking at cognitive functions. For example, Professor Huibert Mansvelder of Free University Amsterdam and his team have looked at the size of dendrites (as explained above, these are the long branched-out protrusions through which each neuron receives signals from thousands of other cells).[55] They concluded that people with higher IQs have long and complicated dendrites coupled with enhanced action potentials. They also showed through computational modelling that neurons with larger dendrites and faster action potentials can process more information and pass more detailed information on to other neurons.

LIMITATIONS OF NATURAL INTELLIGENCE VERSUS AI

Almost all of the current literature talks about the limitations of AI, and those limitations are many and varied. Natural intelligence has its limitations too. These are shown in *Table 1*, which compares the features of natural and artificial intelligence. It illustrates the stark differences between the two in terms of their 'engineering.' We will refer to this table later in the book when we consider how AI should be developed in the future.

FEATURE	HUMAN	MACHINE
Situational awareness	Limited by experiential data	Limited by input data
Data limitations	Limited capacity	Capacity scalable with available technology and resources
Speed of adaptability	Evolutionary speed limitations	Often revised more than once a year
Architecture	Massively parallel processing at the neuron level	Primarily serial processing
Value system	Behavioural and social norms; habits, beliefs and cultural memes	Currently determined by big corporations, nation-states, international frameworks and social governance processes; entirely in the hands of human society at present

FEATURE	HUMAN	MACHINE
Number of inputs	Does not adapt to new sensory inputs	Unlimited – multimode connections including wireless
Age since inception of current model	75,000 years	1 year
Bias	Cultural and clan	Social, data and algorithmic bias (see *Chapter 6*); possible to design out but determined by prevalent cultural values
Time to acquire skills	Years	As soon as appropriate data is published or becomes available
Lifespan	Approximately 75 years	Unlimited, but typically superseded yearly
Data provenance	Easily hackable and intrinsic to evolutionary design for several social and personal reasons	Easily hackable but this can be designed out using data security technologies as they become available
Security	Relatively insecure	Stack dependent
Fault tolerance	Cultural and personal	Determined by underlying hardware and virtualization layers
Activation function	Threshold based; electrical and chemical	Flexible and open to iteratively improved activation designs (discussed further in *Chapter 5*)
Resilience	Massively resilient	Currently mildly resilient
Knowledge and experience transfer	Not fully transferrable from one generation to another (education allows some transfer)	Possible by simply lifting data from one AI system and implementing it in another

TABLE 1: Features of human versus machine-based intelligence

MANIFESTATIONS OF INTELLIGENCE

A few researchers have suggested that intelligence is a single, standard capacity, whereas others accept that it encompasses a range of aptitudes and abilities.[56]

There are various definitions of intelligence. While these definitions can vary considerably from one set of theories to the next, current conceptualizations tend to suggest that intelligence involves the level of ability to do the following:

- **Learn** – The procurement, maintenance and use of information is a critical component of intelligence
- **Recognize issues** – To put information to use, individuals must distinguish potential issues within the environment that must be addressed
- **Solve issues** – Individuals must, to the best of their ability, establish valuable links between what they have learned and issues in the world around them

Intelligence involves various cognitive (mental) abilities, including logic, reasoning, problem-solving and planning. On the one hand, intelligence is among the most heavily researched topics; on the other, it is one of the topics that creates the most significant controversy.

Researchers have proposed a spectrum of theories to explain the nature of intelligence. *Figure 9* shows some of the major aspects of intelligence that have emerged during the past century and the following subsections look at some of the key theorists in greater depth.

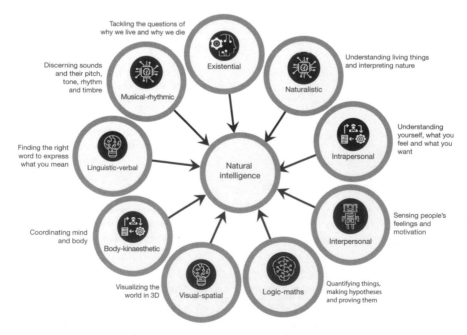

FIGURE 9: Aspects of natural intelligence

CHARLES SPEARMAN: GENERAL INTELLIGENCE

Charles Spearman (1863–1945) was a British psychologist who coined the term 'general intelligence' in his seminal 1904 paper, published at a time when psychology was just starting to be treated with scientific rigour rather than approached via philosophical speculation.[57] Spearman examined mental aptitude tests using factor analysis techniques and concluded that scores on these tests were remarkably similar. Individuals who performed well on one cognitive test tended to perform well on other tests, whereas those who scored poorly on one test tended to score similarly on others. While this theory of general intelligence was met with controversy at the time, Spearman introduced the significant theory that there is an underlying cognitive capacity driving aptitude and that cognitive capacity could be measured and numerically expressed.[58]

LOUIS L. THURSTONE AND HOWARD GARDNER: BASIC MENTAL ABILITIES

Psychologist Louis L. Thurstone (1887–1955) developed a more nuanced theory of intelligence from his work on multiple factor analysis. Rather than seeing intelligence as a single quantifiable capacity as Spearman had, Thurstone's hypothesis centred on seven distinct groups of intelligence factors, which he referred to as primary mental abilities.[59] The abilities that he described were:

- Verbal comprehension
- Reasoning
- Perceptual speed
- Numerical ability

- Word fluency
- Associative memory
- Spatial visualization

Building on Spearman and Thurstone's theories, Howard Gardner (b. 1943) developed the theory of multiple intelligences (see *Figure 9*). He rejected the idea that intelligence could be quantified numerically, as with IQ tests, because that did not represent the complete capacities of human intelligence. Instead, as a model of intelligence, Gardner proposed eight types of insight based on distinct capacities that are valued across cultures.[60] The eight kinds of intelligence Gardner outlined are:

- Visual–spatial intelligence
- Verbal–linguistic intelligence
- Bodily–kinaesthetic intelligence
- Logical–mathematical intelligence

- Interpersonal intelligence
- Musical intelligence
- Intrapersonal intelligence
- Naturalistic intelligence

ROBERT STERNBERG: THE TRIARCHIC THEORY OF INTELLIGENCE

Psychologist Robert Sternberg (b. 1949) characterizes insights as mental action coordinated in order to determine, influence and make purposive adjustments to real-world situations significant to one's life. Whereas he agrees with Gardner that intelligence is much broader than a single, common capacity, he proposes that a few of Gardner's theorized types of insight are better seen as personal abilities. Sternberg proposed what he called 'effective insights,' which include three diverse components:

- **Analytical intelligence** – Our problem-solving abilities
- **Creative intelligence** – Our capacity to negotiate new circumstances using past encounters and current skills
- **Practical intelligence** – Our capacity to adjust in a changing environment[61]

MACHINE INTELLIGENCE

Machine intelligence began from a humble primordial soup of mechanical gears and levers used for calculating and code-breaking, and it progressed to where we find ourselves today. The move to the digital world has enabled rules-based engines to speed up many tasks and processes. We are now in the realm of implementing humanlike capabilities of sensing, learning, adapting and acting. Indeed, with the evolution of certain new capabilities – such as the IoT, elastic computing (automated computation capacity scaling, such as Amazon Web Services' EC2) and storage scalability, open-source and democratized learning, reuse of novel algorithms, and borderless and globalized exchange of ideas and innovations – we are entering an era of hyper-convergence. This hyper-convergence relates not only to technologies and tools but also to people, processes and methods. We deconstruct these broader, interrelated concepts in the next four chapters.

State-of-the-art machine intelligence is currently based on artificial neurons that try to mimic biological processes that scientists were first able to observe in the brain during the mid-20th century. The concept behind artificial neurons implemented in digital code is that it is possible to mimic certain parts of neurons, such as dendrites, cell bodies and axons, using simple mathematical models of what we perceive to be their functions.

Machine intelligence is not as well understood as natural intelligence. Consequently, studies of natural intelligence – as made possible by computational neuroscience, neurophysiology and neuroscience generally – will lead to great advances in the way we design machine intelligence. It is a matter of conjecture which of the multiple routes to creating a 'thinking' machine is better. Teaching machines abstract problem-solving skills (such as playing chess) might involve giving them senses and teaching them like a child. This route has been tried, and machines can easily outdo humans in most of those types of tasks. That still does not make the machines intelligent, but there is a perception in the popular media that machines are on the march.[62]

The purpose of ML is to enable relationships to be established between inputs and outputs without explicit programming. For example, if someone has trained a system with enough data, when they give it a new input, the system should be able to independently classify that input. Examples include video and audio recognition, unlocking smartphones based on fingerprint or facial recognition, cancer detection, automated student assessments and chatbot assistants.

There are four main approaches in this field (which we will cover in *Chapter 5*): unsupervised learning, supervised learning, semi-supervised learning and reinforcement learning. Within the four main approaches, there are many ML algorithms, but these variations revolve around the particular problems that we face as humans and in businesses. Many of the ML methods are based on artificial neural networks (ANNs). ANNs contain neurons analogous to the biological neurons introduced earlier. *Figure 10* shows two schematics of ANNs.

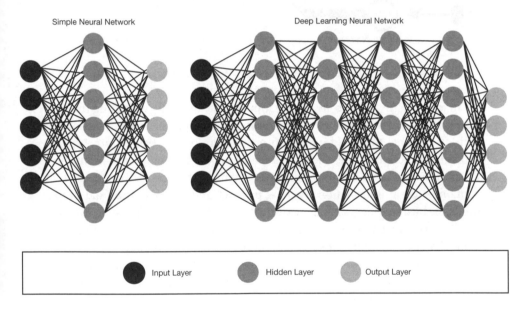

FIGURE 10: Simple and deep learning neural networks

One subset of ML is called deep learning (DL). In DL, the artificial neurons are ordinarily organized into multiple layers. Neurons of one layer interface with the neurons of the adjacent layers (see *Figure 10*). The layer that receives external information is the input layer, while the layer that produces the result is the output layer. All layers between the input layer and the output layer are called hidden layers, and the depth of a DL neural network is determined by the number of layers that are hidden. The layers can be associated with one another in numerous ways. For example, they can be completely associated, with each neuron in one layer interfacing with a neuron in another layer. When 'pooling' is used, a group of neurons in a one-layer interface is associated with a single neuron in a deeper layer, decreasing the number of neurons in that deeper layer. The way the neurons are connected to each other determines the topology of the network.

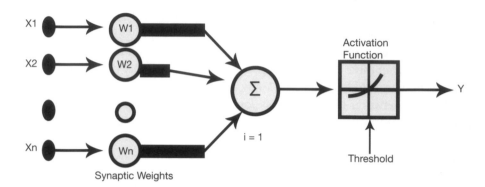

FIGURE 11: Simple neural network schematic

In a simple ANN, neurons receive inputs, scale them (by weighting the neural signals), combine them (simple addition) and apply an activation function with an optional threshold or bias to produce an output (see *Figure 11*). The activation function defines the output based on an input or a set of inputs, in a way not dissimilar to the neuron action potential in *Figure 8*. The inputs may contain external information, such as pictures and records. The final output fulfils the business task, such as answering a question about a picture. For technical reasons that will become clearer in *Chapter 5*, the activation function's main characteristic is that it should be smooth and differentiable.

In DL, each neuron is connected to another through synapses and each association has a designated weight that represents its relative importance. A neuron can have various input and output associations.[63] A simple function computes the input to a neuron from the outputs of its precursor neurons. These outputs may include weighted inputs from some or all of the neurons from the previous layer. As a result of the input propagating through further synapses, the weighted sum of neural signals and an activation function threshold can be accounted for in further computations.

Neurons can carry out more complex behaviour than just transforming input into output: they implement logic gates, incorporate some aspects of memory about previous computations, have a probabilistic element associated with their outputs, are noisy and so on. These give rise to an array of ANN topologies such as the following list (with some visually represented in *Figure 12*):

- Feed forward neural network (FFNN)
- Radial bias function (RBF) network
- Recurrent neural network (RNN)
- Long- and short-term memory network (LSTM)
- Gated recurrent unit (GRU)
- Bidirectional variants of the above three types (BiRNN, BiLSTM, BiGRU)
- Autoencoder (AE) and variational autoencoder (VAE)
- Denoising encoder (DE) and sparse encoder (SAE)
- Markov chain (MC) or discrete time Markov chain (DTMC)
- Hopfield network (HN) – where every neuron is connected to every other
- Boltzmann machine (BM) and restricted Boltzmann machine (RBM)
- Deep belief network (DBN)
- Convolutional neural network (CNN) and deep convolutional neural network (DCNN)
- Deconvolutional network (DN)
- Generative adversarial network (GAN)
- Liquid state machine (LSM)
- Extreme learning machine (ELM)
- Eco state network (ESN)
- Neural Turing machine (NTM)
- Capsule network (CapsNet)

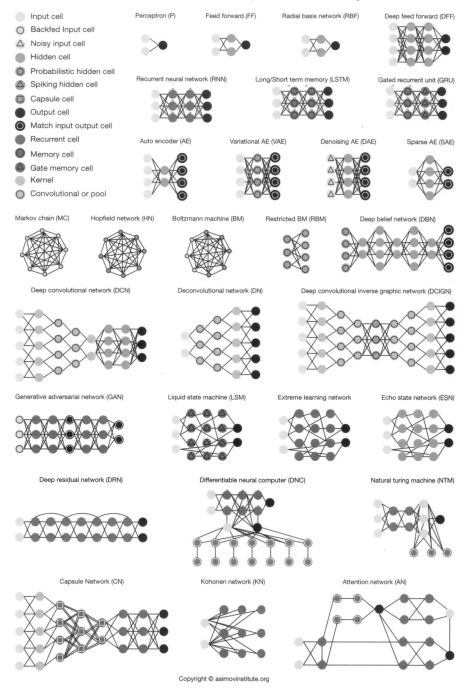

FIGURE 12: The Neural Network Zoo from the Asimov Institute[64]

We refer the reader to the Asimov Institute's Neural Network Zoo (see *Figure 12*) to explore these and other topologies. Readers can design their own topologies and see whether they might offer better solutions to some business problems. Although many of the topologies have names that hold promise, almost all of the features of natural neural networks are absent from such topologies at the moment. Despite this, even rudimentary and ridiculously simple topologies have proven their use in many business problems, which we will discuss later in this chapter.

With any of these topologies, some key parameters are set before the learning process starts. These are called 'hyperparameters' and their values are derived via learning. Some examples of hyperparameters include learning rate, the number of intermediary computation layers and batch size. The values of different hyperparameters can be interrelated.

For most people, machine intelligence is strange. The use of paradigms created by the movie industry is often not helpful (in that movies use artistic licence to pander to human prejudices, albeit this is sometimes exciting and thought provoking). So, whether it is via the evil HAL 9000 in *2001: A Space Odyssey*, *The Terminator*'s Skynet, Maria from *Metropolis*, Quorra in *Tron: Legacy*, David in *Prometheus*, Robby in *Forbidden Planet*, Ava in *Ex Machina* or Agent Smith in *The Matrix*, the writers and directors enable a conversation between technology and society. These films and many other projects, ideas and endpoints in terms of social, political, economic and ethical consequences pander to the human consciousness in terms of scenario simulation and alternative reality planning.

AI is in its infancy, but it has already amazed many people with its possibilities. Presently, we see AI as a simple matrix of algebra and calculus with which to handle data. As AI progresses to become more sophisticated and capable, society faces many issues around data security, provenance and ethics.

To help clarify the relationship between humans and AI, let us consider that AI can be better than humans where:

- Enough examples and training data are digitally available to remove ambiguity
- The solution to the problem is clear (enough labelled data is available) or it is possible to clearly define preferred states or long-term goals that should be achieved

Applications of different types of ANN topologies are covered in *Chapter 5*. In this chapter, we need to be able to classify different types of AI systems in terms of their relationship to human intelligence and capabilities, so we can articulate which of those human capabilities have been implemented in AI and which have yet to be researched and applied. One classification for such a comparison has four types of AI or AI-based systems:

- **Reactive machines** – Reactive machines are the oldest of all AI systems and have a shallow cognitive capability. They emulate the ability in nature to respond to different kinds of stimuli. These machines do not have any memory-based functionality. They cannot use information from the past to inform their present actions, which means they cannot learn and improve their operations. They are only used to autonomously respond to a limited set of inputs. A well-known illustration of a reactive AI machine is IBM's Deep Blue, which beat chess grandmaster Garry Kasparov in 1997.
- **Limited-memory machines** – Limited-memory machines build on a reactive machine's capabilities by learning from verifiable information to guide choices. All present-day AI frameworks, such as those that make use of learning, are prepared using expansive volumes of stored information to create a reference for understanding future issues and problems. For example, an image recognition AI uses thousands of images and image names to instruct the AI to identify the objects it is intended to recognize. When such an AI analyses an image, it uses the training images as references to understand the image's contents. Consequently, it can improve its accuracy as it works with new data. Most present-day AI applications, from chatbots and virtual assistants to self-driving vehicles, are driven by limited-memory machines.
- **AI with theory of mind** – The two types of AI mentioned above are increasingly common, while this one and the next are primarily considered conceptual models and works-in-progress. AI with theory of mind is the next level of AI systems research. An AI with theory of mind would incorporate and understand the entities it interacted with by discerning their needs, expressions and thought processes. The artificial emotional intelligence industry is growing daily. It has intrigued a range of prominent AI analysts, although the current conclusion is that AI theory of mind will need more innovations in understanding cognitive neuroscience. This is because to understand human needs accurately, AI machines will have to perceive humans as individuals (virtually 'understanding' humans) whose minds can be shaped by multiple factors. This is hugely predicated on putting humans at the front and centre of AI's application to add business value and emphasize the mind.
- **AI self-awareness** – Self-awareness is the last step in AI's development, and until recently it existed only hypothetically. This form of AI (when fully realized) will have evolved to be so like the human brain that it will have developed self-awareness. Creating such an AI will require significant research, although some of its central building blocks have already been established. For many, this is the ultimate objective of AI research. Self-aware AI will be able to understand and evoke emotions in those it interacts with and have emotions, needs, beliefs and potentially desires of its own. Once self-aware, AI will have self-determination, self-preservation and intentionality, which poses serious identity issues for humanity. Doomsayers would contend that

such an entity could easily outmanoeuvre any human intelligence and consequently pose an existential risk to the natural order of things.[65]

Our currently constrained machines are more capable in their own specialties (and hence, more valuable to humanity) than their biological 'ancestors' seem to have been (consider the horse versus train comparison from earlier in this chapter). It is easy to draw skewed conclusions about the conceivable outcomes of AI research by anthropomorphizing deep neural systems. Still, artificial and natural neurons do vary in more ways than we perhaps currently admit.

Increasingly, we see headlines such as "Wielding Rocks and Knives, Arizonans Attack Self-Driving Cars" and "Attacks Against AI Systems Are a Growing Concern."[66] There are even worries that people will devise AI systems to attack AI. Scholastic heavyweights such as Tim Berners-Lee and Stephen Hawking and industry titans such as Elon Musk and Bill Gates have all weighed in with their concerns about an AI transcending human control. Features such as "Elon Musk's Billion-Dollar Crusade to Stop the AI Apocalypse" in *Vanity Fair* do not offer a balanced debate, saying, "[Musk] thinks you should be frightened too. [This article looks] inside his efforts to influence the rapidly advancing field and its proponents, and to save humanity from machine-learning overlords."[67]

In this book we discuss ideas relating to general human and artificial intelligence, but we know that AI is already superior in several very specific tasks (see the examples in *Chapter 5*). As AI is already incorporating intentionality and adaptability into algorithms associated with cognition and decision-making, we cover some of the issues around the ethics of machines in *Chapter 4*.

TYPES OF MACHINE INTELLIGENCE

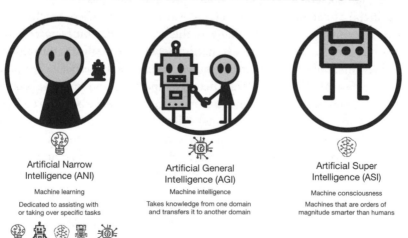

Artificial Narrow
Intelligence (ANI)

Machine learning

Dedicated to assisting with
or taking over specific tasks

Artificial General
Intelligence (AGI)

Machine intelligence

Takes knowledge from one domain
and transfers it to another domain

Artificial Super
Intelligence (ASI)

Machine consciousness

Machines that are orders of
magnitude smarter than humans

FIGURE 13: The three stages of AI

In addition to the different classifications of machines, some people argue that machine intelligence has three categories (as represented in *Figure 13*):

- **Artificial narrow intelligence (ANI)** – ANI is the only type of AI we have achieved. It is designed to perform narrow tasks, such as facial and image recognition; language, sound and speech recognition; language and document processing; and automation. Other examples include driverless cars, playing games (such as chess), process automation and optimizations, and recommendation engines, where in many cases AI can far exceed human capabilities. These algorithms need lots of data to train (often vastly more than a human would). ANI relies heavily on traditional data science techniques (statistics and logic), machine learning and deep learning.

- **Artificial general intelligence (AGI)** – AGI replicates human intelligence with the ability to solve any problem. Achieving this type of intelligence requires a machine intelligence to be indistinguishable from a human intelligence in all cases. This broad and holistic view of all aspects of human intelligence is referred to as generalized intelligence, and achieving AGI requires a machine to have similar characteristics to a human in terms of overall human consciousness. This may seem an impossible task to many as consciousness is not really understood in humans. However, as will become clear later in this chapter, this possibility may not be as nebulous as many people think. If consciousness can be achieved, it is easy to conceive that there will be a route to machines experimenting with code and possibly even requesting forms of action, such as activating sensors and motors. Later in this chapter, we briefly cover the neurobiology and neurophysiology of consciousness and contend that those features that make us human (consciousness and problem-solving) are possible for machines too.

- **Artificial super intelligence (ASI)** – ASI is a realm where machines surpass human intelligence and ability. In this scenario, machines possess forms of expression (akin to emotions, needs, beliefs and desires) and fulfilment (achievement of goals and directives). Machines will theoretically be millions of times faster in the speed of their neural connections and will solve problems better and faster (because of the response speed difference between biological systems and advanced ANN circuits). Also, the evolution of intelligence will not be governed by natural biological selection but by a multifaceted algorithmic evolution of hyperparameters (as explained above, hyperparameters are used to control the learning process in AI). The difference between AGI and ASI is that AGI assumes that humans are the pinnacle of intelligence and that no intelligence can supersede ours, whereas ASI sees further potential. This may sound rather fanciful as we are peculiarly suited to the environment in which we live and are not aware of comparable intelligences. A core distinction is perhaps that AGI serves humans while ASI could see the emergence of rivalry, as ASI machines would gain the concepts of purpose, intentionality and consciousness. The leap of intelligence between AGI and ASI would be huge, as it would involve the emergence of planning and machines being proactive rather just being reactive. Even the smaller jump between ANI and AGI seems remarkable; it is akin to the jump between inorganic earth and the emergence of the first reactive organic life forms.

MEASURING INTELLIGENCE

How does one measure intelligence? It might be determined by any of the following:

- Speed of operation
- Complexity of problems solved
- Adaptability to unfamiliar environments and scenarios
- Interoperability and cooperation
- Ability to affect the environment
- Ability to handle more diverse data

Generally speaking, measures of human intelligence tend to be oriented around intelligence quotients.[68] These tend to be derived using standardized tests that are age-dependent and oriented toward academic and logical problem-solving. To develop these tests, psychologists have researched human nature and the influences on and effects of intelligence.

The main objective of most intelligence tests performed around the world is to measure 'general intelligence' (see the section on Spearman above). Many intelligence tests are reliable (meaning that they yield consistent results over a long time) and have validity (meaning that they accurately calculate intelligence rather than something else). Many psychologists worldwide have put a great deal of effort into creating and improving intelligence measures. To understand intelligence, it is necessary to be aware of the norms and standards in a given population of people at a given age. The 'standardization' of a test requires that it must be updated regularly as the overall norms and intelligence in each population evolve.

The intelligence tests that most people encounter are aptitude tests. These are specially designed to measure a person's performance in a given task. However, it is also possible to measure the more generalized intelligence quotient (IQ). The most commonly used test for IQ is the Wechsler Adult Intelligence Scale (WAIS), which measures broad cognitive ability and intelligence, primarily in adults. This scale yields an IQ score across four domains: verbal, perceptual, working memory and processing speed. This test is reliable and valid, and it is correlated positively with other types of IQ tests. The WAIS also serves as an indicator of cognitive functioning among people with brain injuries and psychiatric illness.

EXPLAINING INTELLIGENCE

Presently, the differences between human and artificial intelligence are stark and sweeping. The numbers shown in *Table 2* for machines are changing rapidly whereas they are relatively static for humans. Moore's law states that computer speed doubles every 18 months, and this has been confirmed for the past 50 years.[69]

FEATURE	HUMAN	MACHINE (e.g. a current-generation HPE Cray EX supercomputer)
Weight	70 kg	c. 150,000 kg (excluding power generation grid)
Power consumption	80 W	10 MW
Number of neurons (cores)	86×10^9	0.5×10^6
Processing type	Massively parallel	Serial or sparsely parallel
Number of floating-point operations (FLOPS)	<1	0.2×10^{15}
Number of different types of sensors in host	Around 10	Hundreds
Number of sensors	Millions	Millions
Memory size	1 petabyte	Unlimited (24 petabytes in some standard configurations)
Memory type	Associative	Address based
Processing power	10^{18} ops (operations per second)	10^{16} ops
Volume of the brain or processors	1.3 litres	Millions of litres
Lifetime	c. 75 years	Unlimited, but usually superseded by new models within a few years
Time to become operational	Years	Minutes

FEATURE	HUMAN	MACHINE (e.g. a current-generation HPE Cray EX supercomputer)
Bias	Considerable: impossible to design out (or learn)	Embedded in data and policies
Main inputs	Data (through sensory mechanisms), embedded evolutionary connections and memes	Data and training data
Features and limitations	No transfer learning – the brain cannot be transplanted from one person to another	Transfer learning; also, inputs and outputs can be completely duplicated and transferred to different models
Material	Carbon (and other crucial elements)	Silicon (and other crucial elements)
Processor unit	Neurons	Transistors
Internal operating temperature	33–40°C	0 to 100°C
Speed of operation, i.e. seconds to switch between tasks (context switch)	0.5×10^{-3}	0.1×10^{-6}
Primary medium for internal signal transmission	Chemical and electrochemical	Electrical
Creation	Reproduction and natural selection	Scientists and engineers: created by humans for humans
Purpose	Exploration, discovery, survival and expression	Presently, to enable humans to achieve their aims
Time to get to the present state of maturity	Billions of years	c. 50 years
Downtime	Considerable: around 8 out of every 24 hours	Not necessary: only limited by engineering
Computational method	Analogue	Digital (binary)

TABLE 2: Human versus AI: specifications

It is worth elaborating on a few points in *Table 2*:

- **Size** – The human brain contains about 86 billion neurons with around 125 trillion synapses. The complexity and utility of this arrangement becomes obvious when one realizes that in AI, the number of neurons (cores) is typically less than 1,000. This should be distinguished from the number of cores in a supercomputer, which is typically around half a million at present.
- **Topology** – In AI the layers generally compute sequentially, while in natural neuronal nets all nodes compute asynchronously. This is not to say that computation in AI neural networks cannot be asynchronous for different layers if the requirement arises, but it is sequential in all the current topologies. Natural networks have neurons that fire asynchronously and in parallel, and they have a small-world nature with a small proportion of highly connected hubs and many lesser connected ones. Also, the different types of neurons and different neuronal structures are a source of great mystery and constitute an active field of neurophysiology, computational neuroscience and neurobiology. You may find it surprising that there are similar diagrams available for natural neuronal networks as the ones shown for AI topologies in *Figure 12*.[70]
- **Speed** – The fastest biological neurons can fire around 200 times per second, and the speed of the impulses is around 1–100 metres per second. In AI, the advent of highly optimized graphics processing units and optical processors has enabled some processes to take place at nearly the speed of light (300 million metres per second). Highly parallel architectures in hardware allow for breathtaking performance and it is reasonable to assume that signals in ANNs will be around a million times quicker than signals in a natural neural network.
- **Learning** – While research is advancing our understanding, many aspects of the way we learn and the way we store and recall information are largely unknown. We still do not understand how the brain learns or how redundant connections store and recall information. Learning involves making use of information in the brain as well as using it to inform information we can or want to learn. In AI, we start with a predefined model with a fixed number of neurons, and only the weights of the connections and the activation function thresholds can change during training – in essence, calibrating the hyperparameters of AI. This calibration or 'learning' will only instil the AI system with one of the many approximations in vast solution spaces. This multidimensional calibration, or AI learning, involves the use of tensor calculus to optimize weights and activation function thresholds, ultimately aiming to minimize the difference between observed and expected outputs. Democratized and pretrained algorithm exchanges (have a look at diffbot.com, for example) between AI developers offer some way

of trying to relate natural learning to artificial learning, in that these activities enable AI learning to build on the successes in optimization of past efforts. This can be thought of as analogous to researchers distilling years of scientific work into briefer texts that other experts can read and understand with much less time and effort.

- **Other aspects** – Factors such as fault tolerance, power consumption, signal processing, neuronal topologies and diverse neuronal microstructures deserve special mention too. There are many areas of research into the inner workings of the brain and the location and utility of conscious and subconscious memory. Fault tolerance in biological and neuronal structures is a unique feature of their topology, associated with how the functions of one region of the brain can be transferred to some degree to another when the need arises (e.g. due to an injury). The brain does not have one central part – that is, its functions are distributed to various parts.

WHAT IS CONSCIOUSNESS?

Machines (algorithms) can perform better than humans in an increasing number of fields. They can recognize sounds and visual imagery, process control machinery, and classify, cluster and make logical deductions better and more quickly than humans. Task-based performance is one thing, but what about the forces directing that performance? Many people argue about whether, as their capabilities advance, machines will come to have consciousness, purpose and intentionality.[71]

Consciousness is everything you experience. It is the love who jilted you, the unwavering addiction that you cannot quench, the tune stuck in your head, the sweetness of your first kiss, the bitterness of a feud with your peers or elders, the fierce love for your child, and potentially a sinking feeling toward the end of your life – perhaps everything was in vain.

The origin and nature of these experiences (sometimes referred to as 'qualia') are mysteries that many philosophers and scientists have argued and pondered over. Many scholars describe consciousness as a given entity and try to understand its connection to the world through science. Some scholars search for neural correlates of consciousness (NCCs), which are examples of minimal conscious experiences.[72] Other scholars focus on the functions of consciousness to try to find clues that would lead to hypotheses. For example, humans are able to create counterfactual representations – in other words, alternative scenarios – using generative models of the environment and the self. Such representations allow us to interact with previously stored data (memory) and to plan ahead through mental simulation of possible futures. This capacity invokes a range of cognitive phenomena, such as intention, imagination, planning, short-term memory, attention, curiosity and creativity.[73]

An important implication of this ability of consciousness to generate world views is that it leads scientists to move away from considering the brain as a passive and reactive information processor. Rather, consciousness is modelled as an active reconstruction of reality. This abstraction of consciousness as a generative process, beyond a mundane product of the brain, enables us to deepen our understanding of the relationship between consciousness and general intelligence. This view of consciousness as a generative process is hereafter referred to as the generation hypothesis.

To understand how consciousness itself may be an emergent property, we can more closely examine some common features of emergence. An emergent phenomenon has the following characteristics:

- **Novelty** – it has features not previously observed in systems
- **Coherence or relationship** – it is a coordinate whole that maintains its group dynamics over meaningful periods of time (i.e. groups emerge that have meaningful coexistence – a collaborating hunting community, for example)
- **Broad applicability** – there are broad components that become characterized by the emergent property (in the human case, the ability to write is a good example)
- **Evolution** – it is the product of a dynamic process
- **Ostensive** – it can be perceived

We might say that the mind is an emergent property of the brain. There are some aspects of behaviour and entities in societies and big cities that cannot be seen in a small village or an individual. These properties too can be considered emergent, and this hints at how much emergence shapes many of the significant features in our lives.

The systems engineering concept of emergence, the generation hypothesis and NCCs provide us with sufficient ways of experimenting with generalized intelligence. Additionally, the generation hypothesis enables us to implement and experiment with mechanisms for AI to generate alternative world views, as the generation hypothesis is a key to achieving overall AGI.

ABSTRACTING INTELLIGENCE INTO A PERIODIC TABLE

Given the complex aspects of intelligence and of AI's development, we propose an AI Periodic Table as a framework for organizing these concepts. There are many areas of technology and management where periodic tables are created to convey complex concepts to diverse audiences.[74] In these periodic tables, complex concepts are arranged in terms of elements and groups of elements.

The purpose of the AI Periodic Table is to educate, inform, engage and steer those involved in applying ML and AI. This conceptual resource enables a forward-looking narrative for business value (as an alternative to the often-used regressive narrative). This framework also helps us to make data alchemy a reality as opposed to conceptual magic, by organizing our toolkit so to speak. The AI Periodic Table can act as a go-to resource for best-of-breed options in creating AI solutions.

The underlying inspiration for the AI Periodic Table is human and natural intelligence. It articulates some of the complexity above in terms of cognition, intelligence and consciousness to enable the reader to visualize the end-to-end elements and groups that drive cognition and adaptation to an environment. The AI Periodic Table is an evolving resource and can be extended to include horizons where humans themselves become neurons in a larger entity (such as a smart megacity) with the emergence of new and unexpected abstractions and expressions. Even beyond that, we can imagine a collection of smart megacities where each one becomes a 'neuron' in a super-connected smart earth. The collective cognitive functions of earth would then enable it to become the fabled Gaia, which thus far has been seen more as a paradigm than as an actualized reality. Before getting too far ahead of ourselves in further abstractions and hypothetical iterations, let us restrict our flight of fancy and start with a basic version of the AI Periodic Table.

WHAT IS THE AI PERIODIC TABLE?

As described above, the AI Periodic Table is a collection of the essential elements required to achieve AGI. These include data, data security, data governance, engineering services (including programming languages, flexible ecosystems and frameworks, community resources, and software libraries, all of which are used to create solutions), environmental adaptation, and the evolutionary aspect of changing cognitive functional values.

The AI Periodic Table connects broader elements to more detailed implementation frameworks and specific technologies, including 'full-stack' DevOps (referring to a suite of DevOps tools that vertically integrate – as in a 'stack' – to enable broader capabilities)[75] and specific cloud frameworks.[76] Through the strategic use of combinations of these implementation frameworks, low-level functions and software development processes can lead to higher-level abstractions. This is akin to basic biochemistry enabling neurotransmitters to alter cognitive functions and drive adaptation, for example. The DevOps stack enables the implementation (at a basic programming level) of collaboration, cloud architectures, data-processing services (both their orchestration and automation), software systems configuration, monitoring, security services, continuous improvement, testing and delivery, and so on.[77] These are essential elements of building data pipelines and advancing them toward intelligence. That intelligence will come with iterations, evolving in response to the ever-changing environment. In the case of biological entities, that iterative intelligence is found in the activation of motor neurons and consequential real-world action, and it is about adapting in order to survive. In the case of AI, it is a data-enabled solution to a problem, using iterative intelligence that adapts in order to achieve optimization.

One of the points to note about our periodic table is that the elements are not really 'elemental' in the sense of the periodic table of chemical elements. In that case, the placement of the chemical elements is determined by electron configuration, atomic number and common chemical properties. In our case, the elements are very much technology dependent; this of course is changing very rapidly and consequently the names of the elements will change. Indeed, this is true of any of the other periodic tables that we have referenced. What does not need to change for the AI Periodic Table is the groups, as they are based on higher-level features of intelligent systems, related to features found in nature that have evolved over billions of years.

WHAT ARE THE GROUPS AND ELEMENTS OF THE AI PERIODIC TABLE?

The groups have been constructed in reference to human cognitive functions and how they are connected to the environment. This mapping between natural intelligence and AI was determined through the following components:

- **Sensations, sensors and perception** – These consist of sensory data sources and connections (e.g. connections in ML are provided by cloud and on-premises architectures; for humans these connections are provided by chemical and electrical signals between neurons).
- **Motor functions and coordination** – These involve the generation of actions from intelligence by interpreting both internal and external data. In the case of AI, these functions are actionable insights that can be implemented as automated system responses or as a data layer for humans to interpret and act on appropriately.
- **Memory** – This is a way of remembering past actions and their results, to improve future actions. In the AI Periodic Table, memory is represented as types of algorithmic parameters and storage architectures.
- **Language and speech** – The communication of information between independent natural intelligences has driven the formation and evolution of language and speech. Presently, AI communicates information based on the computer programming capabilities we use to develop AI, and everything in AI related to language and speech revolves around understanding natural language, sound and speech. Accordingly, a focal point of this component for AI is natural language processing and voice analytics. These areas of development can result in both speech semantics and voice sentiment recognition and application.

- **Intuition** – For natural entities, intuition is an abstraction of the best possible solution to a given problem based on experience. In the case of AI, intuition can be represented as the use of pretrained algorithms that solve specific problems in order to solve similar problems in another space. As a conceptual example, some aspects of employee retention intelligence could be applied to customer retention problems. Currently, AI does not have these capabilities in any robust sense, but companies are beginning to apply such abstractions using manifold mapping (see *Chapter 5*).
- **Consciousness and a clock** – This complex abstraction of environmental awareness and cognition by natural intelligence presents a significant challenge for AI, and there are a range of views as to whether AI will ever achieve this level of sentience. Currently, AI does not have these capabilities. In considering the possibilities, we need to look beyond current algorithms related to ML.
- **Learning and problem-solving** – Every creature with normal cognitive functioning has the ability to learn and solve problems. Without these features of intelligence, life simply cannot adapt to the changing environment. In the domain of data, people have been approaching this feature of AI by using simple data analytics and statistics to optimize solutions. As data becomes more pervasive, many problem-solving solutions will be driven by data alone using ML technologies. As AI development moves from mathematical approaches to statistical approaches and then to approaches predicated on data inputs alone, there will be an expansion of the types of problem that can be solved.
- **Identity and personality** – The determination of self and character is central to higher intelligence. Every type of algorithm can be uniquely identified, but that is primarily from the perspective of human curators. The idea of an algorithm having a sense of self and a character is a radically different prospect.
- **Evolutionary aspects** – In nature, evolution is primarily represented through natural selection. In AI, evolutionary aspects are in their infancy. The most advanced form of evolution in AI lies in the creation of genetic algorithms and adaptive hyperparameter optimization. (Hyperparameters are parameters that control how an algorithm learns, as discussed earlier in this chapter.)

Some of these aspects of general intelligence will be unknowns in the AI Periodic Table, because AI has not yet reached anywhere close to natural levels of intelligence. When AI does reach the stage of adapting to dynamic contexts, it will be through intelligent and democratized data exchange that enables data from different sources to be consumed in an integrated manner, allowing AI to proactively engage with the environment via data synthesis and hypothesis generation. For example, present-generation natural language generation (NLG) models, such as GPT-3 and Turing-NLG, enable automatic generation of natural language text based on contexts provided as inputs. This technology is beginning to get widespread use in cases such as automatic summaries of texts and semi-creative generation of new stories, poems and captions for images.

For AI mechanisms to achieve the many aspects of general intelligence, we need to concentrate on the various ways of connecting neurons into topologies of AI.[78] The fundamental aspects of natural intelligence are sensory data and the actions performed in response to that data. Much of this response involves aggregating multiple sensory inputs and responding to them in a proactive and contextualized manner. To appreciate the types of intelligence AI must provide, consider the complexity of how we use our natural senses.

Humans are traditionally recognized as having five types of sensor: visual, auditory, gustatory (taste), olfactory (smell) and somatosensory (touch). However, we can also detect other stimuli, and these sensory modalities include thermoception (temperature), proprioception (kinaesthetic), nociception (pain), equilibrioception (balance) and mechanoreception (vibration). The sensors in other creatures are different in their sensitivities. For example, some animals can sense electrical and magnetic fields, while others can detect currents and pressures. The meaning of 'sense' is a matter for discussion as it is such a varied phenomenon, and this creates trouble in characterizing precisely where the boundaries lie between reactions to related stimuli.

A sense could be a physiological capacity of living beings that gives information that allows a being to discern something. The senses, their operation, their classification and hypotheses about them are intersecting aspects considered by an assortment of fields of study, notably neuroscience and the philosophy of perception. The nervous system includes tactile nerves and sense organs. These points reinforce the lesson that the processes of collecting information are as crucial as the information one collects for understanding the extent to which AI has achieved AGI. Yet, there are obvious difficulties in drawing a parallel between AGI and human general intelligence.

What would an AI Periodic Table cover if it were representing human intelligence, in terms of specific groups and elements? It would need to include the brain, the sensory perceptions and perhaps a mechanism for enabling improvements in the brain. Beyond these functions, we would be into the respiratory, lymphatic, urinary and reproductive systems. The reproductive system gives us pause for thought as the context of an evolutionary aspect of AI. As a reminder, the evolutionary aspect of AI could take the form of hyperparameter optimization using an evolutionary approach to data. Or it could be an evolving neural network with competing algorithms that could test the network's own performance and have some heritability and mutations of traits between iterations, so that local optimizations did not necessarily lose the algorithm best suited to a task at hand.

Additionally, the security and integrity aspect of the brain requires consideration. Until recently, the issue did not even arise as it was believed that nobody could know what another person was thinking. To 'hack' into a brain is to fundamentally affect its purpose. We now know that we are vulnerable to hackers. Science and technology are already allowing marketers and devices to read people's thoughts and even plant new ones in the brain.[79, 80] Intelligent systems require protection, and AI systems can be made more secure than the human brain. This feature has to be a vital part of the AI Periodic Table. The AI Periodic Table must cover elements of AI (and all that term implies), data, security and mechanisms by which intelligence can evolve or be iteratively refined.

THE 14 GROUPS OF THE AI PERIODIC TABLE

The AI Periodic Table is organized as a set of groups with different properties. Each group contains specific elements that have similarities. We have come up with 14 distinct groups, as shown in *Figure 14*.

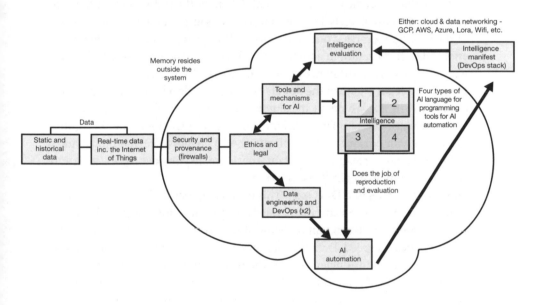

FIGURE 14: The 14 groups of the AI Periodic Table

There are 14 groups:

1. **Static and historical data** – This represents the central nature of data in any intelligence and in models. There are vast and expanding data sources, as described in *Chapter 4*.
2. **Real-time data, including the IoT** – This group embraces all data that has a real-time aspect to it. This might be data from in situ sensors (e.g. in farm fields, buildings and infrastructure) or from sensors within mobile networks and other data infrastructure.
3. **Security and provenance** – It is crucial for digital intelligence that data and its sources are unhackable. If data comes from unproven sources then any intelligence gained from it will have a dubious value. While the nonlinear human mind does not safeguard against being hacked (i.e. selective reinforcement of ideas by external parties), it handles its internal data with a bias toward its own evolving mental and value models. In other words, the human mind's map of its data and the value of that data are prone to change in a way that is predicated on the mental state of the individual. In the case of digital data, we need to be able to trace the origins of data and the history of the processing carried out on that data. This group contains elements that enable decentralization in a manner that is secure. The way decentralization works means that provenance of data comes as a by-product.
4. **Ethics and legal** – One of the key elements in the development of AGI concerns trust in AI. We detail these issues in *Chapter 6*. Corporate, national and international regulatory frameworks and principles are becoming increasingly important as the application of AI begins to extend to all areas of life and commerce. It is important, therefore, to consider the existing and emergent frameworks in the scope of AI.
5. **Data engineering and DevOps** – This is in its infancy and generally not well understood. When considering parallels with natural intelligence, the building of cognition is dependent on being able to recognize data and its parameters at scale and speed. Data democratization is a multifaceted problem. Just having the data is insufficient, as it is the relationships of data objects to each other that can enable appropriate intelligence to be gained. In addition, there are issues related to looking at data through different lenses to ensure that it is fully used. In the case of the human ear, for example, we know that the audio spectrum that it can analyse is limited and that there are sounds beyond that spectrum that can have useful information too. With data DevOps, issues such as parameterization, quality, curation, cataloguing, exchange, provenance, security and monetization are crucial in optimizing data's utility.
6. **AI automation** – AI automation, which we refer to as machine learning operations (MLOps), is a set of best practices to enable AI to be implemented and executed successfully. MLOps is fundamentally different from

mainstream DevOps. Mainstream DevOps is fundamentally intended to enable an iterative and agile view related to continuous software improvement, integration, deployment and product lifecycle monitoring (see *Chapter 7* for more on DevOps). MLOps is more nuanced around issues that face the productization and deployment of AI models. MLOps includes significant aspects related to the technicalities of ML: data collection, validation, labelling and versioning; server architectures and infrastructure (e.g. GPUs); data governance (including privacy, security, lineage); model versioning, model features (such as explainability) and model parameter versioning; etc.

7. **Ether: cloud and data networking**– This group of AI elements is analogous to the electrical connections and chemical signals between neurons in natural intelligence. In the case of AI, the pipelines for data and the methods of integrating them with MLOps, DevOps and user interfaces are provided by cloud and on-premises data storage and processing architectures.

8. **Intelligence manifest (DevOps stack) – User interface (UX) DevOps –** Aesthetics is a fundamental part of the way nature derives and consumes intelligence. This enables aesthetically pleasing entities to have a considerable evolutionary advantage. For AI, the same argument applies. The best results do not necessarily mean that an algorithm is going to be chosen for use; additionally, its value must be clear and appealing. Therefore, presently, there is a need in UX DevOps to align AI's functionality with human needs, both fundamentally and in a user-friendly appearance. The value is conveyed through the user-facing presentation layer. While the presentation layer for most business problems tends to be built using technologies such as Looker, Power BI, Qlik Sense or Tableau , there are many other technologies that can be used for AI-enabled UX DevOps.

9. **Intelligence evolution** – This, in natural and artificial intelligence, is environmental adaptation. There are mechanisms for enabling AI to take on a life of its own by becoming increasingly useful, including model validation, parameter tuning, model evolution and others. These mechanisms can affect whether humans use AI and how they interact with it, or they can use various bits of data to improve upon AI's prime directives (which could be similar to our own prime directives of survival, exploration, discovery, change and expression).

10. **Tools and mechanisms for AI** – This refers to any additional tools, frameworks and processes that relate to AI that are not captured in the AI Automation and Intelligence Evolution groups. So this can include aspects such as divergence of AI algorithms due to the different ecosystems in which the algorithms 'live'. This can mean that the same set of ethics and environmental constraints may not apply to one set of AI as they do for another AI. This group is for a generation of AI that is much more like natural intelligence with different species being differently dependent or connected to the environment and ecosystem.

11. – 14. **Four types of AI** – These cover the evolution of ML from traditional statistics to deep learning and machine learning to artificial general intelligence (AGI) to artificial super intelligence (ASI). They include aspects such as cognition, problem-solving, language and speech. Aspects of AI and ML that we are aware of but that remain unarticulated and unknown can just be represented as missing elements in the periodic table for now (i.e. they can be added when they are discovered). For the moment, we can include all of these undiscovered elements (related to AGI and ASI) as one element, labelled 'xx.'

These four AI groups can be broken down into elemental entities – specific data science approaches already discovered and also those that are undiscovered. The AI Periodic Table also covers aspects related to supervised and unsupervised learning, ML reinforcement and some elements alluded to in the discussions above related to intelligence, consciousness and problem-solving. What is clear from the discussions above around the natural neurons and their types, density and location is that we perhaps ought to consider generating a topological model for the collection of neurons and interfaces to data from other collections of neuronal structures to start building up levels of abstraction of cognition. So in essence neural structures, akin to those seen in nature, may form some aspects of the type of elements that enter the realm of the AGI and ASI groups.

Due to the fact that our understanding and traction related to the 'tools and mechanisms of AI' group is non-existent, we have chosen to replace it in the full AI periodic table with more primitive functions that we call 'languages and libraries for programming AI'. It acts as the basis for all programming at the moment:

Languages and libraries for programming AI – Development of AI and ML is dependent on a number of interrelated languages, libraries and frameworks that have developed over time. Currently, the major programming languages of choice for these resources are Java, Python, R and Scala. Software development frameworks in this domain include Apache MXNet, Keras, PyTorch and TensorFlow. The languages and libraries of AI development can almost be thought of as being akin to natural languages and information libraries.

With this background established, let us explore one iteration of an AI Periodic Table (see *Figure 15*).

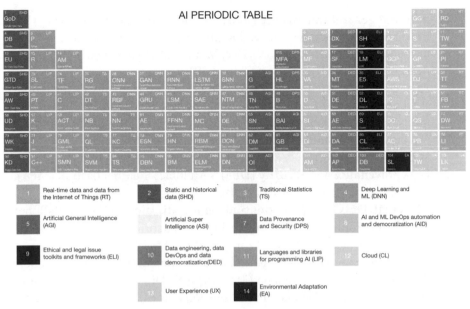

FIGURE 15: The AI Periodic Table

For each of the 14 groups, here is our selection of the 'elements':

1. **Static and historical data (SHD)** – Google Open Data (GOD), DBpedia (DB), EU Open Data Portal (EU), GitHub Open Data (GTD), Amazon Web Services Open Data (AW), UK Government Open Data (UD), Wikidata (WD) and Kaggle Data Sets (KD).

2. **Languages and libraries for programming AI (LIP)** – Python (P), R (R), Scikit-learn (SL), PyTorch (PT), Keras (K), Julia (J), C++ (C++), Apache MXNet (AM), TensorFlow (TF), Café (C), Azure Cognitive Toolkit (ACT), Google AutoML Framework (GML) and Amazon Web Services SageMaker Neo (SM).

3. **Traditional statistics (TS)** – Regression (RG), Decision tree (DT), Naive Bayesian (NB), Q-Learning (QL), Support vector machine (SVM), Nearest neighbours (NN), K-means clustering (KC) and Time series prediction (TS).

4. **Deep learning and machine learning (DNN)** – Convolutional neural network (CNN), Radial bias function network (RBF), Generative adversarial network (GAN), Gated recurrent unit (GRU), Autoencoder (AE), Echo state network (ESN), Deep belief network (DBN), Recurrent neural network (RNN), Liquid state machine (LSM), Feed forward neural network (FFNN), Hopfield network (HN), Boltzmann machine (BM), Long- and short-term memory network (LSTM), Sparse encoder (SAE), Markov chain (MC), Restricted Boltzmann machine (RBM), Extreme learning machine (ELM), Spiking neural network (SNN), Neural Turing machine (NTM), Denoising encoder (DE), Deep convolutional neural network (DCN) and Deconvolutional network (DN).

5. **Artificial general intelligence (AGI)** – GPT-3 (G), and Turing-NLG (TN). In addition, there are several vendors that are at the forefront in this field, including SingularityNET.io (SN), DeepMind (DM), OpenAI (OI), the Beijing Academy of AI (BAI) and Google Brain (GB).

6. **Artificial super intelligence (ASI)** – There are no elements in this group as we are unaware of any framework, algorithm, vendor or institution that meets the test for super intelligence. For us, there is little doubt that there will be a large number of elements here, and we represent them as a whole as Undiscovered (xx).

7. **Data provenance and security (DPS)** – Multifactor authentication (MFA), Hyperledger (HL) and Blockchain (B).

8. **AI and ML DevOps automation and democratization (AID)** – DataRobot (DR), Mind Foundry (MF), Vertex AI (VA), Databricks (D), Sensory Intelligence (SI), Dataiku (DI) and Azure AutoML (AM).

9. **Data engineering, data DevOps and data democratization (DED)** – Dawex (DX), SnowFlake (SF), Matillion (MT), DataEX (DE), Amazon Web Services Data Exchange (AE), Denodo (DA), Azure Purview (AP) and Databricks (DB).

10. **Ethical and legal toolkits and frameworks (ELI)** – SHAP (SH), LIME (LM), ELI5 (E5), DeepLift (DL), Skater (S) and ChatterBox Lab (CL).

11. **Cloud (CL)** – Microsoft Azure (AZ), Google Cloud Platform (GCP), Amazon Web Services (AWS), IBM Cloud (IC), Digital Ocean (DO) and Alibaba Cloud (AC).

12. **Environmental adaptation (EA)** – Seldon.io (SL).

13. **User experience (UX)** – ggplot (GG), Seaborn (S), geoplotlib (GP), D3JS (DJ), Tableau (T), Qlik Sense (QS), Power BI (PB), TensorWatch (TW) and Looker (LK).

14. **Real-time data and data from the IoT (RT)**– Reddit (RD), Twitter (TW), Pinterest (PI), TikTok (TT), Facebook (FB), data.world (DW) and LinkedIn (LI).

The AI Periodic Table gives us a way of forming a holistic view that includes an array of technologies, programming languages, frameworks, methods, tools and vendors. It enables us to understand the complexity of AI by relating the groups of the periodic table to natural systems (in terms of data acquisition, deriving intelligence from that data, determining its value and enabling software-based systems to be created that are cognizant of and adaptable to their environment). It can also point to aspects of problems that we may have missed – for example, often people write algorithms in a way that does not take parallels from nature and may consequently miss the importance of issues such as environmental adaptation, ethics, security or governance frameworks.

A good example to demonstrate the use of the AI Periodic Table in articulating data related issues is to consider the technologies, processes and frameworks that were necessary in our response to the COVID-19 pandemic. Many of the groups of the AI Periodic Table and a selected number of elements from each group were necessary in a concerted end-to-end response by the UK's data science and AI community.[81] Specifically:

- **RT and SHD Groups** – Google Open Data (GOD)[82] as well as Facebook (FB) Data for Good, and other data sources such as those involving Twitter (TW).
- **Data security and provenance (DPS)** – through the use of Hyperledger (HL) and Multifactor authentication (MFA) as well as Blockchain (BL) technology[83, 84] for COVID passporting, data provenance and vaccine distribution.
- **Data ethics (ELI)** – in terms of diversity and inclusion through better data analysis (SHAP and template-driven governance in data engineering tools).[85]
- **Data engineering and democratization (DED)**– by using data engineering to better share data across different technology stacks (e.g. use of Kaggle and various cloud platforms, such as Azure, to data share, and also the use of data pipelines, such as Databricks.)[86]
- **Traditional statistical analysis (TS)** – use of regression, classification and clustering as well as the use of DL neural nets to model the spread of the virus (R coefficient) and provide comparisons with historical flu data.[87]
- **Deep Learning Network (DNN)** for many aspects of COVID-19 data available. For example, the study[88] by researchers in China applied transfer learning on COVID-19 testing using CT images and demonstrated strong generalizability. Their proposed model provides an accuracy of 99.2% while detecting the COVID-19 cases.
- **User Experience (UX)** – The ability to consume results from data intelligence and enable human understanding of that data has been crucial. This may be for public information or for governmental policy discussions. An example is that of the Capita COVID Dashboard[89] – this provided real-time user experience (via Power BI, Twitter, Databricks and UK Government Open Data). This implementation made use of AI MLOps (Azure AutoML) as well as languages (Python) and frameworks (TensorFlow and PyTorch) to enable an agile continuous improvement and continuous integration of solutions that spanned data, ethics, governance, AI and UX. This all sat on top of frameworks enabled by cloud and cloud architectures.

One of the groups that is missing in the above argument is that of Environmental Adaptation (EA) and we have seen that we need to really look at the data yet again to build models for the evolving nature of the virus[90] and perhaps build intelligence to enable us to tackle it. Clearly, this will not be the only pandemic and we need to be better prepared for it with that data that has been collected and is being collected. The next chapter focuses on the foundation stones of AI: data, data engineering, data ethics and data security.

CHAPTER 4

DATA: SOURCES, COLLECTION AND ENGINEERING

Let us begin with some heretical statements to set the scene and appreciate the challenge facing us. Data is the legendary alchemical substance. It is the Philosophers' Stone. Without it, the universe would be empty. It is the elixir, nay the creator, of life as we know it. The reason for these very words is data; there would be no intelligence without it. As we have observed in the previous chapters, data is the *prima materia* (first matter) and the *anima mundi* (the world soul) – to quote Jake Poller on the alchemist Thomas Vaughan with a bit of literary licence, "the first matter of data is the very same with the first matter of all things."[91] People generally mean different things by the term 'data,' so it is incumbent on us to articulate what data is precisely, before we collectively elevate it to a god-like position and effectively worship it, subconsciously and naturally, with our hearts and souls.

Let's begin to understand data by looking at nature, considering the way natural intelligences consume data, the processes that are hardwired into the senses, the filtering that goes on, and the way the neural pathways connect to different cognitive structures to enable decisions and reactions based on learned experiences, memory and adaptations. In human-organized businesses, we face similar decisions about the data we need to sense and consume as are faced by natural intelligences. In the natural context, our senses and sensors have only changed gradually and are tuned to our prime directives (survival, exploration, discovery, change and expression). In the case of machine learning (ML), however, the intake and processing of data have changed an enormous amount in a relatively short time – consider the advent of mobile and connected devices, the generation of diverse business data that is sometimes for one-off use in a rapidly evolving business ecosystem, the ability to consume a broad array of data (some of which is not even related to the problems we need to solve in specific cases) and so on. We must think deeply about data, its lineage, its provenance and what it represents. When we divorce data from its context, we run into tricky problems relating to determining its taxonomy and its relationship to business objects. Contextualizing and objectifying data in nature is easy; in business, it can be difficult. It depends on engineers being able to form and preserve the connection between data and its context and ensure that those objects still exist. This is why many people and businesses get confused about the taxonomy, ontology and lineage of data, especially when all the senses are flooded, and most people end up with data swamps where everything is as clear as mud.

This chapter tackles definitions, concepts and processes around data and its various types (including big data and data from the IoT); the topics of security and privacy, and the ethical and legal issues necessary to make sure that the societal impacts of data use are in keeping with our collective social expectations; data engineering, including the taxonomy, topology and characterization of data; the mining (i.e. extraction), transportation and cleaning of data, including processes needed to get from raw data (our alchemical lead) to value-adding data (our alchemical gold); the use of social contributions to data systems (i.e. data democratization); and then finally the future directions we face to handle increasingly valuable data in our progressively more digital and virtual society.

DATA

WHAT IS DATA?

Data is a collection of information that is used to arrive at a particular decision. In public policy, data assumes the shape of facts and numbers. Computers generally process data in electronic form and store or transmit it according to users' needs. This is a relatively narrow definition and it revolves around digital data. More generally, data is known or assumed facts that form the basis of reasoning, calculations or decisions. This more expansive definition is more accurate and precise about the way information is perceived and used in nature. Analogue data can be a rich source of information, a catalyst for change and a way of driving value – just as much as digital data. Digital data, of course, is the only thing that AI currently consumes.

The most fundamental building block of digital data is a byte of binary digits. A byte represents an 8-bit integer from 0 to 255. This is the most basic digital data type we work with. All other data types require some inference on the part of the programmer or user. For instance, we need protocols simply to represent negative numbers – we agree that the first bit in the byte will represent a negative number (this is called 'two's complement'; when we work with two's complement, an 8-bit byte can represent any number from −128 to 127). For numbers outside the byte range, multiple bytes can be stacked. Characters are mappings of bytes to represent symbols of languages – for example, the UTF-8 character standard maps bytes to letters. Strings are a type of data made from sequences of characters. Floating-point numbers, a common data type used in a range of mathematical applications, are more complex to represent in comparison with characters and strings, and these decimal-carrying numbers require specifications such as the IEEE Standard for Floating Point Arithmetic (IEEE 754) to function. Hence, we see 'floating-point operations (FLOPS) per second' quoted as a performance metric for computation hardware; FLOPS are both a necessary and a limiting factor in computation.

These building blocks of data form more sophisticated data, and data is related to its context – it may be sensor data (including from IoT devices), application programming interface (API) data, images, videos, audio, written words, graphics in diverse formats and so on. All forms of data are based on the small number of types described above; what differentiates them is their context, how they are stored and collated, and how we view and interpret data relative to a specific problem (categorically versus regression, for instance).

Everything we know of is data in one form or another. A tree and an image of it are data; thunder and its manifestations are data; an event is data; emotions are data; feelings are data; even love is data. The perspective from which one experiences such data makes it subjective, but then subjective data is also data. Because so many of these things are subjective and have variability, we often do not see them as data. Remember, everything is data and data is everything. Metaphysical discussions aside, data can be collections of inputs, algorithms and their outputs. Often all three lumped together can (and increasingly will) be considered as data.

GROWTH OF DATA

Since we started scribbling on the walls of caves in our prehistory, we have been record-keeping. Before that, we collectively learned by trial and error, by natural selection, and by context, culture and nurturing. All data (knowledge and record-keeping) was kept in an analogue form (primarily paper, samples, artefacts, etc.). The human invention of digital technology changed that. It has been estimated by Professor Martin Hilbert that the collection of all data in 1986 comprised 2.6 exabytes, of which only 1% was digital.[92] By 2007, analogue data (paper, film, audio and videotapes, vinyl, etc.) accounted for 19 exabytes, while digital data accounted for 280 exabytes. We estimate that by the end of 2021, analogue data will account for less than 0.5% of all data. At the time of writing, the amount of data captured in a single year was around 74 zettabytes (a zettabyte is 1,024 exabytes).[93]

The explosion in the computational power available and the amount of data being generated by people, individually and collectively, have enabled the digital revolution, which is this book's central theme. More data has been created in the past few years than in the entire history of humankind (see *Figure 16*).[94] Consequently, an effective data strategy needs to be put in place to develop and deploy intelligent systems. Most people are trying to develop ML-based approaches as the primary solution for handling data (as discussed in the section related to the quaternion of issues around data in *Chapter 2*; see especially *Figure 5*).

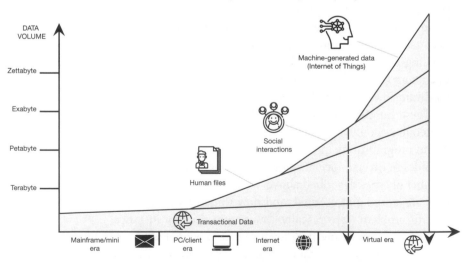

FIGURE 16: The growth of digital data from 1980 to 2020

Data begets data. Take, as an example, the new supercomputer announced for the Met Office in the UK in 2020 to replace the current supercomputer.[95] It will take 215 billion observations from all over the globe per day and carry out atmospheric modelling. The modelling process will produce more data, which needs to be structured and stored in the computer's 24 petabytes of memory before it is checked and used in other models. The current models used in this work are based on traditional numerical methods. Future models (which will implement the form of ML referred to as deep learning, or DL) will take even more data storage to execute. Much of the Met Office's data is consumed by various agencies and ends up supplying information consumers. These include aviation, transportation, farming, defence, communications, utilities, retail, health, media, research and educational establishments. Each of these takes the supercomputer's results (data) and runs their models to generate whatever they need: predictions of power generation demand, routing of flights and transport schedules, sales and logistics information, farming cycle plans and yield prediction, and so on. As consumers, the supercomputer enables us to plan whether we need to carry an umbrella when we go out. As data-logging and data-collection methods have become automated, their frequency and diversity have continued to change and the amount of data we can collect has kept on increasing.

To give you a feel for the enormity of data, in 2019 the World Economic Forum estimated that the following occurred every single day:

- 65 billion messages on WhatsApp
- 650 million Tweets
- 300 billion emails
- 150 billion spam emails
- 5 billion searches on search engines
- Four petabytes of data on Facebook
- Four terabytes of data from each network-connected car
- 800 million photos on Snapchat
- 6 billion YouTube video watches
- 11 billion photos taken
- 67 million photo posts on Instagram
- 18,000 new profiles created on LinkedIn[96]

Around 90% of all data that is currently being created is in the form of record-keeping and messaging. To put this in perspective, if all humans on earth jointly wanted to consume this information somehow, we would each need to read about 3,000 newspapers per day, and these newspapers would all need to be different from what anyone else was reading. It would be impossible to consume that amount of information. We ignore much of the information we get from people close to us, plus much information out there that might be of the utmost relevance. For a long time now, we have been inundated by new information, research, thoughts, and ways of thinking and handling data.

INFORMATION, KNOWLEDGE AND WISDOM

Let us consider some terms that have tremendous importance in natural intelligence.

The word 'information' has its etymology in the Latin word *informare*, which means 'to give form to the mind.'[97] The idea of information is considered to entail resolution of uncertainty, whereas data just represents those arts that help us to resolve a matter at hand. Concerning cognition and sensory data, information is any pattern that leads to constructing other patterns or their transformation to other patterns. Information, as the social scientist Gregory Bateson (1904–1980) suggested, is a "difference that makes a difference."[98] Information does not require consciousness. As an example, the path followed by a river is determined by the topology of the land and its hydrogeology. In another example, in information theory, we take an input sequence and map it to an output sequence.

There are words in human experience that extend the contents of data to information, then extend information to knowledge and knowledge to understanding. If raw data is symbols, then information is the interpretation that provides answers to 'who,' 'what,' 'where,' and 'when.' Knowledge provides answers to 'how' and understanding provides answers to 'why.' 'Wisdom' as a word has somewhat fallen out of vogue, but it conveys another property of data. It implies an evaluated, predictive and intuitive understanding.

Increasingly, most people do not make a distinction between these terms, and data is supposed to contain all those levels of abstraction. It is difficult, but not impossible, to understand the workings and abstractions that experience creates through the various cognitive processes.

DATA ENTROPY

Scientists and engineers generally focus on quantifying things and looking at relationships between causes and effects. Wouldn't it be good if we could measure the amount of data in data? That is quite a different question from 'What is the value of this data?' The value of data can have tangible and intangible measures, and this tells us something about our first question, 'What is the amount of data in data?' The answer to this question is generally termed 'information entropy' and has its roots in signal processing and data compression. Measuring the amount of data in data involves the ways data can be packaged into bits and bytes and the extent to which the data in question offers something unique that is not drowned out by noise. David MacKay states that:

Information theory and machine learning still belong together. Brains are the ultimate compression and communication systems as the tools used by both data compression and error-correcting are the same as used by machine learning.[99]

The driver behind information theory is that a low-probability event has a higher data value than a high-probability event. In nature, we are drowned out by noise. We are particularly tuned toward things that carry a high predictive value for us. However, when we look at the horizon, we are generally more aware of the more unusual and thus important changes compared to the things that remain the same. In an audio signal or a radio signal, we want to detect those things that are not just background noise.

Entropy is defined as:

$$\log_2(p)$$

In quantitative terms, entropy simply measures the number of bits required to represent data. Imagine a standard die. The probability of getting any of the six numbers is one in six. So, the entropy of the die is:

$$\log_2\left(\frac{1}{6}\right) = 2.585 \; bits$$

If the die were to roll such that, say, the number 6 came up only half as many times as expected, the surprise of seeing 6 come up would be:

$$\log_2\left(\frac{1}{12}\right) = 3.585 \; bits$$

So, the lower the probability of an event, the higher the importance of 'observing' that data.

The importance of entropy in AI cannot be overstated. Both cognition and information theory are about data. Many studies have been conducted to determine the relationship between cognition and data entropy. Claude Shannon points out that "the hardcore of information theory is, essentially, a branch of mathematics, a strictly deductive system," while induction is an essential aspect of science.[100] Information theory uses a quantitative approach while analyses of cognition tend to be qualitative.[101] The primary ideas of information theory are related to data in bulk, whereas cognition theory analyses the data in a single message. Although both theories talk about information and data, they deal with different kinds of data, which has made applying one theory to the other somewhat problematic. With the advancements in digital technology, the relationship between cognition and information theory has become relatively flexible. Over the past decade, formulations have been developed to apply information theory in the context of cognition theory and vice versa.

When we apply information theory to cognition, we are mostly interested in analysing information content results related to cognition but with a different yardstick than that used for data itself. The first problem is defining what we mean by 'cognition' in a measurable and quantifiable sense. It would be unjustifiable to indiscriminately use information theory in any context relating to standard communication theory. However, the justification for applying an investigative tool is based on the types of questions that can be answered using that tool. Information theory is a key tool for understanding a range of questions pertaining to data, cognition and AI; however, as it is a broad field, we only touch on its specifics as needed throughout this book. For readers interested in exploring the topic more, we note that the use of multivariate theory in the dynamics of neural ensembles is fascinating and hugely encouraging. Beyond any one theory, we increasingly see the need to use a combination of different quantitative properties of data to understand cognition. The implications for AI of advancements in these theories are considerable. The reader is generally referred to the *Journal of Computational Neuroscience* for inspiration in this field. We believe it will be crucial in the construction of AI consciousness and related next-generation intelligence.

TYPES OF DATA

Data can be qualitative (descriptive) or quantitative (measurable). Quantitative data can be discrete (such as the number of pets someone has) or continuous (such as a person's height). Qualitative data has three main categories: binomial (e.g. true/false, big/small, good/bad), unordered (just a record of each entity without any implied structure or order) and ordered (ordered in some way). From the perspective of data in engineering and algorithms, it is necessary to start with very primitive blocks (integers, real numbers, characters, strings and Boolean values) and build up structures that suit the context. The complexity of these structures will vary depending on the programming language, but in Python it is possible to use built-in structures (List, Dictionary, Tuple and Set) or create user-defined structures (Stack, Queue, Tree, Linked List, Graph and HashMap).

STRUCTURED, UNSTRUCTURED AND SEMI-STRUCTURED DATA

Structured data is generally highly organized and easily consumed in a programming language context. It is generally easy to search and manipulate structured data. Such data generally represents easily recognizable objects, entities and their relationships. The formats for this data include comma-separated values files (.CSV), XML files (which can be useful for hierarchical data) and Excel files (.XLSX). Much structured data tends to reside in relational databases, and Structured Query Language (SQL) is used to interrogate it.

Unstructured data is everything else. It is not organized using a predefined set of rules. This data may be generated by humans or machines, and it is generally stored in a non-relational database such as a NoSQL (not only SQL) database. Examples of unstructured data include video, pictures, sound and social media posts.

Semi-structured data is data that does not have a strict structural framework but does have a loose organizational framework. Semi-structured data includes text that is organized by subject or topic or fits into a hierarchical programming language that is open-ended, with each segment of text having no structure itself. Such data includes emails (e.g. sorted into sent mail, drafts and received mail), files (sorted into folders) and tweets (sorted using hashtags).

ANONYMIZED DATA

The intention of anonymization is privacy protection. Anonymized data is private and personal data that has been permanently modified such that the individual described by the data is no longer identifiable. Most people involved in data science are not able to see the data types of anonymized datasets, and many algorithms are created explicitly to only work on anonymized data, given the importance of anonymization in data governance (a topic elaborated on later in this chapter). Therefore, this category of data is of some importance, and the way it is stored and managed is procedurally different from how its precursors (i.e. private and personal analogue data) are handled.

The European Commission defines personal data as:

> Any information that relates to an identified or identifiable living individual. Different pieces of information, which collected together can lead to the identification of a particular person, also constitute personal data.

It also says:

> Data that has been de-identified, encrypted or pseudonymised but can be used to re-identify a person remains personal data and falls within the scope of the GDPR [General Data Protection Regulation].

> Data that has been rendered anonymous in such a way that the individual is not or no longer identifiable is no longer considered personal data. For data to be truly anonymised, the anonymisation must be irreversible [i.e. end-to-end encrypted].[102]

TRANSACTIONAL DATA

In data management, transactional data is used to record a particular transaction at a specific instant in time. In simple words, it is information acquired through transactions. It records a transfer or exchange between two parties. Transactional data includes the following types:

- **Financial** – orders, invoices, payments, dividends, sales, interest, purchases, etc.
- **Work** – plans, activity records, etc.
- **Logistics** – deliveries, storage records, travel records, etc.

WEB DATA

Web data is the most widely used and best-known source of big data today. Large corporations all over the world integrate customer-level data into their data analytics environment. In simple terms, web data is the detailed data collected from websites. Many organizations integrate detailed, customer-level data sourced from their websites into their organization-wide analytics environments, and this practice has been proven to provide previously untapped sources of corporate value. This data can be used in conjunction with all the other relevant information about customers.

Web data should not be confused with the concept of the data web – the interrelationships between subsets of data on the web. The main objective of a data web is to coordinate large clusters of data.

BIG DATA

Big data can be defined as an amount of data that will not practically fit into a standard database for analysis and processing. This data generally arises from the vast volumes of information that are created by human- and machine-generated processes.[103] Definitions of big data vary, but at the root of them all is the idea of a large, diverse dataset that includes structured, unstructured and semi-structured data, from diverse sources and in varying volumes. These datasets are so large and diverse that it is difficult, and undesirable, for traditional databases to capture, manage and process them at speed.

While the concept of large amounts of data goes back about 50 years, it was only in around 2005 that computer scientists started pondering the data that had begun to be generated by social media companies and mobile phones. This data was beyond what people had previously imagined. At the same time, non-relational forms of storage (such as NoSQL) were gaining considerable traction and other technologies were enhancing our capacity to work with big data. For example, with elastic scalability in cloud computing, clusters of data storage and processing capacity can be made available on the fly for engineers handling subsets of big data.

Big data can be more comprehensively understood through the six Vs, as depicted in *Figure 17*.

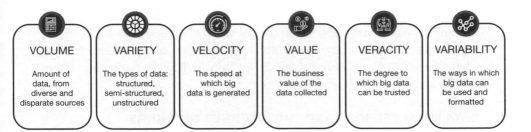

FIGURE 17: The six Vs of data

- **Volume** – With big data comes a large amount of low-density and unstructured data in need of further processing. This can include newsfeed searches on Facebook or Twitter, geospatial locations of people, or the internet searches of a community. This data can range from thousands of gigabytes to millions of petabytes, depending on the organization's relationship with the community.
- **Variety** – Big data comes in many different forms, including structured, semi-structured and unstructured. Traditional datasets were structured in a relational database. Unstructured datasets have become a necessary component of handling big data. Additional data processing is required with unstructured and semi-structured data to derive its significance and extract metadata.
- **Velocity** – This can be described as the speed with which data is received and processed. Data flowing into computer memory, without being written and read from permanent storage devices, has the fastest velocity. Immediate and rapid processing is sometimes required to respond to real-time events that generate big data.
- **Value** – This is the holy grail of big data. It refers to the ability to turn a flood of data into a tangible business asset.
- **Veracity** – This refers to the certainty, accuracy, availability and reliability of data. To provide a solution to big data problems, decision-makers must rely on their data's veracity, which can be absolute or uncertain.
- **Variability** – This refers to situations where the meaning of data is perpetually changing. In language processing, the generated data is constantly changing, and decision-makers must be aware of this. Microsoft's Turing-NLG and OpenAI's GPT-3 are prime examples. Words don't have static definitions, and their meaning can vary wildly in context.[104]

There is often a seventh V of big data included along with the aforementioned list –visualization. Businesses must be able to decipher and visualize what their big data is revealing. Visualizations can contain dozens of variables and parameters. Through principal component analysis, visualizations can be created that quickly enable presentations that are interactive, engaging and informative.

Impactful graphics are crucial in data storytelling and in effectively communicating analytical insights to create and demonstrate value. Among the many tools available for visualization, useful ones include Chart.js, D3.js, Fusion-Charts Suite XT, Google Charts, JavaScript InfoVis Toolkit, Nanocubes (from AT&T) and Power BI (from Microsoft).

DATA FROM SENSORS AND THE INTERNET OF THINGS

Data can be generated from dedicated sensors or embedded sensors built into smart devices as part of the IoT. As a broad source, this kind of data comes from devices that have sensory contact with things in the physical environment. Such sensory contact acts as an input and generates sensory data as an output; this data can then be fed as an input to any other device for processing. The importance of connected devices in the explosion of big data cannot be overestimated.

The IoT is a transformational technology as it can connect the internet to anything that can be connected. We are now in an era when data analytics, connectivity and automation are creating innovations that were previously out of reach. As the internet continues to gain a significant foothold in our lives, we will see the emergence of new IoT technologies and frameworks, such as Industry 4.0. The Global Standards Initiative on the Internet of Things defines the IoT as "a global infrastructure for the information society."[105] It is a complex network containing devices that link humans, animals and plants, which can interact without physical contact. These interconnected wireless systems are linked over a network, through which data from the various participants, sensors and processors can be shared.

The IoT is built upon the foundations of micro-electromechanical systems (MEMS), the internet, wireless technologies and microservices. It will affect every sphere of life as it will become the eyes and ears (senses everywhere) of intelligent systems related to infrastructure. Examples of how the IoT will transform our connections and everyday interactions include:

- **Smart manufacturing** – Manufacturing is a multi-trillion-dollar industry. This is an industry where robots transfer goods from one place to another and sensors track every action (e.g. metal-stamping machines in an auto-parts factory on an assembly line). Otherwise known as industrial manufacturing, this sector has seen exponential growth over the past few decades. Data collected from various processes can help to prevent unplanned downtime and/or predict supply needs based on sales forecasts. It can also be used to optimize maintenance logistics by using devices connected to the IoT and monitoring every aspect of operations.
- **Smart agriculture** – Farming and agriculture can reap significant benefits from IoT technologies. These technologies have helped farmers to increase their crop yields through better data management. Drone technology allows better and more frequent surveys of the land. Crop data sensors can monitor

crop growth and livestock. These advancements – coupled with aspects around data exchanges (whereby data from different devices and owners can be consumed in an appropriate model of governance and monetization) – come together to create what is known as 'precision farming.' These technologies will help farmers keep up with the rising demand for food.

- **Smart transport** – Smart vehicular systems will revolutionize transport systems. The introduction of driverless vehicles has set this phenomenon into motion. According to Gartner, driverless vehicles will represent approximately 25% of passenger vehicles in mature markets by 2030.[106] Driverless cars may initially have a steering wheel due to their design legacy and to allow for a 'machine override' option , but ultimately there will be no manual controls in cars at all. All conventional controls (e.g. gear systems, steering wheel, ignition, brakes and clutch) are being replaced by artificially intelligent systems capable of taking passengers to their desired destination through GPS, satellites and ML technologies. This impressive technology focuses on controlling cars and communication between other vehicles on the road. These vehicles communicate through internet-based technologies, which allow them to share their status and calculate routes.

- **Smart energy** – Electric power grids started to be operated in the 1890s, but they were highly centralized and isolated from one another. However, as the transmission network was extended in subsequent years, load-shifting technologies were employed to control power sourcing and distribution in order to strategically avert power outages or power generation shutdowns where those would be most costly or harmful. Many small power-generating units (such as windmills and solar energy parks) now generate electricity at varying capacities, depending on the conditions. Today, electrical distribution networks contain many more sources, as households themselves are also generating electricity; this necessitates adaptation of the grid and makes it difficult to manage the centralized system. Depending on system conditions, energy grid operators can decide which energy source is the cheapest in the moment and shut down coal- or fuel-based energy sources to avoid unnecessary power generation and cost. Similarly, smart meters, which currently bill the client based on their precise electricity usage, will decide the cheapest energy sources in the future through their network-connected sensors.

- **Smart wearables** – Wearable technology has tremendous potential as has long been promised by smartwatches, smart medical devices and virtual reality headsets. However, for a considerable amount of time, these products did not live up to the hype. The use of fitness trackers increased because they were simpler to develop and use. Now, technology has evolved to match the possibilities and create a new reality. The current generation of wearable devices comes with a longer battery life as well as increased functionality and new sensor capabilities. Wearable technology is now moving beyond the wristband into smart jewellery, clothing, tattoos and even implantable devices. Indeed, many of these devices can now be used in pets and wildlife to facilitate caretaking and conservation.

- **Smart homes** – A smart home is a modern residential system that contains lighting, security cameras, air-conditioners, TVs, entertainment devices and other technology. All these devices are interconnected and controlled remotely from any place in the world. A significant innovation in smart homes will be inventory management. This will allow home appliances to keep a record of essential items and automatically order them if the quantity reaches a minimum threshold. Also, entertainment and security devices will contact the relevant service provider in case of a fault or security breach within the smart home. Imagine smart rubbish bins that automatically notify rubbish collectors that your trash cans are full so they can pick them up on an as-needed basis.
- **Smart cities** – The smart city is an exciting application of the IoT. Smart homes can be connected across cities and interface with smart cities' IoT sensors and services. Consumers can draw several benefits from these technologies. Data from the IoT coupled with other big data enables performance to be optimized in many areas, such as streetlight efficiency, pollution control, automation of traffic movement, transport infrastructure, improved sustainability, etc.
- **Blockchain** – In conjunction with the IoT, blockchain technology can help with supply chain management. The distinctive feature of blockchain is that the technology allows for a fixed ledger for traceable transactions. This characteristic makes it ideal for use in several situations, such as in inventory management (as noted above) or in counterfeit mitigation, where the supply of currency needs to be traced. As an example of another application, it will be possible for a consumer to know which seed and which farm the food they are about to eat came from and under what conditions it was grown.

The point of the above list is that everything around us will become driven by data as we move toward smart adaptive systems. We will see the emergence of stem-IoT devices. In nature, stem cells are cells with the potential to develop into many different types of cells in the body. Their main function is as a repair system for the body, and there are several different types of stem cell (embryonic, adult and induced pluripotent).

We see stem-IoT devices being able to reconfigure themselves in response to the environment and even order their own upgrades and replacements through data-democratization platforms. In our view, they will do this in such a way as to develop their utility and system resilience in a manner that optimizes function and return on investment. The emergence of self-adapting IoT systems is already beginning to be mentioned in the literature.[107]

OPEN DATA

Data that is freely available without any restrictions relating to copyright, patents or other mechanisms regarding its use is called 'open data.'

In 2012, the Open Data Institute (theodi.org) was founded with the mission to show the importance of open data and create awareness of the creative use of open data, which can positively impact the world. Open data must have the following features to be workable:

- **Availability and access** – The data must be available to all and it must be possible to download it without any restrictions. Also, the cost of reproducing open data (i.e. copying, verifying and distribution) must be reasonable and must not work against any particular interest or industry.
- **Reuse and redistribution** – The data must have terms of use that enable other datasets to incorporate or redistribute it.
- **Universal participation** – There must be universal reuse and redistribution allowed for open data without discrimination against any particular user group. For instance, there cannot be barriers that would preclude commercial use or establish restrictions for specific sectors (e.g. education).

Another organization worth mentioning is the Open Knowledge Foundation (okfn.org), which advocates for open data and works closely with a project it started, the Comprehensive Knowledge Archive Network (CKAN) (ckan.org). CKAN is an open-source portal for open data. It helps users to access, manage and publish collections of open data.

Open data is a complex topic and cannot be covered fully in this book. It is worth noting that there are multiple problems with democratizing open datasets, including issues with data quality, cataloguing, lineage, taxonomy and ontology. Further information on open data is available from the organizations referred to above.

DATA GOVERNANCE

Data governance determines how an organization will handle data, with the aim of maximizing value and minimizing risk. As an organizational approach to handling data, data governance planning raises high-level questions about data quality, such as:

- What is the data handled by the organization?
- Where and when is that data collected, stored, processed and acted on?
- Who handles the data at its different stages?
- How will data be deemed acceptable, in terms of filtering for accuracy or other parameters of validity?

Data governance asks these questions and gathers answers from a broad range of stakeholders within, and sometimes beyond, the organization. The high-level nature of data governance is key to efficient and effective use of data throughout an organization's activities, given the risks of using standards and requirements inconsistently or omitting to use them at all. More specifically, data governance must address issues relating to data reliability, utility, compliance and security across all segments of an organization's data lifecycle.

Data governance must guide the organization through the quaternion of issues around data mentioned earlier – trust, cost, relevance and strategy (see *Chapter 2*, especially *Figure 5*). Data management and decision-making tools can help organizations to rise to the challenge of effective data governance. Data management can provide insight and processes to determine data quality needs, identify and organize key data assets and interfaces, and produce useful meta-data. AI can assist in data governance, as many problems in data governance arise from human shortcomings. It is possible to assess the validity and probability of success for different business processes – including data governance strategies – using AI techniques such as unsupervised learning (which will be introduced in *Chapter 5*). When implemented appropriately, these technologies can highlight where major processes fall short of requirements and can be a central guide for data governance development.

DATA SECURITY

Data security measures protect sensitive information, intellectual property rights and commercial interests from unknown sources that are not the primary creators or owners of the data. Data security methods include data encryption, tokenization, hashing, and management practices that protect data assets across diverse applications and platforms.

Data security arrangements need to be proportional to the nature of the data and the risks involved. Across the globe, various countries have enacted data protection laws that bar any state agency or private corporation from collecting users' data without their consent. Therefore, data related to personal information must be treated as sensitively as possible. In the UK, the Data Protection Act 2018 stipulates that personal details must only be accessible to relevant people. Personal data contains sensitive details such as home addresses, signatures and patient records. It may be digitalized or non-digitalized. Care must be taken to prevent its wrong usage, including by anonymizing data (as discussed earlier in this chapter).

Data security can be improved by:

- Segregating the data into multiple files in a way that makes it difficult to steal personal details – for instance, patients' sensitive records and their names must be kept in separate files

- Encrypting data containing personal information before it is stored or transmitted
- Following best practices in data storage security when data files are to be destroyed (e.g. overwriting data with noise multiple times)

PHYSICAL SECURITY
Physical security involves:

- Controlling access to buildings, rooms and cabinets where data, computers, media or hardcopy materials are held
- Controlling access to data archives or necessary hardware through logins and passwords
- Ensuring that data is not transported to any place outside the organization other than in exceptional circumstances – for instance, giving sensitive data sources to an untrusted technician for repair can pose serious data security threats

NETWORK SECURITY
Implementation of network security involves the following considerations:

- Sensitive data, such as that containing personal information, must not be stored on external computers connected to any open servers – the threat to personal safety is compounded when personal details are stored on a host computer
- Introduction of viruses and malicious code must be avoided through the use of firewall protection and security-related upgrades and patches to operating systems
- Computer systems must be locked with well-managed permissions and password systems
- Computer software must be up to date
- Line-interactive uninterruptible power supply systems and power surge protection should be used to keep servers operating as expected
- Password protection, encryption and controlled access to data files should be implemented using appropriate permissions settings – for example, setting files, folders and drives as 'no access,' 'read only,' 'read and write' or 'administrator only,' as appropriate
- Any person or entity with access to personal details must sign a nondisclosure agreement

DATA SECURITY AND CLOUD STORAGE
Certain cloud storage platforms (including Dropbox and Google Drive) store data in foreign jurisdictions that are not covered by the UK's Data Protection Act 2018 or its other privacy laws. Storing personal information on such cloud platforms

makes information more vulnerable to misuse. It is generally advised that personal details must not be stored on these cloud platforms to protect privacy.

Intellectual property and data of commercial value must not be stored on cloud platforms. It is generally said that data encryption protects data from misuse. This is true to some extent; however, encryption does not necessarily fulfil all of the requirements of data governance laws, such as the GDPR.[108]

Alternative systems must be set up to migrate and/or restore sensitive data in case of network breaches. File Transfer Protocol (FTP) or Secure File Transfer Protocol (SFTP) servers and secure content management systems should be set up in secure workspaces.

DATA ETHICS

When considering data use, it is not enough to ask 'Can we do this?' Instead, you must ask, '*Should* we do this?' There have been several high-profile controversies surrounding the use of data – most often concerning the use of personal data. These examples – which differ in their motives, purpose and impacts (including threats to human rights and a lack of transparency) – have been analysed in myriad other sources.[109] Here we want to consider the efforts needed to avoid such situations occurring in the first place. Managing data 'on the ground' in both the public sector and the private sector is not a trivial matter. Hence, organizations are increasingly making attempts to ensure their activities are compliant with data protection legislation and pressure from governments or citizens.

Almost every organization must handle data in some way. Most organizations just want to make sure they are obeying the law (i.e. in the UK, by adhering to the Data Protection Act 2018). However, today, when an organization – in any sector – is handling data for novel purposes or more complex technical applications, employees need to think beyond the law and consider ethics. The fundamental question for individuals and organizations using data in novel applications is how they consider ethics from day to day. It is not enough to say a company or government body strives to act ethically. The main question is: how does this translate into the organization's policies and objectives, and how do individuals, inside and outside the organization, perceive those ethics on the ground?

ETHICS ON THE GROUND

Ethics is not only what we are doing and why but also how we do things, and it involves continuous improvements and value assessments of what we have put in place. When considering potential negative impacts of data use, we may immediately conjure up ideas around purposefully nefarious applications, such as surveillance and manipulation of consumer behaviour. However, the need for ethical data collection and use is about much more than examples of that kind. If we recognize the broader context of data ethics, projects and new applications can be thought of in terms of practice and objective (see *Figure 18*).

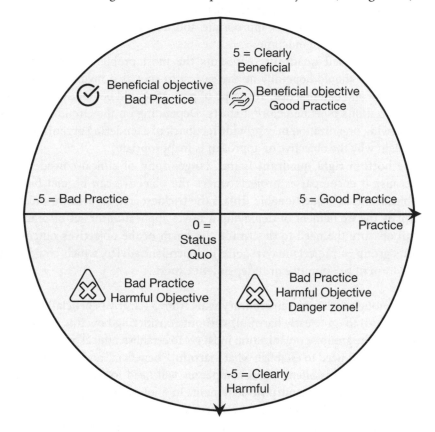

FIGURE 18: Measuring ethics

Figure 18 shows the ethical quadrants that all projects fall into, based on their data ethics in terms of objectives and practices:

1. Most organizations' projects fall into the **top right quadrant**. These organizations are actively pursuing products, goods and services that align with responsible business practices and sustainability. Their objectives are clearly defined and accepted as being beneficial. The practice used to deliver on these projects can vary and will be determined by the expertise present and the project's context.
2. The **top left quadrant** represents projects that have a beneficial outcome but use questionable approaches. These could include an absence of appropriate expertise, a rushed approach, or a lack of quality assurance or transparency. In substantial projects, there tend to be many opportunities for

team members and leaders to address problematic areas that are not being approached ethically or securely. Still, as data becomes more critical and the stakes become higher, there must be systems and procedures in place to ensure that a project is appropriate and uses data ethically in order to achieve its intended outcome.

3. The **bottom left quadrant** represents the most problematic set of projects but it should hopefully be the easiest to spot as it involves a harmful objective and bad practice. This type of project should be removed from an organization's pipeline before it starts. Depending on the circumstances, a reviewing organization may provide feedback to a tendering organization to explain why the objective or approach is inappropriate.

4. The **bottom right quadrant** is the 'danger zone' of ethical consideration because it encompasses projects where the objective can be met but the objective itself is questionable. This is the trickiest area to measure and control as the excitement of deploying a novel application or set of practices can obscure the need to determine the harm of the objective's outcomes. This group of projects may require independent advice, which could take the form of a committee or independent expert.

It is not enough to draw up an arbitrary scale from 5 (clearly beneficial) through 0 (status quo) to −5 (clearly harmful) without considering how this is assessed. This means the group or organization must try to establish ethical oversight of its project, and will need to establish what 'harmful', 'beneficial' and 'good practice' mean for them. This often means companies will need to work from a set of principles or values, or a purpose statement. In a lot of fields, good practice is generalizable, so seeking guidance from trusted sources is possible. To establish good practice for a holistic process, it is useful to draw up a framework of all the competencies typically needed when developing new uses of data (including service design, data analysis and ML skills, operational skills, legal skills, and policy development and implementation skills). Each competency will have its own role to play in ensuring responsible use of data. Establishing 'what good looks like' for each will allow for self-assessment within teams. This enables consideration of both objective and practice as distinct but interdependent variables.

Although consideration of ethics can appear inherently subjective, many societal norms are widely accepted, at least nationally, which means we have the opportunity to discuss what we think is acceptable. However, how we go about this is critical. Having a diverse and multidisciplinary team is key to any consideration of ethics. For exceptionally high-stakes projects, diversity of thought, background, gender and political stance will help to elucidate how an objective might be perceived by the public at large, thereby helping to determine whether it is 'ethical'. If there is not diversity within a team or organization, it will be necessary to seek it externally via non-governmental organizations, civil society bodies and community groups.

We can think about this more practically by considering two high-profile examples from recent years:

- **Use of the Northpointe algorithm for parole decisions in Florida** – In 2016, ProPublica analysed risk assessment software (powered by ML) known as COMPAS. Judges in Florida were using COMPAS to aid parole decisions. ProPublica showed the algorithm was biased against black defendants, falsely flagging them as future criminals and wrongly labelling them in this way at almost twice the rate as white defendants. In addition to having racist outputs, ultimately the algorithm didn't fulfil its objective of accurately predicting prisoners' risk. This application failed in its practice, leading to unethical outputs.[110]
- **Use of personal data on Facebook to develop political microtargeting** – In 2017, links between the infamous data-insight company Cambridge Analytica and multiple high-profile electoral votes, including the 2016 Brexit referendum and the US presidential election in the same year, were revealed by *The Guardian* and *The Observer*. Cambridge Analytica had used personal data from Facebook's users to develop a sophisticated ad-targeting methodology. The precise effectiveness of microtargeting is hard to measure empirically. Still, it is widely accepted that this instance affected some political votes and the use of Facebook user's data broke data protection law. In this case, the use of the data produced a satisfactory result – for those seeking to use the application to influence votes – but it is questionable whether this level of individual manipulation belongs in a healthy democracy. Cambridge Analytica has since been found to have obtained the data illegally, and the practice of microtargeting is still awash with ethical concerns. This application was effective in terms of its practice but had a potentially harmful objective.[111]

These examples help us to separate objectives (what purpose do we seek to achieve?) from practice (is a particular measure sufficient or suitable to achieve the given purpose?). Only after both of these aspects have been considered should we layer in the question of the ethicality of a project. This is fundamental when considering the appropriate use of people's data. We need to ask ourselves:

- Are the tasks undertaken suitable to achieve the objective?
- Are the tasks necessary to achieve the objective?
- Would the described use of data be considered appropriate by the entities that allowed its use in the first place?
- Would indirect or secondary uses of data be acceptable based on the original permission granted for the data use?

Importantly, none of these questions can be considered by a data specialist alone. A key component of ethical data use is ensuring multidisciplinary teams of experts are driving the methodology and potential solutions from the beginning. Product, policy, operations and service expertise need to be included, combined with data protection, information assurance and ML expertise to allow consideration of questions about the appropriate use of data to achieve a particular aim. For teams on the ground, deciding on the best course of action will require consideration of transparency, reproducibility, testing, appropriate measures, and ways of adapting and improving models.

For many uses, especially those in public service, it is very important to determine what is acceptable in terms of false negatives and false positives within the intended system. This has a direct impact on the type of model and metrics chosen. What the model is used for will determine the threshold for potential errors. Some false negatives or false positives can bring disastrous consequences, while others will simply waste resources.

For example, an ML model used to scan images to make a cancer diagnosis could have a higher tolerance for false positives (an indication that a patient has cancer when they do not). In contrast, a false negative (an indication that a patient does not have cancer when in fact they do) would be extremely detrimental to a patient. This means that the tolerance for the model outputs must be designed within a holistic process. In most cases, we would still want a human to have some sort of oversight of the assessment, ensuring automation is aiding decision-making rather than replacing it. In other applications, the stakes may be lower and a wholly automated process may be tolerable. The accuracy, reproducibility and continuous improvement of an application will help to determine the best approach.

The desired objective will determine the acceptable loss function (meaning how far an algorithm's output is from the correct intended value), the type of algorithm and the metrics used to gauge the results. As assessed by these attributes, the model's performance should be compared to a null model (i.e. a default value, as compared with the modelled value and intended value), a competing model or the current state of play. You must consider how you can explain the relevant options or decisions to the rest of your organization, users and society at large (to ensure accountability), depending on the application's scale.

AN ETHICAL CULTURE NOT ONLY *DOES* GOOD, IT *FEELS* GOOD

Ethics is not just good for outcomes – it's good for your workforce, clients and the public. Unethical behaviour can ruin reputations, deliver bad results, harm employee morale and decrease revenue. It can even increase regulatory costs. More importantly, it damages public and client trust in a business or government and, at worst, has direct negative impacts on citizens and their families.

When your organization is considering its practice, you will need a set of agreed values; otherwise, individuals will have nothing to work from. Therefore, it is helpful to have principles that lead to organizational norms and establish desired behaviours and expectations for new entrants. Individuals need to know what is expected of them before they can assess whether they are taking the right approach, as individuals and as part of a team.

Principles and norms often appear to point out the obvious, but how we interpret them is not always obvious. For example, a common starting point for ethical principles might include the statement 'do no harm.' Harm in most contexts is obvious – for example, don't develop a new use of data or technology that actively hurts people. However, what if the new technology is intended to be punitive and meet democratically elected governments' needs? People's subjective interpretation of harm and their political views might skew how they judge a certain objective. This is where ethics can become tricky in practice and why an organizational or governmental framework is useful. The framework must aim to provide actionable advice – that is, it should not simply say 'do no harm' but should also provide advice on what 'harm' specifically means in the particular context or how a team can minimize harm using generalizable standards and guidelines. An organization's principles or norms should flow from its purpose statement.

PURPOSE AND LEADERSHIP

Even with all the frameworks, measurements and quality assurance possible, if the leadership of an organization is intent on following questionable objectives, there is little hope of ethical outcomes on the ground. Conversely, if a purpose is noble and the leadership is fully bought into the objectives, with a clear understanding of how the objectives translate into their day-to-day work, this will permeate the whole organization.

This means ethics goes hand in hand with culture. Leaders must set the bar for what the organization plans to achieve. Moreover, individuals must feel empowered to speak openly, question and critique approaches. This will draw out useful feedback on whether what the organization is doing seems reasonable to most people. Commercial and security factors will prevent a wider discussion of many projects outside the organization, but this doesn't mean it's impossible to have rational processes in place to gain feedback. While most data ethics matters can be managed internally in a responsible organization, when designing a potentially contentious new use of data, user research or discussion with civil society and experts is key to determining whether the approach is suitable. Any good process for developing new technology will involve robust user research. This user research should help to elicit any potential fears from users, clients and citizens (as relevant).

DATA SOURCES

In nature, the data sources are the senses, the motor functions and the cognitive functions. They are all primary sources. More specifically:

- **Senses** – This data source is obvious. Data elicited through the senses can include all the data originating in the outside world. We perceive it in some way and then may choose to make use of it, or sort it and note it if our cognitive functions deem necessary.
- **Motor functions** – This data source is not so obvious as we generally think that our motor functions are outputs. However, our motor functions have feedback mechanisms. When we try lifting something, it may be too heavy, and that data about weight is derived from our motor functions.
- **Cognitive functions** – This data source consists of things we might traditionally class as information, intelligence, knowledge, creativity, wisdom, experiences, or innate or learned prejudices and biases.

When building artificially intelligent systems, the picture is a bit more convoluted. We are often not the masters of the data we get, and we have not quite mastered the art of iterative refinement and trust of data. We either need to find a way of collecting new data (primary data) or rely on others to provide us with it (secondary data). *Table 3* shows some examples of these two types.

	PRIMARY DATA	SECONDARY DATA
Sources	Research, surveys, observations, interviews, experiments, data from connected devices	Books, journals, articles, blogs, open data, web pages, commercial data, data from connected devices, customers
Pros	Authentic, reliable, focused, current, control	Cost, time, scale
Cons	Cost, time, complexity, scale	Reliability, accuracy, relevance, control, bias

TABLE 3: Primary versus secondary data

There are many ways of collecting and analysing data, and it is beyond the scope of this book to detail them all. There is also a lot of free data, but it can be challenging to find and use efficiently. One example is Google's Dataset Search tool (datasetsearch.research.google.com). This enables users to search through over 25 million publicly available datasets, and anyone can add their dataset (on a free or licensed basis). The tool enables searches to be conducted by type of data and usage license. Many agencies, institutions and enterprises also provide data that can be integrated into data science projects; this class of sources will become increasingly important in integrated models (i.e. models that combine multiple dimensions and sources of data and analysis to reach an output).

Table 4 provides a list of some free datasets, and there are many more examples. Data providers and data integrators often offer programmatic interfaces (e.g. API access) to enable access to their data. Finding data of any type is becoming easier and cheaper. There are, of course, datasets that will continue to be expensive and those that are impossible to collect now or are very costly. Historical datasets concerning farming and financial markets are prime examples in this category, as older records are either nonexistent or inaccessible. Nonetheless, the main point to remember is that it is no longer so valid as it was a few years ago to claim that there is a lack of data available to train diverse sets of cognitive models.

Dataset	Description	Website
Amazon Web Services Open Data	A huge resource of public data, including the 1000 Genomes Project (an attempt to build the most comprehensive database of human genetic information) and NASA's database of satellite imagery of Earth.	http://aws.amazon.com/datasets
Canada Open Data	Provides many of Canada's open datasets.	https://open.canada.ca/en/open-data
CIA World Factbook	Provides information on the history, population, economy, government, infrastructure and military of 267 countries.	https://www.cia.gov/the-world-factbook
DBpedia	Derived from Wikipedia and distributed under the same licensing terms as Wikipedia. Wikipedia is composed of millions of pieces of data, structured and unstructured, on every subject under the sun. DBpedia is an ambitious project to catalogue and create a public, freely distributable database allowing anyone to analyse this data.	https://www.dbpedia.org
European Union Open Data Portal	Based on data from EU institutions.	http://data.europa.eu/euodp/en/data
Facebook Graph	Although much of the information on users' Facebook profiles is private, a lot isn't. Facebook provides the Graph API as a way of querying the huge amount of information that its users are happy to share with the world (or haven't hidden because they haven't figured out how the privacy settings work).	https://developers.facebook.com/docs/graph-api
Gapminder	A compilation of data from sources including the World Health Organization and the World Bank, covering economic, medical and social statistics from around the world.	http://www.gapminder.org/data

Dataset	Description	Website
GitHub Open Data	Contains a huge amount of data on diverse topics as well as models and algorithms. Junar is a data-scraping service that also includes data feeds.	http://www.junar.com
Google Finance	Provides 40 years' worth of stock market data, updated in real time.	https://www.google.com/finance
Google Public Data	Provides a large range of data related to world development.	https://www.google.co.uk/publicdata/directory
Health Data	Contains 130 years of US healthcare data, including claim-level Medicare data, epidemiological information and population statistics.	https://www.healthdata.gov
National Climatic Data Centre	Houses an impressive collection of environmental, meteorological and climate data. The world's largest archive of weather data.	http://www.ncdc.noaa.gov/data-access/quick-links
NHS Digital	Provides datasets from the UK's National Health Service.	http://digital.nhs.uk
UK government	Data from the UK government, including the British National Bibliography.	http://data.gov.uk
UNICEF	Offers statistics about women and children worldwide.	https://www.unicef.org/reports
US Census Bureau	Provides a wealth of information on the lives of US citizens covering population data, geographical data and education.	http://www.census.gov/data.html
US government	In 2015, the US government pledged to make all government data freely available online. This site acts as a portal to information related to agriculture, climate, ecosystems, energy, local government, shipping, disasters, oceanography and much more.	http://data.gov
World Health Organization	Offers world hunger, health and disease statistics.	https://www.who.int/en
Wikidata	A free and open knowledge base that can be read and edited by humans and machines.	https://www.wikidata.org

TABLE 4: Examples of free datasets

DATA ENGINEERING

If an ML scientist is someone who looks at how different cognitive systems work, a data engineer is someone who designs how to get data from sensory inputs to cognitive functions. On this basis, a data engineer needs to be good at:

- Creating and maintaining data stores
- Creating and architecting distributed data systems

- Creating reliable connections and interfaces between pipelines
- Combining data sources
- Interfacing and collaborating with ML specialists to provide the right data solutions for them

While applications, tools and frameworks such as Databricks, Python, Scala and Spark are important, it is also important that data engineers understand how data architecture systems relate to the real world. Data engineers fit into one of the following three roles:

- A **pipeline specialist** determines how data gets to the people who consume it or provide it.
- A **database-centric** data engineer is capable of designing and populating databases. They are usually capable of carrying out extract–transform–load and other related activities.
- A **generalist** is someone who can do the whole process from end to end. They are familiar with how to acquire data and provide it to data analysts. They are often capable of building interfaces and dashboards that enable clients to see problems and understand the value of their data in the context of problem-solving applications.

DATA QUALITY

Data quality is becoming an increasingly important topic, for the reasons outlined in the discussion of data's value in *Chapter 2*. As data progressively becomes the new value exchange mechanism, we want to make sure that the goods are of the right quality. This is a difficult concept to unify, as users, consumers, data-exchange traders and custodians of data have different perspectives and requirements. All will have some view on the actual state of a given set of data versus its expected state. These views may relate to various dimensions of data: accuracy, consistency, availability, accessibility, completeness, credibility, relevance, validity, uniqueness and timeliness.

In organizations that collect a lot of data, there needs to be a delineation of the following to enable a framework for improvement to be set up:

- Data collected, uses of data and the purpose for which the original data was collected
- Roles and responsibilities of those trying to establish quality measures
- Rationale and results of using a data quality framework
- Action plan for quality improvement
- Metadata for the dataset(s)
- Any further data related to the data collected, including potential customers, requests and problems

The international standard for data quality is ISO 8000, and IQ International (www.iqint.org) is the go-to professional association for developers and researchers in the field.

When developing a framework, most assessment tools are deprecated quickly as customers' and users' requirements change so frequently. You might start off with good intentions to use a particular dataset that at the outset seems reasonable; however, as the applications making use of the dataset develop, it may quickly become apparent that it is necessary to integrate the data with other datasets. While the quality of the original dataset may have been adequate, it may no longer be delivering the expected value: the requirements and the algorithms have moved on.

Finally, there are increasing amounts of research and literature devoted to the quality of open data sources, such as DBpedia and Wikidata, as discussed briefly in the section on data sources and free datasets earlier in this chapter.

TAXONOMY, ONTOLOGY, META TAGS AND BUSINESS OBJECTS

Data must be collected and documented in a way that relates to business objects, in terms of data quality, structure, metadata requirements and other parameters. Care should be taken so that the parameters accurately reflect the nature of the data objects including contextual information. Some parameters will not sit well with the objects. These additional bits of information can be added to the object data as meta tags. Meta tags can contain information such as lineage, the types of processing already carried out on the data and whatever else is deemed necessary. To increase the usefulness of metadata, it should be standardized. Language, spelling and date format should be covered by the process of standardization. It is not easy to draw comparisons between different datasets if one standard differs from another.

A key component of metadata is the schema. The schemas designed for metadata define their complete framework, including what kind of metadata will be included and in what form. Schemas are of vital importance as they explain what can be expected within metadata. Moreover, they are commonly useful in dealing with simple standards such as dates, names and places. Discipline-specific schemas may be used when dealing with specific subjects. Meta tags are often useful in creating a dataset's taxonomy, but they have real implications for its ontology too. Some schemas can contain dynamic parameters (such as date of use) to conform with regulatory requirements.

Taxonomy, generally, is the science of classifying concepts and objects. There are established structures in natural sciences, business, computing, education, safety and other fields. A data taxonomy is a hierarchical structure that enables data to be separated into classes with common characteristics. For example, we could separate user-created artefacts into word-processed documents, spreadsheets, presentations and so on. The documents could be further divided into departmental categories or whatever is relevant. To ensure that these taxonomies work, there must be some enforcement and standardization within companies. These practices enable reuse and are efficient in data resource management. Most companies are not organized enough to create such taxonomies effectively in a way that endures.

As contextualization and personalization increasingly become essential through the growth of the semantic web (i.e. those parts of the World Wide Web that follow standards to ensure the contents are machine readable) and other interfaces with data consumers, data ontologies will become more and more critical. Ontological models enable the organization of structured and unstructured data through their entities, properties and relationships. These models enable discovery and searches of data relationships. Ontologies establish relationships between classes and attributes. While class hierarchies can be created manually, with the application of some intelligent models and the adoption of some meta-tagging rules, they can be established and validated automatically. With sufficient semantics (i.e. machine-readability of online content), we believe that the process of establishing business objects can be automated, and consequently so can the process of establishing hierarchies. This will then enable a powerful automated data contextualization method and the possibility of applying manifold mapping and learning techniques.

The key difference between data taxonomy and ontology should now be clear: taxonomies are static and one-dimensional while ontologies are dynamic. Ontologies also enable multidimensional relationships to be established between taxonomic objects. Ontological considerations are particularly important for user experiences, where the contextualized response can only be provided by multidimensional and dynamic relationships between taxonomic objects.

DATA WRANGLING AND PREPROCESSING

Data wrangling (also called data munging) is a process in which raw data is transformed into a clean dataset. Data gathered from different sources is generally not ready for analysis. Various steps need to be taken to convert the raw data into an appropriate, clean dataset as part of data engineering. These steps include data cleaning, data integration, data transformation and data reduction.

Data preprocessing goes beyond data wrangling, in that it involves extra steps to put acquired and cleaned data into the required form for a given application. Data preprocessing is of vital importance as most real-world data has issues with its formatting.

Mostly, real-world data is composed of the following varieties, all of which likely require both wrangling and preprocessing before being used in value-adding applications:

- **Missing data (inaccurate or incomplete data)** – Missing data is collected gradually, with frequent gaps in the data series. Such data also gives rise to technical issues with systems that rely on a complete data series (such as biometric data, which relies on having a complete record across a specific period).

- **Noisy data (erroneous data and outliers)** – Noisy data is collected due to issues with the technological instruments that collect data. It can also result from a human mistake during data entry.
- **Inconsistent data** – Data can be inconsistent due to issues such as duplication, human data entry errors, or mistakes in codes or names, including formatting inconsistencies.

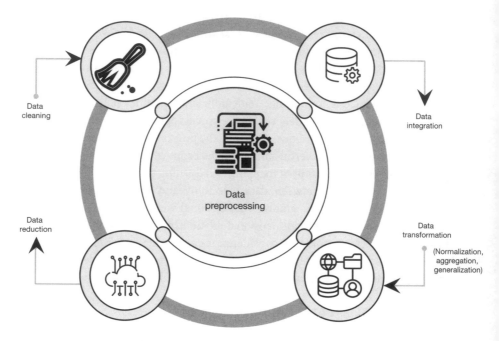

FIGURE 19: Tasks of data preprocessing

Data preprocessing (as shown in Figure 19) is carried out to remove the faults in unformatted real-world data, which we discussed above. Missing data can be handled in three ways:

1. **Ignore missing records** – This method is the easiest of all. However, it should not be performed if the number of missing values is large or if the pattern of data is related to the unrecognized primary root of the cause the missing values.
2. **Manually add missing values** – This method is among the most used. However, it has constraints when large amounts of data are being used, especially in cases when the missing values become important. In such situations, the use of this method is not considered appropriate.

3. **Add computed values** – To obtain missing values, averages or estimates can be calculated from the collected values. These may, for example, involve arithmetical calculations (such as interpolating in a rational manner as to what the most plausible value might have been). More advanced prediction of missing values can also be derived using an ML or DL algorithm. This method can give rise to biases among the computed values as they don't have the same origin as the collected values.

Data wrangling is used when manufacturing an interactive model or data application. Data wrangling enables the conversion of raw forms of data into something usable. The methods of data wrangling follow a range of instructions, often implementing a multistage procedure, including steps such as data extraction, sorting based on a defined set of rules, and then storing organized data in appropriately accessible files for further processing.

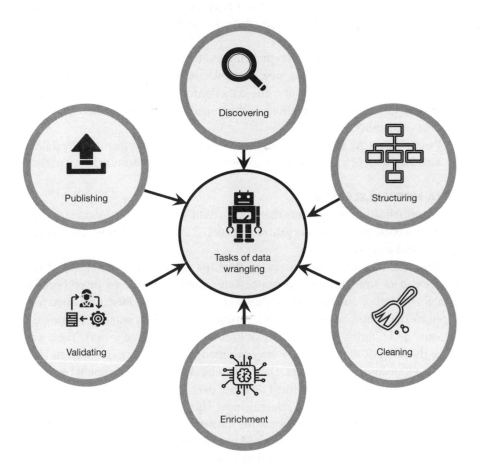

FIGURE 20: Tasks of data wrangling

The tasks of wrangling (as shown in *Figure 20*) are as follows:

- **Discovering** – Data managers must clearly define the context and intended purpose of data to decide on the appropriate method for working with it. For example, when weather data is analysed, the data uses are based on the data's spatial and temporal patterns, and those facts will guide the search and handling of weather data for a given application.
- **Structuring** – Data that is collected from various sources will carry the various features and standards of those sources. This creates a need for formatting to be done correctly so that the collected data can be put into a consistent and useful state.
- **Cleaning** – This process of cleaning of data is carried out to avoid inefficiencies when the data is later analysed. Data cleansing involves: the removal of duplicate or irrelevant data; the possible filtering and removing of outliers that are obviously erroneous; fixing structural flaws in data including missing values; validating the data and ensuring appropriate quality assurance is carried out on the data.
- **Enrichment** – To increase the efficiency and functionality of models and applications that will use the data, new elements are extracted or derived from it.
- **Validating** – This step ensures the data conforms with standards and rules needed for data transformations and application-specific verification of the data's suitability.
- **Publishing** – As all of the wrangling steps above are performed, the data is saved for later, in a manner that is consistent with uses of similar forms of data.

DATA NORMALIZATION

Data normalization is a process that allows data stored within a data structure (such as a database) to be reorganized in such a way that it can be used to run queries and analysis.

The data normalization process involves the achievement of key objectives. Whereas data wrangling and preprocessing apply similar steps more broadly, data normalization focuses these steps toward a specific aim. First, unwanted (e.g. duplicate) data must be removed from various datasets. This entails analysing the database and filtering out values (e.g. eliminating any redundancies). These can affect the analysis of data as they are unwanted. Second, there is a need to classify data into appropriate groups. Data that relates to each other should be stored together, and data that is dependent on other data should be stored in close proximity or with properly defined relationships. This process of data normalization creates a well-organized dataset ready for the intended analysis or processing.

Considering the state of big data today and how much of it is unstructured, data organization is of vital importance in restructuring and enabling analysis of unstructured data. This is done using data normalization tools.

Data normalization enables organizations to make effective use of the big data they collect. Big data that has not been normalized can fail to offer value to an organization, due to the increased burden of handling it in terms of volume, velocity (see *Figure 17*) and other factors. Data normalization is a key tool in overcoming fundamental challenges with big data (such as data storage), as it shrinks the storage space needed and creates opportunities to run analyses, even if they are only simple ones. This is only the beginning of the benefits of data normalization, as it can have more advanced uses in building efficiency and value for a given service or analysis.

It is worth noting the similarities between the processes here and processes found in the natural environment. A good example is data processing in the visual cortex. This is a marvel of nature. The neurons are organized by learned efficiencies, and rules are effectively embedded in the cortical architecture to filter and relate the vast amount of raw visual data we sense. The resulting output is a more compact yet functional visual dataset for our mind to use in various applications. Neurons become specialized for typical visual patterns and can self-organize to process these patterns more efficiently. Similar approaches in data engineering – where intelligence is embedded at the data-collection and recognition end of data engineering – are crucial for the future of data democratization. The visual cortex model suggests that it should be possible to create general high-performance systems for processing real-world data, using techniques such as advanced data normalization. Such an approach would begin to eliminate the complexity of creating convoluted artificial taxonomies and ontologies, as the pattern recognition system would end up with a level of recognition that is embedded in the data-collection (engineering) architecture, following the example of data processing by our very own eyes.

DATA PIPELINES

A data pipeline (diagrammatically shown in *Figure 21*) is a set of tools and activities for moving data from one system – with its own data storage method (source) and processing – to another system in which it can be stored and managed differently (sink). We can think of data pipelines in nature as visual, audio and other sensations that we are constantly streaming and on which we carry out various types of filtering and transformation, to make the data ready to be consumed (i.e. to gain knowledge and subsequently take action). A data pipeline may have the same source and sink.

Business data sources are diverse, and an effective pipeline allows for automatically wrangling data from many disparate sources, then preprocessing and normalizing it into one high-performing dataset in formats that are ready for consumption. Typically, the inputs will be in many different formats (e.g. CSV files, Extensible Markup Language (XML) files, email, databases or JavaScript Object Notation (JSON)) and the outputs will be in any desired format.

The operations in the pipeline (e.g. validating, filtering, transforming, and looking up and adding operations related to data governance) are determined by business use cases. Increasingly, these use cases are around ML.

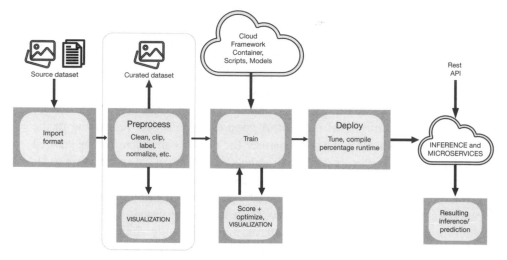

FIGURE 21: A data pipeline

Because pipeline operations are business dependent, companies generally end up building their own pipelines. There are various evolving technologies that are used in data pipeline workflows, storage, processing, maintenance and monitoring. Data pipeline toolkits and infrastructure systems are dependent on organization size and industry, data volumes, use cases for data, budget, governance and trust requirements. Increasingly, these technologies and tools provide for out-of-the-box connectors to enable code-free connection to diverse sources and sinks. Among the building blocks of data pipelines are:

- **ETL (extract–transform–load) tools**, including data preparation and data integration tools (e.g. Alooma, Apache Spark, AWS Glue, Informatica PowerCentre, Matillion, Stitch and Talend Open Studio).
- **Data warehouses**, which are central repositories for relational data that is transformed (processed) for a particular purpose. The main users are business analysts and the most common use case for data warehouses is business intelligence. Examples of warehouse tools include Amazon Redshift, Azure Synapse Analytics, Google BigQuery, Oracle and Snowflake.
- **Data lakes**, which provide storage for raw, structured and unstructured, and relational and non-relational data. This data can extend to petabytes in size and may be replicated from operational sources, including databases and software as a service (SaaS) platforms. Data lakes make unedited and unsummarized data available to any authorized users. They are mostly used

by data scientists for ML projects. Data lakes provide diverse interfaces, APIs, endpoints for loading and accessing data, sophisticated access control mechanisms, cataloguing and search mechanisms, and support for connections to analytics and governance engines. Data lakes can be built on top of cloud platforms (e.g. Amazon Web Services, Azure, Google Cloud Platform or IBM) or can be located on the premises.

- **Batch workflow schedulers** (e.g. Airflow, Azkaban, Luigi or Oozie), which allow users to programmatically specify workflows as tasks with dependencies between them, as well as automate and monitor these workflows.
- **Tools for processing streaming data** that is continuously generated by sources such as machinery sensors, IoT devices and transaction systems (e.g. Apache Spark, Flink, Kafka or Storm).
- **Programming languages** (e.g. Java, Python or Ruby) to define pipeline processes programmatically (i.e. using computer code).

SYNTHETIC DATA: GENERATION, USE AND LIMITATIONS

The lifeblood of AI is data. Collecting data and meeting the regulatory requirements related to ethics and privacy can be burdensome. Consequently, generating data that can be used to train ML algorithms sounds like the right step to take. However, generating this 'fake' data is not an easy task.

Nature handles problems around data by hardwiring various cognitive networks and establishing different brain regions to handle different data types so that each new generation inherits some embedded built-in training from its parents. To a large extent, the taxonomy of the data is well reflected in these cognitive structures. In contrast, in computing, algorithms have to start afresh every time with new data and new learning, or at least with a new design and adaptation of existing methods.

Synthetic data generation aims to make use of a small subset of real data and then mimic that set. When the synthetic dataset and the real dataset are indistinguishable, even by subject-matter experts, the synthetic dataset can be used to train ML algorithms. The advantages of using synthetic datasets are many and varied:

- They enable development and testing of algorithms
- They make data cheap to produce once it has been correctly tuned to the operational requirements
- They enable evaluation of new data as it comes in and determination of which sets are adding most value
- They allow us to discuss results with subject-matter experts and test various hypotheses
- They enable proof-of-value discussions to determine whether further expenditure is justified (on data or development)

Privacy and legal concerns around obtaining or using available data are often reasons why a data engineer might not have access to extensive real-world data. Anonymization of data to remove personally identifiable information (PII) is commonly required by internal policies and external regulators. In most cases, PII needs to be deleted (see the sections above on anonymized data and data ethics), and in such cases it may be that desired insights (e.g. about a group of people who are of interest to the client) simply cannot be derived. Consequently, anonymized data is quite often not as useful and it may even be entirely stripped of meaningful information. There are additional complexities relating to such data, of course. It may be possible for anonymized data to be deanonymized unless the engineering is done diligently and rigorously.

Good synthetic data engineering allows engineers to follow privacy guidelines while following processes that mean the synthetic data matches the original data's statistical properties. It can be difficult to strike a balance between the loss of important information and ensuring no privacy leakage. Privacy can also be mathematically guaranteed using techniques such as differential privacy. These techniques allow companies to access large datasets for research without breaching privacy and they also automate privacy processes via cloud-sharing communities across the globe.

There are at least two ways of generating synthetic data:

- **Neural networks** – While there are many methods of generating synthetic data using neural networks, generative adversarial networks (GANs) are increasingly becoming dominant. GANs have two neural networks that work in competition: one is a generator and the other a discriminator. During this process, eventually the generator overcomes the discriminator by creating data that is like reality.
- **Bayesian networks** – These networks use directed acyclic graphs that model the conditional probabilities of attributes and adequately represent the correlations between them.[112]

It should be noted that models used for synthetic data generation have security vulnerabilities, and the original data may be exposed. If an ML model is accessible to adversaries, private data can be uncovered through model inversion attacks. For example, if the attacker has all facial-recognition information, they can elicit the majority of the original data. However, differential privacy is a solution to this problem. If differential privacy is included in the generative model, it will enable data leakage to be quantified. However, it requires a trade-off between privacy preservation and the quality of the artificial data.

As models can be exposed and stolen, model inversion attacks[113] must be taken seriously. Given that AI is increasingly democratized and it is now easier to access the exact models that someone might be using, it is now a reality that model inversion attacks in white-box settings (i.e. where the model code itself is available) can be used to reconstruct training data from model parameters.[114] This is also possible even if only black-box access to the model (i.e. only the compiled application is available, without its source code) or the synthetic data itself is available to an attacker. Membership inference attacks can determine whether a given data point was part of the training dataset, even without assumptions about data distribution training. These attacks can be mitigated only to some extent by reducing the overfitting of the model (see *Chapter 5*), as overfitting parameters can enable attackers to more easily identify model idiosyncrasies, which are keys to model inversion attacks. This is because models that overfit give a lot of clues as to how they work.[115]

DATA DEMOCRATIZATION
AND DATA EXCHANGE

The most challenging component in the application of data alchemy is data itself. Data is often siloed, difficult to make sense of, and poorly collected and curated. In addition, much data comes from inefficient business processes and is of poor quality.

As the volume of data has increased and the consumers of that data have more commonly become intelligent systems, the need for automated data provenance has expanded. Not only that, but companies also need to democratize data through decentralization and have an appropriate framework for monetizing their data. This is a problem that several companies are now in a race to solve, and it will involve overcoming problems related to data democratization's scale and speed, and various issues related to trust.

The quaternion of issues around data (as explored in *Chapter 2*; see especially *Figure 5*) – that is, trust, relevance, cost and return on investment and strategy – constitute the next wave of revolutionary change in the use of data.

There are three aspects of the journey toward data democratization:

- **Data parameterization** – resolving issues around trust, relevance, cost and business strategy
- **Data monetization** – providing frameworks for data to be evaluated and shared appropriately, thus making data akin to a new currency
- **Data exchange** – enabling data to be discovered and used appropriately

There are exchanges that are appearing (such as Amazon Web Services Data Exchange, DataEX and Dawex) but the journey ahead will be long. This is due to the fact that issues around data parameterization involve disparate and conflicting interests. Also, the mechanisms for valuation and decentralized exchange mechanisms need international cooperation. Every big corporation faces similar problems with data and the value that can be extracted from it.

THE FUTURE OF DATA

The sensing devices (cameras, microphones, geolocators, etc.) of computers and smartphones are constantly gathering personal information. The coming years will bring the widespread adoption of new data-collection devices, such as smart speakers, implants, sensor-embedded clothing, smart cars and wearables. Avoiding engagement with such sensing devices is increasingly difficult, as sensing devices (such as security cameras with facial-recognition technology installed in public spaces) have become ubiquitous parts of society's infrastructure and norms. This future of data sensing is unfolding now, as digital assistants and internet-connected devices become more common in homes and public spaces.

As a society, we increasingly talk about improving outcomes in schools and making education less about the buildings and more about the students. Should we be collecting data through chatbots and other means (such as automated assessments) to ensure that we can improve resources and teaching? Is there a need for health insurance companies to track us through our social media and our wearables? What about chatbots that nudge us (either through messages or sensory devices) such that they improve us in a way that our partners cannot, or possibly alert various services if they detect behaviours that may indicate a risk of suicide?

As technology pushes the boundaries of what's possible with AI, there will be a need to reassess what is personal and what is not. We will also need to learn to make sense of personal data that is not even real, at least in that it did not come from humans – for example, algorithms that generate synthetic and fake data in order to train the next generation of proactive algorithms. Deepfake technology allows propagandists and hoaxers to leverage photos shared on social media to make videos depicting events that never happened but that can produce the same effects as if they had. AI can form faces that have no identity but appear real. Increasingly, as virtualization of humans takes place, we will assume personas that suit the context. Trying to discern whether a Tinder match or a person you follow on Instagram actually exists will become impossible.

Whether data is fabricated by computers or created by real people, one of the biggest concerns will be how it is analysed. Society's problems related to data and data monetization continue to grow, while governments and corporations lag in their data governance strategies. Indeed, the issues around data privacy are as crucial as the issues around democratizing some of that data. How many pandemics will it take to ensure that we share data that is crucial for the well-being of many at the expense of a few? It is now widely known that personal data is used by algorithms that can determine someone's health benefits or their probable next purchase. But those decisions can lead to unacceptable bias in a society that measures itself by rules and norms that keep evolving.

There is no doubt that there should be strict regulations around personal data. These rules should cover the monitoring of individuals in public and personal spaces through the use of biometrics and other sensors. The need for individuals to license (i.e. intentionally permit use of) or sell their data as they see fit is seen by some as a reasonable move forward (through appropriate models of decentralization). This raises many issues. Individuals' preferences change with time. Generation Z is perhaps more willing to share their private and personal lives than the previous generations. So, we are in a novel situation as the use of data evolves, but we have a variety of understandings, abilities and opinions between individuals, generations, cultures and nations. Indeed, there are nations that will not offer some of these protections and may end up leading some of the great innovations that may be possible in the efficient functioning of connected things.

The use of personal data for social engineering raises debates about models of democracy and the roles of businesses, dictators and media barons. The Cambridge Analytica scandal (see the section above on data ethics) and some of the practices around internet search tracking raise easy-to-understand points relevant to these debates. Complex practices related to nefarious activities at state level are perhaps the bigger unknowns in relation to freedom of thought and lawful expression – especially given that lawful expression will increasingly be determined by AI and some of that expression may be in virtual spaces.

The future of data lies in decentralization and democratization, with appropriate models for AI-mediated governance. The future must also lie in intelligent data, as humans cannot work at the pace that is required to handle big data in the arena of national security. We may start to restrict access to some personal data in specific cases, but there is no doubt that there are some benefits to be had for society in creating intelligence from personal data. Societies that can tread the fine line between privacy and public benefit will be hugely advantaged in their response to national and global problems.

CHAPTER 5

ARTIFICIAL LEARNING SYSTEMS

Before diving straight into what AI is, it is worth contemplating what we want to achieve from our digital data and recalling some analogue parallels in nature. These parallels enable us to develop some models and strategic directions for AI and ML. The purpose of intelligence and learning is that by interacting with the data there should be an improvement (survival, performance, accuracy, capacity, adaptation, dominance, etc.). The improvement should be observed in a learning environment. This chapter is about such cognitive processes and how to implement some of the very basic ones in digital machines.

We learn, we adapt, we flourish. The whole purpose of education is to enhance our abilities and to make the world a better place for us to live in. We are, by nature, implicitly and innately selfish.[116] Life itself is a paradigm of selfishness, a vector of selfishness. We look at the world around us, and there are things we know and things we do not know. We remember some past experiences. We learn from trial and error, from experimentation, through challenging our opponents and learning from their strategies, through deductive and inductive reasoning. Increasingly, we learn by using machines, by playing games and through virtualization. Indeed, there are aspects of learning that are innate and do not need to be taught. There are some hardwired primordial cognitive processes in nature that enable an organism to 'boot-up from its kernel': suckling of milk, crying to reflect a need, and the connection of neurons to experience the environment. There is hardwiring in our senses, and there are some memes we pick up while still in the womb.

We process the information we get in a variety of ways, and those ways reflect aspects of natural intelligence, as discussed in *Chapter 3* (naturalistic, intrapersonal, interpersonal, logical–mathematical, visual–spatial, bodily–kinaesthetic, verbal–linguistic, existential, and musical). These words related to natural intelligence are imbued with context and meaning and are not mutually exclusive. An excellent way to think about what we want machines to do is to look at what we do and the processes we go through to make those decisions and choices. Most of the decisions that we make are not deterministic – given the same data and same context, we would probably make different decisions at different times in our lives. As we briefly touched on in *Chapter 3*, the cognitive systems that enable us to do all this are conceptually simple, but there are many detailed aspects that we do not understand.[117] The desire of humanity to collectively understand the nature of the universe, along with the limitations of a human lifespan, allows for a dynamic and evolving approach to environmental adaptation. That is the challenge of this chapter – to build a learning and value system that has similarities with naturally inspired learning systems. As evident in *Chapter 3*, even though the cognitive system is capable of gaining various experiences (relating to the senses, processing information, and reacting to the environment meaningfully), we have not yet considered an overall integration of those experiences.[118] We can talk about models of consciousness and how they can be implemented, but there remains a hard problem related to intentionality – the missing piece is understanding 'wanting to live' or 'the reason for being.'[119] The point is that, as we begin to create machines that outdo us in tasks that only we could previously perform, we need to understand what this means for us as humans.

After providing a brief history of data science, this chapter tackles the deep learning (DL) aspect of ML. Not surprisingly, most people tend to confuse the terms and use them interchangeably. It is crucial to be able to distinguish them and use them appropriately.

OVERVIEW OF MACHINE LEARNING

A BRIEF HISTORY OF MACHINE LEARNING

ML is a relatively new concept and is linked to researchers' work in fields such as mathematical logic, statistics, neurobiology and cognitive science, computer science, and electrical engineering. It was established in 1956 as an academic field. As in many fields, military and nationalistic factors have been the primary motivations for some key projects and research funding. The Second World War provided an impetus for several digital technologies, and, against this backdrop, humans endeavoured to translate their natural experiences into ML algorithms. The resulting advances were in fields such as electronics, automation, control systems, communication (and some aspects of information entropy) and general systems engineering.

As an example, consider the work of the mathematician Norbert Wiener. In 1940, he worked with engineers to develop an automatic rangefinder for anti-aircraft guns. Such systems need to be able to use past histories to make improvements. Scientists who are familiar with human feedback mechanisms should be able to incorporate previously recorded data and, in some cases, account for their own inherent instability. Wiener and his colleagues realized that there were similarities between the human brain and their intelligent system. They worked to establish cybernetics.

One of the first documented mentions of artificial neural networks (ANNs) was by Warren McCulloch and Walter Pitts in 1943.[120] Their work inspired Marvin Minsky, who in 1951 built the first neural network machine, the Stochastic Neural Analog Reinforcement Calculator (SNARC). The second half of the 20th century saw Minsky become one of the great exponents of the field.[121]

Alan Turing and John von Neumann were active in the field of binary logic in the 1950s.[122] At that time, Turing dared to predict that "in about 50 years time it will be possible to programme computers ... to make them play the imitation game so well that an average interrogator will not have more than 70 per cent chance of making the right identification after five minutes of questioning ... [and] one will be able to speak of machines thinking without expecting to be contradicted."[123]

Turing's theory showed that any form of computation could be described digitally. He also proposed what became known as the Turing test to gauge machines' intelligence and empirically prove whether a machine could think like a human. The empirical evidence and ongoing research agreed on the possibility that intelligent machines could make decisions on their own.

AI was gaining momentum in the mid-1950s. Scientists were developing models to calculate, store and process numbers through machines. Their initial successes suggested that if these machines could manipulate numbers, they could also process symbols linked to how human cognition works. These ideas led to the development of machine intelligence.

In 1956, Allen Newell, Herbert A. Simon and Cliff Shaw created the Logic Theorist program.[124] The program would eventually prove several theorems in Bertrand Russell and Alfred North Whitehead's *Principia Mathematica*. Simon posited the idea that things composed of matter can think and have developmental faculties. He was venerated for solving the mind–body problem and argued that computers could develop the capacity to think.

The Dartmouth Summer Research Project on Artificial Intelligence of 1956 marked the formal birth of AI and was organized by Minsky, among others.[125] The programs developed in the years after the Dartmouth workshop were to most people, simply astonishing. Computers were slowly creeping into every field of life. They were used to generate mathematical models, predict meteorological events, and prove mathematical theorems. It was the start of a new 'enlightenment.' Scientists were sure that they would be able to develop intelligent electronic systems within the next 20 years. Government agencies, such as the Defence Advanced Research Projects Agency (DARPA), were pouring money into the new field.

In 1967, Minsky predicted that "within a generation, the problem of creating 'AI' will be substantially solved."[126] Those were rather unfortunate words as the tide was turning and AI was about to face its first dark age, which lasted from 1973 to 1980. The reasons for this were many. In 1967, an attempt to achieve machine translation failed. Then, in 1970, a move in the direction of connectionism (the ability of ANNs to explain cognition) failed due to a lack of computational power and memory at the time. On top of this, Lord Lighthill produced a report in 1973 for the Science Research Council that argued against the possibilities of AI and essentially emboldened European research centres, as well as DARPA, to end much of the funding for research in the area.[127] The metaphor for taking inspiration from nature was challenged. People argued that a plane does not flap its wings like a bird and that relating biological neurons to artificial neurons was equally invalid.

During the 1980s, however, AI boomed as expert systems became popular. An expert system is divided into two subsystems: a knowledge base and an inference engine. The knowledge base represents facts and rules. The inference engine generates new facts by applying existing knowledge to existing data. Inference engines can also have explanation and debugging abilities. They became popular primarily due to the advent of the first microprocessors at the end of the 1970s. Also in the 1980s, the Japanese were heavily funding their researchers' AI initiatives and accelerating toward the development of fifth-generation computers. Another encouraging event in the early 1980s was the revival of connectionism through the work of John Hopfield. Around the same time, Geoffrey Hinton popularized a method for training neural networks called 'backpropagation.'

ANN technology rose to prominence in the 1980s. Research into metal oxide semiconductors (MOS), in the shape of complementary MOS technology, aided the invention of new ANN technology. However, by 1988 there had been a drop in spending on new AI by the Strategic Computing Initiative (in the United States) due to the collapse of the market for the Lisp language and the emergence of traditional computing architectures from IBM. In 1987, AI entered a new winter, which lasted until 1993. The reasons were that personal computers attracted talent from AI, as well as the complexity of algorithms created by architectures due to the memory requirements and developments in the older operating systems [HB1]. The increasing power of the new computers and their versatility meant that machines explicitly designed for Lisp disappeared almost overnight. A decade after its launch in 1981, Japan had yet to complete its fifth-generation project due to these issues. It wasn't until the 1990s that neural networks began to appear on the horizon. These programs were employed in optical and speech recognition in smartphones and engineering devices. On 11 May 1997, Deep Blue became the first computer chess-playing system to beat a reigning world chess champion, Garry Kasparov. The event was broadcasted over the internet and received over 74 million hits.[128]

In 2005, a Stanford robot won its developers the DARPA Grand Challenge by driving autonomously for 131 miles (unrehearsed) along a desert trail.[129] In 2007, a team from Carnegie Mellon University won the DARPA Urban Challenge by creating a vehicle that autonomously navigated 55 miles in an urban environment while avoiding traffic hazards and adhering to all traffic laws[130].

These successes were not due to some revolutionary new paradigm; rather, they resulted mostly from the tedious application of engineering skills and the tremendous increase in computer speed and capacity that had been achieved by the 1990s. This dramatic increase is measured by Moore's law,[131] which predicts that the speed and memory capacity of computers doubles every 18 months. Transistor counts (based on MOS technology) were doubling every two years. The fundamental issue of 'raw computer power' was finally being solved.

Researchers from every field were trying to develop models to solve problems of daily life. Mathematicians, economists, engineers and researchers all made progress in their respective fields, with the result that AI became a small part of an immense superstructure. AI solved several problems. It opened avenues for new fields in computer sciences, such as data mining, industrial robotics, logistics, speech recognition and medical diagnosis.

However, the field of AI received little or no credit for its successes in the 1990s and early 2000s. These successes were gauged using the same yardstick that was used to evaluate such innovations in other fields. The research work published in the 1990s was mostly labelled as anything other than AI. Scholars were publishing their results under titles such as 'computational intelligence', 'cognition' and 'knowledge-based systems.' It was believed that many researchers were doing this to show that their field of research was distinctive from AI, to help them procure funding.

In the commercial world at least, the failed promises of the 'AI winter' continued to haunt AI research into the new millennium. *The New York Times* reported in 2005 that "computer scientists and software engineers were afraid to use the term AI because whoever was associated with AI was termed as a wild-eyed dreamer."[132] However, the role of AI as the forbearer of this technological revolution eventually came to be identified.

In the first decade of the 21st century, the proliferation of new technologies and social media gave us the concept of big data. This phenomenon, coupled with easy access to supercomputers and advanced ML algorithms, led to AI and ML being employed for the benefit of the public. Frequent use of AI in public policy made it a popular tool among government agencies. Particularly noteworthy events of this period included the following:

- **2006** – Geoffrey Hinton, Simon Osindero and Yee-Whye Teh published "A Fast-Learning Algorithm for Deep Belief Nets," in which they stacked multiple restricted Boltzmann machines together in layers.[133] This enabled the training process to be much more efficient for large amounts of data by solving the curse of dimensionality: as the number of features or parameters (dimensions) grows, the amount of data needed to generalize grows exponentially; one quickly gets to the realm where there is just insufficient data to generalize.
- **2008** – With the advent of general graphics processing units (GPUs) around 2007, when Nvidia introduced its CUDA development environment, Andrew Ng's group at Stanford started advocating for the use of GPUs in training deep neural networks, arguing that this would substantially reduce the training time.[134] This made DL on huge volumes of data more efficient and practical.
- **2009** – Finding enough labelled data has always been a challenge for the DL community. In 2009, Fei-Fei Li, a professor at Stanford, launched ImageNet, which is a database of millions of labelled images. It continues to grow and serves as a benchmark for DL researchers every year.
- **2011** – The ReLU activation function was introduced by Xavier Glorot, Antoine Bordes and Yoshua Bengio in their paper "Deep Sparse Rectifier Neural Networks."[135] This avoided what is known as the vanishing gradient problem. As a result, DL experts avoided issues relating to very long and impractical DL training times.

- **2014** – Ian Goodfellow and colleagues developed the generative adversarial network (GAN), in which two neural networks compete. This opened new doors in the application of unsupervised DL.

By 2016, the global market for AI-related products, hardware and software had reached more than USD $8 billion, and *The New York Times* reported that interest in AI had reached a "frenzy."[136] The applications of big data began to reach into every field of study, including the social sciences.

SUBDOMAINS OF AI

There are various names for the processes that can be performed on data. These depend on what one does with the data, the technologies and the mathematics employed, and the way one collects and consumes the data from data-processing systems. The three most used names are 'AI,' 'data science,' and 'machine learning.' We then divide these further into subcategories with additional specificity. For instance, 'deep learning' (DL), which currently is entirely a subset of ML, makes use of ANNs and parallels from biologically inspired neural networks (see *Figure 22*).

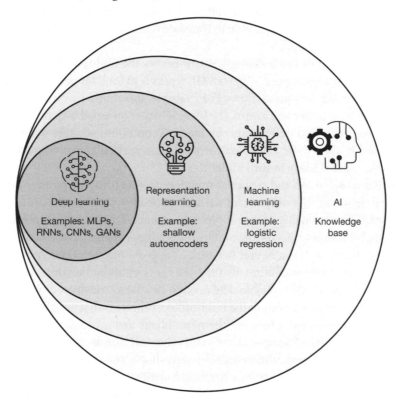

FIGURE 22: Some subdomains of AI

Increasingly, people forget that there is huge room for improvement in the use of traditional statistics, and in analytical and numerical algorithms that were not inspired by neural networks. In addition, it is surprising how much debate there is even among professionals about the differences between AI, ML, DL and data science. There does not appear to be a common consensus about the definitions.

AI is the capacity of a machine to emulate human thinking, or the imitation of human cognition by computers. Andrew Ng, a co-founder of Google Brain, defines it as "a huge set of tools for making computers behave intelligently."[137] Others define it differently. Zachary Lipton, the editor of *Approximately Correct*,[138] characterizes it as a target in motion based on those qualities that humans have but which machines cannot adapt. So, for some people, the meaning of AI has changed over time. Those things that we would have termed AI at one time would not be termed as AI now. The most common example is that chess-playing machines are now not considered AI. Currently, AI-based technologies include self-driving cars that can sense their surroundings; digital assistants and smart speakers such as Alexa, Cortana, Google Assistant and Siri, which can understand the words spoken to them; biometric identity recognition (e.g. disease diagnoses from tissue and blood samples, such as cancer); and language translators, which are able to translate one language into another more effectively than most people.

ML is the field of study that gives computers the ability to learn without being explicitly programmed. The way ML works is to look for patterns in existing data and make new predictions. For example, this might involve determining whether a customer will 'churn' (be lost), whether an email is spam, whether a given image contains indications of a medical condition, whether a monetary transaction is likely to be fraudulent or whether a particular evolving scenario in a public place is likely to turn violent.

DL is a subset of ML and creates abstractions in data using a layered approach to neural networks. The deepness of a neural network typically reflects the complexity and dimensionality of the problem. In essence, DL creates a function that maps inputs to outputs. According to the universal approximation theorem, deepness is not necessary for a neural network to approximate arbitrary continuous functions. The need for continuous functions is obvious as functions with singularities cannot be differentiable. The need to be able to construct any arbitrary function is also necessary due to the multitude of problems that need to be solved and solutions optimized. There are many problems that are common to simple networks (such as overfitting; see later in this chapter) that deep networks help to avoid (see *Figure 10* for the differences between simple and deep networks). Deep neural networks can generate much more complex models than simple ones. That is not to say that DL does not have its own problems. One problem that is common for some topologies (determined by how the neurons are connected to each other) is the aforementioned vanishing gradient problem, where the gradients between layers gradually shrink and disappear as they are rounded off to zero. There have been many methods developed to approach this problem, such as long short-term memory units and changing the activation function.

In many areas of business, there are examples where even quite simple DL can rival human capabilities. In other areas still, some more state-of-the-art DL architectures can even rival human accuracy in computer vision fields, specifically on datasets such as the Modified National Institute of Standards and Technology (MNIST) database and traffic sign recognition.[139] Chatbots powered by natural language processing engines (such as IBM Watson and Azure LUIS) can easily beat humans at answering general questions. Recent developments in DL have produced astounding results in competitions with humans in games such as Doom and Go.

Various definitions of **data science** exist, with some including all aspects of big data and DL. We prefer to label data science as a field of study where data and inferences from that data are processed based on rules, albeit with significant emphasis on statistical data analysis. The data can be structured or unstructured. In this definition, data science has significant overlaps with big data, data mining and some topologies of DL. Data science is an old branch that continues to evolve, but its main role is to connect storytelling and data visualization. Some people view data science as an extension of the field of statistical analysis, while others regard statistics as a nonessential part of data science.

Data science, ML and AI are all about data, making sense of it and creating an experience that is affected by it. They differ in the amount of data, its attributes, and the toolkit available to the specialist analysing the data. Fundamentally, the internet has democratized toolkits to a large extent.[140] A considerable number of (sample) problems have been solved and shared on GitHub, Kaggle, Keras.io, Stack Overflow and TensorFlow.

TYPES OF INPUTS AND OUTPUTS

The type of tools that we use depend on the problem that needs to be solved. It is best to understand the basic terms and how they are used, as this affects what names we assign to algorithms and techniques.

Inputs and outputs can be quantitative (continuous or discrete) or categorical (binary, nominal or ordinal):

- **Continuous** variables are things like volume, speed, distance and time
- **Discrete** variables are things like number of trees or number of people (they are normally integers)
- **Categorical binary** variables include win/lose, cancerous/non-cancerous and yes/no
- **Categorical nominal** variables include class names, colours and species
- **Categorical ordinal** variables include ratings and position in a group

Over and above these, other terms include:

- **Confounding variable** – a variable that masks the true effect of another variable
- **Latent variable** – a variable that cannot be directly measured
- **Composite variable** – a variable made up of more elementary variables

Understanding AI begins by understanding how data-driven intelligence works. Natural intelligence is about classifying things (e.g. this is better, heavier, prettier or longer than something), predicting things (e.g. it might rain, or I might outrun that) and clustering things (e.g. this is my tribe, or you are from that clan). There is then a need to measure the accuracy of predictions and the speed of our decisions. Among these will be how much data was used to make predictions and decisions.

Nature and artificial intelligence differ in intuition, mechanisms of learning, the bootstrapping of new brains, the embedding of memes and cultural enforcements, and the evolutionary embedding of the cognitive hardwiring. This differs in the senses, sensory data processing, connections between the sensory data and neural cortex processing, as well as evolved motor neuron activations.[141]

MACHINE LEARNING

The purpose of ML is to acquire skills or knowledge from experience. This is done using several different ways of learning depending on the nature of the problem to be solved:

- **Supervised learning** (see *Figure 24*) can be categorized into classification and regression, which are quite similar. In supervised learning, there is some form of supervision of the algorithm – that is, relating previously observed outputs to previously observed inputs. We provide the algorithm with a raw dataset, and a target. The latter can be a single variable or multiple variables. Then, the algorithm attempts to understand how to match the input to the output. Every time the algorithm makes a mistake, the supervisor tries to correct it.
- **Unsupervised learning** (see *Figure 24*), in the context of ML, usually refers to clustering. In this case, we provide the algorithm with raw data, but instead of providing a target, the algorithm is essentially allowed to do its own thing and identify patterns in the data provided. It tries to find any regularities that seem significant, but there is no supervision involved. This type of learning is very difficult because it involves ill-defined problems and almost always requires a human for interpretation, usually in the final stage of the pipeline. For example, the algorithm might identify patterns that are irrelevant to what we are trying to do, so we might need to drill down into

the results and then define the problem a little better. Unsupervised learning can be particularly important in contexts where human prejudices need to be eliminated, as it can create machine-generated clusters that a human might not even have thought of as somehow being related.

- **Semi-supervised learning** is a type of ML that sits between supervised learning and unsupervised learning. It uses both labelled and unlabelled data to fit a model. In some cases, unlabelled data can improve the accuracy of the model, but generally this is not the case, and labelling data costs money and takes time. Semi-supervised learning has had a resurgence in recent years because it reduces the error rate on some important benchmarks. This type of learning includes self-training, multi-view learning and self-assembling.

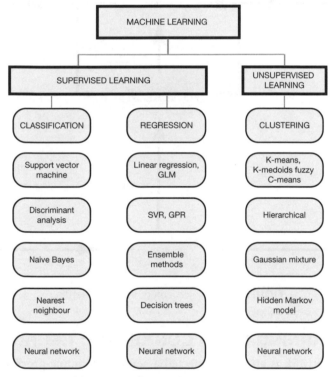

FIGURE 24: Types of machine learning

- **Reinforcement learning** (see *Figure 25*) can be defined as a process in which a computer agent (i.e. a program that acts on its own or on behalf of a user autonomously) learns through the presence of positive and negative reinforcements in an environment. Reinforcement learning's distinctive feature is that it almost replicates the way humans adapt and learn (i.e. human learning processes and cognition). It is quite different from other types of ML (i.e., the supervised and unsupervised types). The main distinction between reinforcement learning algorithms and supervised/unsupervised learning algorithms is the presence of reinforcements. In a reinforcement learning algorithm, a data scientist must ensure the presence of positive and negative reinforcements for the computer agent. No prerequisite 'training data' is required. The only training is based on an iterative process in which the computer agent runs the program up to a desired number of times until the algorithm works in conjunction with the reinforcements.

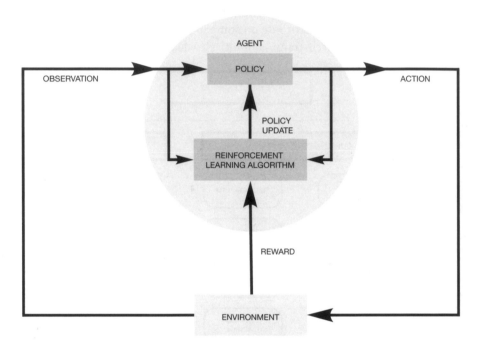

FIGURE 25: Reinforcement machine learning

LEARNING FROM CONNECTED NEURONS

A neural network is an interconnected assembly of simple processing nodes or units whose functionality is loosely based on the natural neuron. The inter-unit connection strength captures the ability of the network to learn. Interunit strength can be obtained through adaptation or running an iterative set of training programs.

In nature, the neurons communicate via electrical or neurochemical signals, which are short-lived impulses or spikes in the cell wall's voltage or membrane (see *Chapter 3*). Their coordination and links are ensured through electrochemical junctions called synapses, which are present on the branch-like cellular structures called dendrites. Each neuron typically receives many thousands of connections from other neurons and is continually receiving many incoming signals, which eventually reach the cell body. These thousands of signals reach the neuron and cause a spike in voltage in the neuron structure. Such a spike is translated as a signal to other neurons.

The behaviour of neurons in response to an incoming impulse is not linear. Neurons can exhibit a spike or remain stagnant depending upon the nature of the incoming signal. Some signals produce an inhibitory effect and cancel a spike in voltage while others produce an excitatory effect and cause a rise in voltage. Neurons behave differently based on their characteristic ability to differentiate, as well as their synaptic connections with other neurons.

This interconnected behaviour in neurons has given rise to a new area of study, called connectionism. It highlights the importance of connections between neurons. This methodology is frequently employed in psychology to study human cognitive functions. In our case, we intend to make use of it regardless of its limitations. Data scientists wish to incorporate connectionism into neural networks to ensure greater efficiency.

In computer science, the equivalent of biological neurons is the nodes in an artificially intelligent system, or unit. AI systems loosely mimic natural neural networks. So, the actions of synapses are modelled by multiplying the network's inputs by a weight. This weight represents the strength of connection or signal between two neurons. Then, the activation signal is sent to other nodes for processing through the axon. Next, the activation is compared with a threshold. The unit then produces a spike (a high-valued output) if the threshold is exceeded, otherwise it produces nothing. This kind of threshold logic unit is the simplest model of an artificial neuron. It was first outlined in 1943 by Warren McCulloch and Walter Pitts.[142] Some of the assumptions of this model need to be noted: the weighted inputs are added in a linear fashion, there is a single simple activation function, and there is a lack of multi-state memory embedding in each of the synapses and the neurons.

Before we delve deeper into the neural aspects of ML and AI, there are some concepts that we should familiarize ourselves with as they turn up time and time again in all industries when dealing with data.

BASIC NOTATIONS AND TECHNIQUES

Consider a basic representation (as depicted in *Figure 26*) of an artificial neuron and a number of observations $(x_1, x_2 \ldots x_n)$ from a sensor. The purpose is to build up some intelligence to be able to predict the output (y_j).

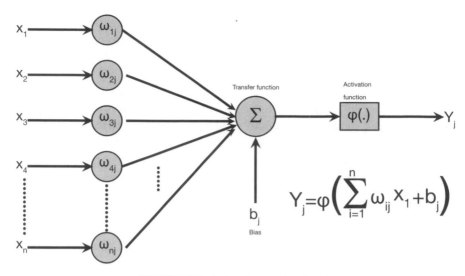

FIGURE 26: A simple neural network

One of the keys to understanding how neural networks work from the simple diagram above is to comprehend the universal approximation theorem. This is a way of determining the disparity between predictions and observations (cost function), gradient descent and activation function, which are discussed below.

THE UNIVERSAL APPROXIMATION THEOREM

You may wonder how a simple linear combination of inputs can enable us to represent *any* output. The assumption here is that the relationship between the inputs and the output is monotonic – that is, there are no discontinuities. In such circumstances, the universal approximation theorem states that in a feedforward network with a single hidden layer of the type shown in the simple neural network (see the section 'Artificial neural networks' later in this chapter), a finite number of neurons can approximate any real-valued continuous function. That activation function can be any continuous function that is differentiable.

There are mathematical proofs of the theorem, and we can almost relate it back to Fourier series analysis, where we can construct any function using sinusoidal waves of varying amplitudes and frequencies. Mathematically, if $F(y)$ approximates the function $f(y)$, then the universal approximation theorem states that $|F(y)-f(y)|$ can be made arbitrarily small with $F(y)$ being represented by φ in the activation function:

$$\sum_{i=1}^{N} = v_i\, \varphi(w_{ij}\, x_i\, x + b_j)$$

Here, N is an integer representing the number of inputs, w are the weights and b is the bias. The big assumption is that the activation function should be continuous and differentiable. This is a big assumption as in real neurons we know that the activation function is a spike and spikes have discontinuities.

ACTIVATION FUNCTIONS

The most common activation functions used in DL are shown in *Table 5*.

Name	Plot	Equation	Derivatives
Identity		$f(x)=x$	$f'(x)=1$
Binary step		$f(x)=\{0, x<0$ $1, x\geq0\}$	$f(x)=\{0, x\neq0$ $?, x=0\}$
Logistic (a.k.a Soft step)		$f(x) = \dfrac{1}{(1+e\text{-}x)}$	$f'(x) = f(x)(1\text{-}f(x))$
TanH		$f(x) = \tanh(x) = \dfrac{2}{(1+e\text{-}2x)} -1$	$f'(x) = 1\text{-}f(x)2$
ArcTan		$f(x) = \tan\text{-}1(x)$	$f'(x) = \dfrac{1}{(x^2+1)}$
Rectified Linear unit (ReLU)		$f(x)= \{0, x<0$ $x, x\geq0\}$	$f'(x) = \{0, x<0$ $1, x\geq0\}$
Parameteric Rectified Linear unit t (PReLU)		$f(x)= \{\alpha x, x<0$ $1, x\geq0\}$	$f'(x)=\{\alpha, x<0$ $1, x\geq0\}$
Exponential Linear unil l (ELU)		$f(x)= \{\alpha(ex\text{-}1) x<0,$ $x, x\geq0\}$	$f'(x)=\{(f(x)+ a, x<0$ $x, x\geq0\}$
Soft plus		$f(x)= \log_e (1+ex)$	$f'(x)= 1/(1+e\text{-}x)$

TABLE 5: Common activation functions

The type of activation function used depends on the nature of the problem. Rectified linear unit (ReLU) is usually the preferred activation for networks that are deep due to a problem encountered during backpropagation. This is the aforementioned vanishing gradient problem, where the gradients between layers gradually shrink and disappear as they are rounded off to zero. This makes it difficult to train a network as the navigation toward an optimal solution becomes slow or impossible. It is easy to see that this is truer for some activation functions than others. It is also important to see whether real differentiators (sorry about the pun) in the value and uniqueness of the data are skewed in the positive part of the curve or in the negative part of it.

COST FUNCTION

The learning process involves minimizing the error between the expected value of the output and its predicted value. For example, we could use a quadratic cost function to represent the penalty of getting a mismatch between the expected output and the actual output and adjust the weights iteratively to minimize the cost function:

$$C = \frac{1}{2N} \sum_{j=1}^{N} \| F(y_j) - f(y_j) \|^2$$

The purpose of learning this is to minimize the cost function. Technically, a cost function can be dependent on any of the previous layers. This restriction exists so that we can use backpropagation. The equation for finding the last layer's gradient is the only one that is dependent on the cost function (the rest are dependent on the next layer). If the cost function is dependent on other activation layers besides the output one, backpropagation will be invalid because the idea of 'trickling backwards' no longer works.

Other cost functions can be used. These include metrics based on cross-entropy cost, exponential cost, Hellinger distance, Kullback–Leibler divergence, Itakura–Saito distance and so on. The cost function we use depends on the nature of the problem.

STOCHASTIC GRADIENT DESCENT

As discussed above, we use a cost function to reduce the difference between the expected outputs and the observed outputs. We are faced with an optimization issue. Clearly, we could take a haphazard brute force approach and try different weights to see which gives the best match between the expected results and the observed results, but that would be computationally prohibitive. Stochastic gradient descent (SGD) is a variant of the classical gradient descent where the stochasticity is from using a random subset of the available data to compute the gradient at each descent. This approach has shown to be highly suitable for a variety of loss functions and as such has become the foundation of deep learning. The above equations give us a way of methodically deciding on the weights. The two parameters that can be controlled in the cost function are the weights and the bias. Stochastic gradient descent (see *Figure 27*) enables optimization of the objective function in a way that is differentiable. The objective function represents the objective of intelligence in the environment. It is a function that represents the relationship between the various parameters and it is this function that we try to optimize. An objective function could, for example, be the relationship between various parameters of a house (floor area, location, number of rooms, build cost, etc.) and its price.

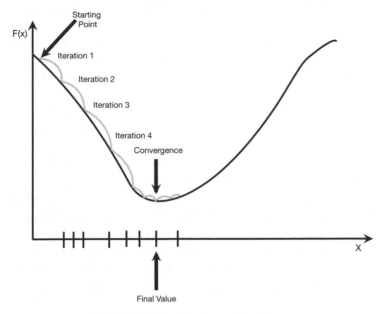

FIGURE 27: Stochastic gradient descent

Consider an objective function, $Q(w)$ that we need to estimate. $Q_i(w)$ is the value of the i-th observation of the dataset.

$$Q(w)=\frac{1}{N}\Sigma_{i}^{N}=_1Q_i(w)$$

The way to work out the new value of the weight (w) is to look at the step size (η, also called the learning rate) and the gradient of the objective at that point:

$$w=w-\eta\nabla Q(w) = \frac{\eta}{N}\Sigma_{i}^{N}=_1\nabla Q_i(w)$$

LEARNING RATE

The learning rate is a measure of how quickly one moves toward the minimum of a loss function. The learning rate is usually a tuning parameter that is measured as the step size taken in the direction of the descent. In addition, the learning rate is changed between epochs or iterations. There are two parameters that are used to determine the change in the tuning parameter, with the purpose being to enable the achievement of the minimum without overshooting or undershooting that mark. These parameters are called decay and momentum.

EFFECT OF THE LEARNING RATE

The key to learning for neural networks is to look for a function that maps inputs to outputs using training datasets. The speed at which models run is dependent on the learning rate hyperparameter. The weights of a model are significantly affected by the learning rate. As the errors are apportioned each time the model's weights are updated, the learning rate gives the most effective approximation of the function at hand. A large learning rate may accelerate the learning process of models, meaning less time is taken to arrive at a suboptimal final set of weights, and vice versa.

Large training epochs undermine the efficacy of a model, as a greater amount of time is required to arrive at the final conclusions. Slow performance is also said to be caused by weights that diverge. On the other hand, a slow learning rate may get stuck on a suboptimal solution or never converge.

The challenge of ML, of course, is that the learning algorithm must be able to perform well on previously unseen inputs. This is called generalization. This is what separates ML from simple curve-fitting optimizations. ML looks at techniques to try to minimize generalization error. Generalization errors are found in natural systems as well, particularly in large, over-parameterized neural networks. However, this statement appears to be in direct contradiction with classical notions of functional complexity, where smaller nodes have an edge.

OVERFITTING AND UNDERFITTING

When training models, we often split our data into two sets (usually three, but explaining the process is easier with two). These are a training set and a testing set. We use all the data in the training set to train our predictive model, and, when we are happy with the performance, we do a single final evaluation of our testing set. We do this to ensure that the model we have created is fit for purpose and can generalize to future unseen data. To see why, examine *Figures 28* and *29*.

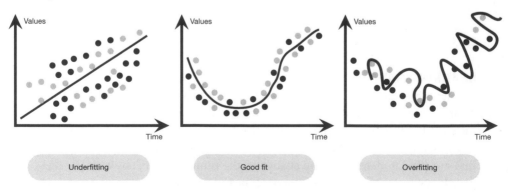

FIGURE 28: Overfitting and underfitting

We want a model that has learned an accurate representation of the under-lying problem we are attempting to solve. An underfitting model is relatively easy to spot – it performs poorly in both training and testing because it is not able to learn a good representation of the problem. Overfitting, on the other hand, is trickier to spot, because a model that shows signs of overfitting has learned how to represent the training set accurately. If we were to put all our data into the training set, we would be misled by the accuracy scores as future unseen values would likely give wrong results. We can almost anthropomor-phize this to human memory. The model has only learned to remember the data it has been shown during training.

By splitting the dataset into a training set and a validation set (see *Figure 29*), we can now train our model on one set, then perform a final evaluation on it with the other. A validation dataset is a sample of data held back from training the model that is used to give an estimate of model goodness while tuning the model's hyperparameters. We can expect these values not to be too far away from each other in a well-learned system. This proves the generalization theory because the model has never seen the examples in the test, so it can't have memorized them; the data is sufficient to train the model and obtain answers to new questions.

HOW DO WE PREVENT OVERFITTING?

There are several techniques that can be used to prevent overfitting while still ensuring a good fit. One of the best methods is called k-fold cross-validation. In k-fold cross-validation, we take a dataset and divide it into k sets, then set up k experiments where one set at a time is left out to be used as the test set while the other $k-1$ sets are used as the training set. By observing the k results metrics, we can see the average accuracy as well as the variance of the accuracy. A high accuracy with a low variance is a good sign that a model can learn a good representation of a problem. High variance means the accuracy of the model is highly dependent on which test set is used – a likely sign of overfitting and a big red flag for our aspirations toward generalization.

What happens when the model is quite complex, though? As is the case in DL, techniques such as k-fold cross-validation become time-consuming and expensive.

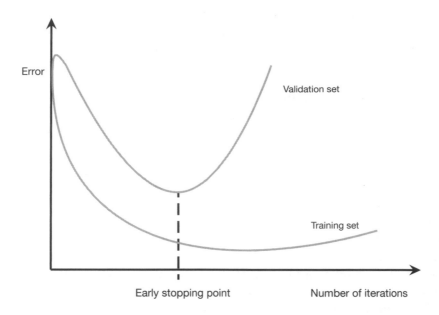

FIGURE 29: Training and validation data

Another way to tackle overfitting is to use ensemble methods. Two of the most popular ensemble methods are called boosting and bagging. Boosting is an iterative technique which adjusts the weight of an observation based on the latest classification. Bagging is a technique to reduce the variance in the predictions by generating additional training datasets using combinations with repetitions to produce multiple sets of the original data. The idea behind ensemble methods is that the combined output of multiple models is better (in a reduced variance or reduced bias sense) than relying on a single model.

This brings us on to the most popular way of preventing overfitting – regularization. In regularization, the aim is to force the model to be simpler, learning more general interpretations rather than ones specific to the training set. The form this takes depends on the type of model we are using. For instance, in regression, we may opt to add something like a penalty to our model coefficients, forcing them to be sparser (so we capture the significant underlying trend). In a decision tree, we may perform pruning by setting requirements such as the minimum number of occurrences a sample must have in the training data before it is placed as a leaf node.

In neural networks, we again have a choice. It used to be the case that we would apply regularization to our model's weight matrix, much like we would the coefficients in our previous models. However, while there was empirical evidence that this helped to alleviate overfitting somewhat, we weren't addressing the real root of the problem in neural networks – co-adaptation. Co-adaptation occurs because all of the weights of the neurons that make up a neural network have learned together at the same time, meaning that due to the makeup of the training dataset, some of the connections will have more predictive ability than others. Through the iterative training process, these more predictive neurons are used more and keep getting stronger while the weaker neurons remain weak. The result is a model where many neurons throughout simply aren't contributing to the predictive power. Once this is understood, the concept of dropout naturally follows. Dropout is a regularization technique for neural networks. In each pass of the training process, neurons are chosen at random with a probability p of being included (thus, a probability of $1-p$ of being dropped). This forces the model not to rely on specific individual neurons to do all of the heavy lifting. Thus, our co-adaptation problem is solved, and we now have a handle on overfitting in neural networks.

GOODNESS OF LEARNING

Evaluating an ML algorithm is an essential part of any project. A model may give meaningful results and have a metric that demonstrates that the data has some clarity of meaning. Several metrics should be used if possible. The following sections focus on the following metrics:

- Classification accuracy
- Logarithmic loss
- Confusion matrix
- Area under a curve and receiver operating characteristic
- F1 score
- Mean absolute error and mean squared error

CLASSIFICATION ACCURACY

Classification accuracy is almost synonymous with accuracy. It can be defined as the ratio between predictions that are correct and total input samples:

$$Accuracy = \frac{Number\ of\ correct\ predictions}{Total\ number\ of\ predictions}$$

For example, if we have analysed 100 English sentences and 92 have been classified correctly into a semantic bucket (such as 'this sentence is about a fruit' or 'this sentence is about an animal'), then our classification accuracy is 92%. The threshold of accuracy that we are willing to accept may be dependent on the problem and a comparison with the level of accuracy humans can achieve. An accuracy of 51% may be acceptable for financial market predictions while an accuracy of 90% may not be accurate enough in relaying to a patient that they have cancer.

LOGARITHMIC LOSS

False classifications are penalized using logarithmic loss, or log loss. This works well for multi-class classification. All the classes must be assigned a probability by the classifier when working with log loss. Consider a situation where N samples are linked to M classes. The log loss is calculated as follows:

$$-\frac{1}{N} \sum_{i=1}^{N} \sum_{j=1}^{M} x_{ij} \log(p_{ij})$$

Here:

- x_{ij} indicates whether sample i belongs to class j or not
- p_{ij} indicates the probability of sample i belonging to class j

The range of log loss is $[0, \infty)$. Higher accuracy is synonymous with a log loss close to zero and vice versa. In general, classifier accuracy is increased when log loss is minimized.

CONFUSION MATRIX

Confusion matrix is a measure of the performance of a classification model. Consider a binary classification problem where we have a sample of data points belonging to one of two classes: yes or no. On testing with our class, the results shown in *Table 6* are obtained.

	Predicted: no	Predicted: yes
Actual: no	40	4
Actual: yes	10	55

TABLE 6: Outcome of the test

The matrix contains:

- **True positives (*TP*)** – a match when a positive (yes) is predicted
- **True negatives (*TN*)** – a match when a negative (no) is predicted
- **False positives (*FP*)** – yes was predicted when the actual output was no
- **False negatives (*FN*)** – no was predicted when the actual output was yes

Accuracy in this case is just a measure of how many results are predicted correctly:

$$Accuracy = \frac{True\ positives + True\ negatives}{Total\ predictions} = \frac{55 + 40}{40 + 4 + 10 + 55} \cong 87\%$$

The confusion matrix forms the basis of some other metrics. These include precision, recall and F_1 score discussed below.

AREA UNDER A CURVE AND RECEIVER OPERATING CHARACTERISTIC

Area under a curve (AUC) is a widely used metric for evaluation (see *Figure 30*). It is used for binary classification problems. The AUC of a classifier is the probability that the classifier will rank as an arbitrarily picked positive example higher than an arbitrarily picked negative example. There are three fundamental terms related to AUC:

- **True positive rate (sensitivity)** – this corresponds to the proportion of positive data points that are correctly considered as positive, with respect to all positive data points; it is given as $TP / (FN+TP)$
- **True negative rate (specificity)** – this corresponds to the proportion of negative data points that are correctly considered as negative, with respect to all negative data points; it is given as $TN / (FP+TN)$
- **False positive rate** – this corresponds to the proportion of positive data points that are incorrectly considered as positive, with respect to all the negative data points; it is given as $FP / (FP+TN)$

The receiver operating characteristic (ROC) is a probability curve. The quicker it trends toward 1, the better, as this indicates that the classifier can be used to classify data correctly. The AUC indicates the degree to which we can separate the two classes.

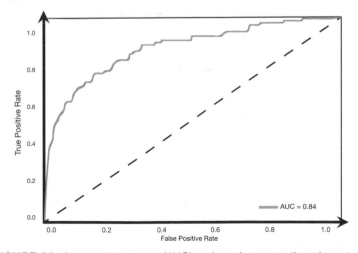

FIGURE 30: Area under a curve (AUC) and receiver operating characteristic

The AUC has a range of [0, 1], as is evident in *Figure 30*. It can be observed that the values are directly proportional to the effectiveness of the model.

F1 SCORE

The harmonic mean (HM) between precision and recall is the F1 score. The harmonic mean is calculated as the reciprocal of the arithmetic mean of the reciprocals of the given set of numbers. So the harmonic mean of 8, 4, 2, and 1 is $\{[8^{-1} + 4^{-1} + 2^{-1} + 1^{-1}]/4\}^{-1}$ is about 2.1, whereas the arithmetic mean is 3.75. It measures a test's accuracy rating and harmonic mean is particularly used when rates are involved. The range for the F1 score is [0, 1]. It is defined by the precision of a classifier (how many instances it classifies correctly) and how robust the classifier is (how many instances it misses). High precision with lower recall means a classifier is accurate but misses a large number of instances that are difficult to classify. The greater the F1 score, the better the model.

$$F1 = 2 \times \cfrac{1}{\cfrac{1}{predictions} + \cfrac{1}{recall}}$$

The F1 score tries to find a balance between precision and recall:

- **Precision** – the total number of correct positive results divided by the total number of positive outcomes evaluated by the classifier
- **Recall** – the total number of correct positive results divided by the number of all relevant samples (identifications of all samples must be positive)

MEAN ABSOLUTE ERROR AND MEAN SQUARED ERROR

These metrics are used to measure the goodness of fit between the original and predicted results. The equation for mean absolute error is:

$$\frac{1}{N} \Sigma_{j=1}^{N} |y_j - <y_j>|$$

and the equation for mean squared error is:

$$\frac{1}{N} \Sigma_{j=1}^{N} (y_j - <y_j>)^2$$

ARTIFICIAL NEURAL NETWORKS

The above building blocks can be built into a network.[143] The term 'artificial neural network' (ANN) is used to refer to any system of artificial neurons, from a single node to a large collection of nodes, in which each one is connected to many other nodes in the net (or even all of them).

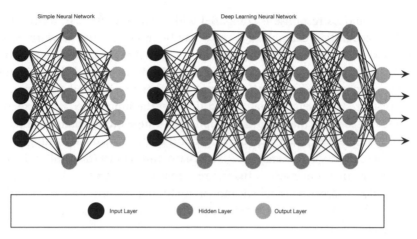

FIGURE 31: Simple and deep learning neural networks

At the most basic level, there are two types of neural networks: simple and deep. Take a look at *Figure 31*, which we began to examine in *Chapter 3* but will now unpack in greater depth. A simple neural network has just one hidden layer. The nodes have an orderly structure in the form of layers. Each signal is generated at a node within a layer and then, after passing two nodes, it dies. This is typically referred to as the feedforward pattern and it is used when an input signal is classified into several classes (i.e. per the desired output pattern). For example, suppose the input consists of an encoding of light and dark patterns in an image of handwritten numbers. In that case, the output layer may contain ten nodes – one for each number (0 to 9) to represent the number class each input character is from. There is usually one node allocated to each output class. Care should be taken that the spike in voltage comes from the output class of nodes as an input signal for the subsequent classes. The number of layers is always a cause of debate. It does require careful consideration depending on the complexity of the problem and the degree of nonlinearity that needs to be introduced. Other issues include whether additional layers would lead to overfitting and the number and complexity of inputs.

The emphasis of all neural networks is an aspect related to learning about the data and the relationships between various bits of data. How does one adjust the weights so that the output(s) can be related to that representation? The answer is experience. Neurons' synaptic strength can be changed so that they adapt or change as per their input signals, as needed. In our case, the fabrication of weight values is equivalent to a change in natural neurons. In terms of processing information, the data related to the strengths of relationships should be stored in weights, which evolve through a process of adaptation to stimulus from a set of examples (i.e. a pattern). In supervised learning, used in conjunction with nets of the type shown in *Figure 31*, an input pattern is presented to the net and its response is compared with a target output. In terms of the number-recognition example, a '1,' say, may be input and the network output compared with the classification code for 1. The difference between the two patterns of output then determines how the weights are altered. The principles of adaptation or change create a learning rule. That rule is based on computing and creating static weights that embed the way the inputs are transformed to outputs. As soon as the weights are updated, a new output pattern emerges, and this is then compared with the target and changes made accordingly. This sequence of events is repeated iteratively many times until (hopefully) the network's behaviour converges so that its response to each pattern is close to the corresponding target. This holistic model (including any ordering of the pattern that is presented, criteria for terminating the process, etc.) is the essence of a training algorithm.

But what happens if the network encounters an unfamiliar program after training? There are two possibilities. If the network is able to understand the underlying structure of the program, then it can learn to generalize. However, if the network fails to decode the underlying structure, then generalization is not possible. In this case, the network's value is reduced to a mere classification table, which has no practical use. Therefore, good generalization is an important characteristic of good neural networks.

Having covered the basic building blocks of an ANN, we will cover variants later in this chapter. The differences between the variants revolve around neuron topologies and learning, feedback and memory mechanisms.

FEATURE ENGINEERING

Feature engineering, as depicted in *Figure 32*, is an important parameter in ML systems but it consumes a lot of time. It makes ML operations efficient by altering the training data and adding supplemental elements to it. One can begin with raw data, which is automatically transformed into elements by the neural networks as soon as they learn it.

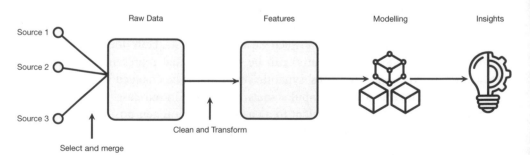

FIGURE 32: Feature engineering

Feature engineering was the most commonly used method in ML and was a manual process; domain experts propose hand-crafted features to help the learning process. DL works differently and efficiently due to its recognition element, which works better than the feature detectors. Furthermore, DL has a learning operation that focuses on classification learning as compared to the old feature design of neural network learning. Therefore, DL has proven to be a complete trainable system that uses raw input, like image pixels, and generates an output of recognized objects.

AUTOENCODERS

An autoencoder is an ANN that is capable of learning various coding patterns. The simple form of an autoencoder is like the multilayer perceptron (a perceptron is a single layer neural network; DL neural networks are composed of multiple layers of perceptions) containing an input layer or one or more hidden layers, and an output layer. The significant difference between the typical multilayer perceptron and feedforward neural network and autoencoder is in the number of nodes in the output layer. In the case of the autoencoder, the output layer contains the same number of nodes as the input layer. Instead of predicting target values as per the outputs, the autoencoder has to predict its inputs. The steps in the learning operation are listed below.

For each input x:

- Do a feedforward pass to compute activation functions provided in all the hidden layers and output layers
- Find the deviation between the calculated values with the inputs using an appropriate error function
- Backpropagate the error to update the weights
- Repeat the task until a satisfactory output is achieved

If the number of nodes in the hidden layers is fewer than the input/output nodes, then the last hidden layer's activations are considered a compressed representation of the inputs; when the hidden layer nodes are more than the input layer, an autoencoder can learn the identity function, and at this point it becomes useless in most cases. Learning the identity function represents extreme overfitting to the training data in that there is only one input to one output, meaning that it has not learned anything that enables generalization.

DEEP LEARNING FRAMEWORKS

There are many DL frameworks. Among the most popular are:

- **Keras** – This is among the most popular open-source neural networks and it is written in Python. It uses TensorFlow, the Microsoft Cognitive Toolkit (CNTK) and Theano as components of its backend. It has good documentation and is easy to use. Thus, it is used in fast-paced environments, especially in research, where the results of experiments need to be ascertained quickly. Keras has a modular element to it, making it extensible and platform independent as it can run on central processing units (CPUs), graphics processing units (GPUs) and tensor processing units (TPUs).
- **TensorFlow** – This is a DL framework developed by Google Brain, originally used for conducting research. It is written in C++ and Python. It has made complex numerical computations faster. It uses data-flow graphs as the data structure at the backend, and the nodes of the graph represent a set of mathematical operations to be performed. The edges of the graph represent multidimensional arrays or tensors.
- **PyTorch** – This is written in C++ and Python. It is one of the most straightforward frameworks to use as a replacement for NumPy arrays, and it speeds up the processing of numerical computations in a GPU environment. It uses tensors to increase the computation speed many times over. This is different from what happens in the two frameworks above, which build a neural network and reuse the same structure again and again. If any modification is present in the network, then the structure must be rebuilt from scratch, which is time consuming.
- **Fast.ai** – This is a learning library that offers high-quality elements that can rapidly and effectively generate results in any standard DL system. It also provides analysts with the opportunity to work with some common standard elements rearranged in an innovative way. It has a layered architecture with some mutual basic designs of numerous DL and data processing methods concerning decoupled abstractions. These abstractions can be communicated concisely and clearly with the help of fundamental dynamics from Python and PyTorch libraries. Fast.ai incorporates an untouched framework for Python along with a semantic sort of progression for tensors. It also contains a GPU-optimized computer vision library that has extensions in pure Python. It includes an optimizer whose purpose is to refactor out the common functionality of modern optimizers into two simple parts. This allows optimization systems to be run by only four or five lines of code. This has led to the creation of a novel two-way callback system that can be accessed through data, models or optimizers.

Using these frameworks enables designing, training and validation of DL using a high-level language. These frameworks offer, using their libraries, high-performance

GPU-parallelized solutions to a wide range of training problems GPU accelerates applications running on the CPU by offloading some of the computer-intensive and time-consuming portions of the code). These problems fall into the areas of natural language processing (NLP), computer vision, reinforcement learning, time series predictions and more.

SPIKING NEURAL NETWORKS

A growing body of research is being directed toward spiking neural networks (SNNs). An SNN is a DL neural network inspired by information processing in biological neural systems, where sparse and asynchronous signals are communicated and processed in a massively parallel manner. In our brains, the neurons talk to each other through spikes. These are very short voltage spikes and not constant signals. This gives the brain the property of energy efficiency.[144]

While models of cortical hierarchies from neuroscience have strongly inspired the architectural principles behind DL, deep down there are significant dissimilarities between brain-like computation and analogue natural neural networks (ANNNs – note that these are not the same thing as artificial neural networks, or ANNs). One obvious difference is that the neurons in ANNNs are mostly nonlinear but continuous function approximators that operate on a common clock cycle. However, biological neurons compute using asynchronous spikes as they can detect any event with the help of digital and temporally precise action potentials.

Researchers from the domains of computational neuroscience, ML and neuromorphic systems engineering have tried to replicate the success of deep learning neural networks (DNNs). (DNNs are a form of ANNs. ANNs can be shallow or deep – they are called deep when there is more than one hidden layer – see *Figure 10*).

AI APPLICATIONS AND THE PROMISE OF SNNS

SNNs are highly efficient because of some of the characteristics they share with real neural circuits like brains, such as analogue computation, low power consumption, fast inference, event-driven processing, online learning and massive parallelism. In addition, they have the potential to integrate natural brain organoids, in which case they might give rise to a whole new field – a topic we cover briefly in *Chapter 6*.

Power consumption is the most significant benefit of SNNs. A 'normal' neural network uses large GPUs or CPUs, which consume hundreds of watts of power. In contrast, SNNs use just a few nanowatts.

With sensors being deployed everywhere (e.g. event-based audio (audio that only gets triggered by specific actions) environmental sensors and vision sensors) and reaching maturity through advancements in the IoT, deep SNNs are among the most promising concepts for processing such inputs efficiently.

Traditional DNNs encounter many difficulties because of their massive hunger for computational resources. DL follows modern-world applications such as automated driving, robotics and the IoT.

STATE-OF-THE-ART SNNS

State-of-the-art SNNs are initially trained on conventional neural networks, and by this means they gain the parameters of those neural networks. There is a loss of a few percentage points of accuracy in predictions due to the transfer of learning, but the result is a system that consumes much less power. Normally, DL is dependent on stochastic gradient descent and error backpropagation, which need differentiable activation functions to run. Specific modifications are carried out to decrease activations to binary values, which are known as spikes. These binary networks share the discontinuity of spikes. However, they do not share an asynchronous operation mode with SNNs. Spikes are only used for asynchronous SNNs; additional effort and time are needed when dealing with the integration of spikes into the training process.

It is possible to train state-of-the-art SNNs with unsupervised learning – for example, spike-timing-dependent plasticity (STDP). However, this can only be done for one layer accurately. The current strategies for training deep SNNs include:

- **Binarization of ANNNs** – Conventional DNNs are trained with binary activation but maintain their synchronous information processing mode
- **Conversion from ANNNs** – Conventional DNNs are trained with backpropagation, and then all-analogue neurons are converted into spiking ones
- **Training of limited networks** – Before the transformation process, the normal DNN training methods are put together with limits that model the spiking neuron models' properties
- **Supervised learning with spikes** – This involves direct training from SNNs using variations of error backpropagation
- **More realistic nature-inspired training** – This involves using local learning rules at the synapses, such as timings and sequences

SNNs are currently an active research field due to the various advantages they will offer, as highlighted above.

AUTOML AND THE DEMOCRATIZATION OF AI

Data science, ML and DL have been around for some time now; their learning has been largely democratized and there is widespread sharing of resources. Moreover, through the huge success of open-source code-sharing platforms, many algorithms have been tested and used in a multitude of scenarios. The consequence of all this is that many of the algorithms that are required are as good as they can get.

Increasingly we see headlines such as "The Death of Data Scientists," with articles expounding the view that we are reaching a stage where the exponential growth in the requirement of data scientists and data engineers will be curtailed, because so many of their tasks are capable of being automated.[145] A typical ML project involves data cleaning, feature selection and engineering, model selection, hyperparameter optimization, model validation, deployment and continuous improvement. The dominant problem in most projects is still around the amount of time that is needed to get data ready for ML.

Companies such as Amazon, DataRobot, Google, H2O.ai and Microsoft offer tools for automating the ML journey, and there are a large number of start-ups that are trying to give these bigger players a run for their money. These include emerging companies such as Mind Foundry and Sensory Intelligence.

The workflow in ML involves the following:

- **Feature engineering** – This involves engineering of the inputs, potentially using AutoML. For example, it must convert text-based values to numbers, impute missing values, and otherwise clean them (e.g. replicate them twice, delete any nulls and blanks, or remove extra characters). There is an assumption, hopefully a valid one in most cases, that the user knows their data well. A lot of this can be done manually, even without formal data science training. It is reasonable, then, for AutoML platforms to require the user to specify features.
- **Algorithm selection** – This involves choosing algorithms, the library or framework to use, and the particular type of algorithm within the library or framework. There are rules of thumb for picking the type, depending on the type of prediction required. This is generally where AutoML can amaze users, even automating a competition between multiple algorithms.
- **Hyperparameter tuning** – Algorithms possess various parameters that can be altered to control their operation and how they are applied to the data. Each one will have a range of acceptable values. Most AutoML tools will pick the parameters automatically and allow a degree of adjustment.

By combining the above aspects, ML begins to be democratized. It becomes available to a broad set of technologists and scientists as well as business executives. It does this in two particular ways:

- **Model competition** – Many tools will pick a set of candidates then build models based on various combinations of those candidates. From there, models are trained and tested to determine which is the most accurate. As soon as the training is complete, a leader board shows which is the most accurate model.
- **Building ensembles** – AutoML deals with the creation and packaging of models to make them look similar. Many AutoML systems want this task to be done by humans. Ensembles are computed more accurately than single models.

However, their scoring takes longer, since it is repeated a number of times before any consensus predicted value can be computed. Much of this work can be parallelized, though the extra infrastructure required to run things in parallel isn't free.

Generating a model through AutoML can be hugely beneficial. The icing on the cake is AutoML's ability to deploy the model to production and then monitor and manage it to maintain its accuracy and efficacy.[146] The tasks here include:

- **Model deployment** – This involves creating a callable web service to score new data against the model, then deploying it to some hosting environment and gaining an endpoint (i.e. a URL).
- **Model monitoring** – In this process the model is monitored by software programming and running new data through it to ensure and maintain accuracy. If the model drifts, the changes are checked continuously. Bear in mind that in a competition between models, the particular standard used for accuracy varies and can be calculated.
- **Model retraining** – Many systems respond to drops in accuracy while managing and retraining models on an automated basis. These systems sometimes just operate at a determined frequency. This type of feature is used with models that work specifically with streaming data. Hence, AutoML systems that manage such operations completely handle the entire process from start to finish.

It should be clear by now that AutoML offers immense value and could enable most companies to apply ML effectively with significantly reduced costs (see *Figure 33*). It has the potential to accelerate AI's adoption.

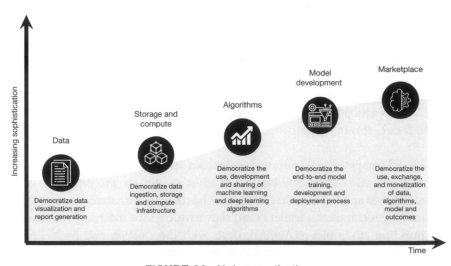

FIGURE 33: AI democratization

GOOGLE CLOUD AUTOML

Google Cloud AutoML (cloud.google.com/automl) is among the most reviewed and universally accepted options, often referred to as the best-of-breed tool in the AutoML category. It is superb at most aspects of automation related to feature engineering and hyperparameter tuning, and claims to perform as well as Kaggle Masters[147] (i.e. people who have been certified as masters of Kaggle).

Google Cloud AutoML starts with your existing model and data. It then implements automatic deep transfer learning and a neural architecture search (meaning that it finds the right combination of extra network layers) in order to run systems for tasks such as language pair translation, natural language classification and image classification. In each area, Google has existing pretrained services based on deep neural networks and sets of labelled data. These may well work for users' data, and using them can result in significant time savings. In addition, Google Cloud AutoML helps users to create a new model without the need for transfer learning or even knowledge of how to create neural networks. Transfer learning has two benefits compared to training a neural network from the beginning. First, it needs less data for training as the majority of the layers are well trained. Second, as it only operates the final layers, it programs quickly.

Google Cloud AutoML has several APIs. For example:

- **AutoML Translation** – This API allows for training against 1,000 two-language sentence pairs using transfer learning. The base neural network, which can be customized, took hundreds to thousands of hours to train from scratch for each language pair, on a large number of CPUs and GPUs. However, the AutoML Translation Beginner's Guide describes the basics of what AutoML Translation can do: it refines an existing general translation model for a niche purpose.[148] No training needs to be done for general translation of about a hundred languages that Google already supports. However, transfer learning is available for specialized vocabulary or usage. General-purpose translation cannot always use the correct terms for niche or new words.
- **AutoML Natural Language** – This API deals with text files and predicts entities, sentiment, syntax and categories (from a predefined list). If a text classification problem doesn't fit any of those, the user can supply a labelled set of statements and use AutoML Natural Language to create a custom classifier. To set up AutoML Natural Language for training, it is necessary to source the data, label it, prepare it as a CSV file. AutoML Natural Language's interface can be used to upload and label the data.
- **AutoML Vision** – This API separates pictures into numerous predefined groups. Furthermore, it identifies individual objects and faces within pictures, and finds and reads printed words. AutoML Vision allows a list of categories to be defined and trained. This has real-life applications, such as detecting faults on wind turbines from drone photos and classifying

recyclables for waste management. Setting up an AutoML Vision dataset requires at least 100 images for each category, and they must be labelled in a CSV file. All of this needs to be saved in Google Cloud Storage.

Google Cloud AutoML also provides customized facilities for translations like customized text and image classification. Each API delivers good performance if it is given sufficient accurately labelled data. Additionally, using these APIs takes less time and skill than building a neural network model from scratch; it is possible to create TensorFlow models without necessarily knowing anything about TensorFlow, Python, neural network architectures or training hardware. The three APIs work to prevent any unnecessary mistakes, as all of them check for the most common errors, such as having too few or too many exemplars for any category. The diagnostics shown after training give a good idea of how well the model works and enables models to be tweaked by adding more labelled training data and rerunning the training.

MIND FOUNDRY

Mind Foundry (mindfoundry.ai) develops automated ML software aimed at technical users with limited data science training. Founded in 2016, the company spun out of the University of Oxford's Machine Learning Research group. Its founders – Professors Stephen Roberts and Michael Osborne – and a group of their researchers combined decades of ML expertise in Bayesian inference to apply principled probabilistic methods to real-world problems. The software now lets users apply that same probabilistic thinking to their data problem, yielding scientifically rigorous models with clear estimates of their confidence bounds and their uncertainty in predicting outcomes.

PLATFORM

Mind Foundry provides an automated ML platform capable of discovering a suitable predictive model for both supervised and unsupervised learning problems, focusing on augmenting the user's domain expertise (e.g. an engineer in a mechanical manufacturing company or a clinical trials analyst in a pharmaceutical company). At its core lies a Bayesian optimization toolkit, used for model selection and hyperparameter tuning. However, the platform takes users through a guided end-to-end data science journey, starting from data cleaning and preparation and ending with a deployed, managed and auditable model that can be directly integrated into any business system. In the following paragraphs, we describe the methods used by the Mind Foundry platform, following the data science journey a user would typically follow.

First, users load data into the platform by uploading flat files in any of the common formats (e.g. CSV, TSV or XLSX); connecting the platform to a database management system (e.g. IBM Db2, Microsoft SQL, MySQL or PostgreSQL); or even connecting to cloud storage from any of the major cloud providers. Data is automatically parsed, with intelligent type and format detection. Moreover, an initial analysis is performed to store additional metadata, which the user can override.

Second, the user prepares the data by putting it into a format suitable for training an ML model. Here, one of the key differentiators of this platform plays an important role: the data adviser. The data adviser uses context-aware analytics to suggest cleaning procedures, feature extraction methods and format conversions. This will lead to better ML models being trained. The user can also explore the data visually, through interactive histograms, word clouds and time series plots that automatically resize to sub-selections of the data.

The third step is the modelling phase, where the platform performs a model search using Bayesian optimization. Bayesian optimization employs a surrogate model, often (as in this case) a Gaussian process, to capture knowledge about a problem's parameter space. The optimizer chooses the next best place to explore in that large, often infinite set of possible model hyperparameters to maximize the information obtained using an acquisition function.

With this method, Mind Foundry can solve several problem types, including binary and multi-class classification, regression, clustering and time series forecasting. The last of these can be tackled either through the general platform interface (which is aimed at a broad set of users) or through a bespoke interface designed for users in the financial sector (which focuses on feature generation and exploration). The platform has settings for advanced users, including several validation methods, data stratification, standardization and stationarization, and model-specific score metrics.

The trained model can finally be deployed into production in one of two ways. At the lower level, this can be done through data preparation and model inference APIs. At a higher or more managed level, it can be done through the use of Mind Foundry's operationalization and governance platform.

PLATFORM

Mind Foundry's operationalization and governance platform provides performance monitoring, automated model retraining, model correction, versioning, governance and third-party integrations, through which alerts and notifications are also delivered. The platform is built in a containerized fashion and deployed via a Kubernetes cluster. It can be hosted on any cloud provider, particularly those that offer a managed Kubernetes service (all the major commercial providers do). It can also be deployed on-premises and managed by a customer IT team.

When deployed on the cloud, Mind Foundry's software can leverage the power of automatic resource scaling (cluster auto-scaling, both in computational resourcing and in storage), requesting the computational resources needed to perform a task only for the duration of that task, and scaling back down when the task completes. This provides large cost savings compared to flat hardware usage and can flexibly handle peaks in demand.

USERS AND USE CASES

Mind Foundry's platform is targeted at a broad audience, with a strong focus on simplifying the data science process and making it accessible to business problem owners. It has primarily been used in three areas: financial services, life sciences and industrial telemetry. In finance it has been used for process automation, for fraud and compliance, for alpha discovery and portfolio optimization, and as a heavy presence in the insurance market. In the life sciences, the Bayesian optimizer lies at the core of several experiment design solutions, at all technology readiness levels. In industrial telemetry, Mind Foundry has had its largest successes in predictive maintenance, data-driven design and accident detection.

The time series forecasting capability has been particularly successful in investment funds, helping users transition from a fundamental approach to a quantitative approach. The primary user of the platform is often the technical expert.

SENSORY INTELLIGENCE

DL for image and video analysis is continually evolving as companies such as Sensory Intelligence (sensoryintelligence.ai), Facebook, Google and Microsoft work non-stop to create bigger and better models for the community. A new state-of-the-art model is one that we can categorize as increasing a performance target, usually lower processing time or higher pure accuracy. For instance, video analysis often requires fast models as frames can be streamed multiple times per second. In contrast, static image analysis is often content to trade off that speed for higher overall accuracy. End users should not have to think beyond this level if a democratization tool can do its job. Based on the problem and the dataset description, Sensory Intelligence's platform will automatically choose the best model for a problem.

Sensory Intelligence's data journey is simple for users, with three main steps. First, it assists the user in creating an unbiased and balanced dataset. Second, the user then guides the platform by labelling examples in the dataset, injecting their actual domain knowledge. Third, the platform trains an AI model to solve the problem. Then, the trained AI model is hosted on the cloud and served globally. Using industry best practices, including access control, it is ready to use in production environments.

Sensory Intelligence's approach is based on the idea of 'bring your own knowledge' (BYOK). As for other democratization tools, users do not need to have a deep understanding of image processing, computer vision or AI. The users understand their images, and the AI helper enables that knowledge transfer in the form of labelling. This democratization process puts the power of years of research and development in image and video AI into the hands of anyone.

EXAMPLE USE CASES

Some of Sensory Intelligence's example use cases are as follows:

- **Medical imaging** – Sensory Intelligence's imaging AI has been applied to many forms of cancer (e.g. lung, breast and skin). The result was that the AI could perform as good as or better than its human equivalent. Imaging AI has also proved useful in classifying heart electrocardiograms (ECGs), scoring 92% versus 79% for doctors.
- **Quality assurance** – Imaging AI has great potential application in processes that are already heavily automated (e.g. automating the inspection of pills or their packaging on an assembly line). Imaging AI could detect the faults and raise issues to be dealt with.
- **Security** – The actual cost of closed-circuit television (CCTV) is not in installing the cameras but having the ability to monitor what is happening 24/7. Instead of having a human attempt to multitask and focus on ten different video streams, imaging AI can run in the background and process them all independently. For example, a building site may need to identify whether any people are on site for health and safety auditing – this can run around the clock automatically.

The recurring theme here is that a computer is much faster than a human, is not prone to bias or fatigue, and can scale rapidly. Many similar arguments were made for the moving assembly line back in the early 20th century. The integration of AI is the next step on our collective efficiency journey, both inside and outside the commercial world.

AUTOMATION AND ROBOTIC PROCESS AUTOMATION

WHAT IS AUTOMATION?

Automation is at the heart of effective, sustained digital transformation. Automation is transforming a wide array of business operations by using software to carry out tasks previously performed by humans – and even, in some cases, tasks that are too complex for humans to perform unassisted. In this way, automation can free up humans' time to focus on value-adding activities and can enable businesses to draw deeper insights into their activities and customers.

BENEFITS OF AUTOMATION

Automation has various benefits:

- **Improved efficiency** – Automation software is typically able to process information and execute tasks far more quickly than humans can. It can run at any time of the day and night, can be rapidly scaled to flexibly manage demand, and can even be programmed to identify and overcome process hurdles.

- **Improved quality** – Unlike humans, software does not make mistakes. Automation provides a means of ensuring greater accuracy and consistency in execution. It is widely used to assure quality (e.g. in regulated industries, where failure in quality control can cause significant financial or reputational damage).

- **Improved customer and client experience** – Automation can significantly improve the customer experience through faster and more consistent service, extensive insight into customer preferences, and the ability to allow self-service. Better quality and predictability of services can also lead to benefits relating to service level agreements, strengthening client relationships, and increasing business competitiveness in rebid processes.

- **Improved operational insight** – Automation technology enables businesses to rapidly process high volumes of data, and complex algorithms can be used to derive deep operational and customer insights.

- **Improved employee experience** – By decreasing the amount of human time spent on administrative tasks, automation allows employees to focus their energy on more rewarding and value-adding activities, leading to better professional development and increased employee satisfaction and retention.

There is a broad spectrum of automation technologies available. These technologies use programmed software to execute the tasks required. Examples include:

- **Robotic process automation (RPA)** – automation of structured business processes
- **Optical character recognition (OCR)** – converting content from paper or electronic documents into machine-readable data
- **Natural language processing (NLP)** – extracting information by processing spoken language

Often, these technologies can be implemented together within the same business to streamline the end-to-end service.

ROBOTIC PROCESS AUTOMATION

RPA uses software robots to replicate manual and repetitive processes and tasks (keyboard or mouse tasks, mass email generation, data reading and entry, database creation, file transfers, etc.). The software robot acts exactly like a human – each robot requires system credentials to be set up for it to use, it needs the same levels of access to the same systems, it moves the mouse where the human moves the mouse and it tabs where the human tabs.

RPA is particularly effective for high-volume, high frequency, repetitive processes that follow simple rules and require limited or no judgment – meaning that software bots will be able to learn the process easily.

BENEFITS OF ROBOTIC PROCESS AUTOMATION
RPA has various benefits:

- **Accuracy and consistency** – RPA improves accuracy and consistency of performance by substituting rules for judgment and eliminating the potential for human error.
- **Time** – By decreasing the amount of human time spent on administrative tasks, RPA frees people up to focus on more value-adding activities, including enhancing the customer experience. This can lead to a happier and more motivated workforce.
- **Processing speed** – RPA also improves processing speeds. Robots operate more quickly than humans, work longer hours, and can be pre-programmed to undertake work out of hours, during times of lower systems utilization or when the office is closed. For instance, an RPA bot can be programmed to perform invoicing overnight, ensuring reports are available to finance teams before the start of working hours.
- **Flexibility** – RPA enables businesses to manage demand flexibly by allocating more bots to processes at peak times (e.g. a product launch) and then removing them (along with the associated cost) once the peak has passed. This capability can be delivered in an agile way to allow businesses to cope with unexpected peaks, such as incidents.
- **Improved quality of data** – RPA can also improve the intelligence-gathering capabilities of a business. RPA robots generate high volumes of structured data, which can drive deeper insights into operations and customer needs, improve decision-making, and ensure safe and compliant service delivery. These processes can be continuously monitored for exceptions and opportunities to improve efficiency.

CURRENT LIMITATIONS OF LEARNING

ANTHROPOMORPHIZING ML AND DATAISM
'Dataism' is a term coined by Yuval Harari to describe the era that we are entering, in which we trust data and algorithms more than our own reasoning and judgment.[149] Take, for instance, the ability of people to trust deepfakes or their GPS. That trust in part comes from our insecurity about asking the question lest we look like fools, and partly from the convenience of the information, which panders to our prejudices and biases. Anthropomorphizing ML and projecting our natural desire to fit our truths on it means we can be led down blind alleys

toward results that are absurd. The problem is that the rigour won't kick in until there is a fatality or severe loss.

DETERMINISM

ML is a stochastic process. There are no natural constraints concerning what algorithms must conform to. It is entirely data driven, and it does not form any closure with the laws of the universe; the solution is never unique as it has bounds and uncertainties. This is primarily because the data is never complete. Data and its permutations are as many as there are grains of sand. When we collect data, we should expect a degree of uncertainty in our results. Through some aspects of feature engineering, feature selection and feature constraints, it may be possible to embed some conformance with the limitations placed by universal laws, but that moment is not here yet.

LOCAL GENERALIZATION VERSUS EXTREME GENERALIZATION OF DATA ISSUES

The problem with data alchemy is that there is not enough data, or that data is not sufficiently pure or clear and it lacks quality. Using data that is not sufficient to train a neural network will introduce a bias that can be fatal. It is like training a baby to eat just pizzas. A better dataset would contain variety (for the baby, complete nutrition). Training an algorithm with images that represent only a small subset will lead to errors. Often, even with tens of thousands of images, errors can occur in ML because of contextual or environmental differences – for example, a fox in a domestic setting may accidentally be classified as a dog. ML has got relatively good in image recognition and classification with human-annotated data. Much of ML is relatively far from human capabilities, and we know the huge limitations of humans in this space.

Another problem revolves around unfairness and bias. Data will reflect the biases that society currently has embedded within it. Many of these will not be palatable or even meet national legislation when one sees them embedded in a machine algorithm.

MISAPPLICATION

Increasingly, we have a flood of people applying AI in a way that is quite blind and without due regard for the actual problem. At the same time, people are creating democratizing tools without due processes for guiding right behaviours during the ingestion of data (i.e. feature engineering). Moreover, from the selection of appropriate algorithms to their manifestation and then to the model's evolution to reflect the changes in the environment (use case or data), there is a danger of misapplication. There are two possible consequences:

- As the amount of data increases exponentially, there is a real danger of creating spurious correlations that will be statistically significant. Say, for example, that we accidentally related the duration of charging a mobile phone to how much water we drank. It just would not make logical sense.

- Statistical modelling is about confirming some hypothesis, while ML is about exploration. We should be cognizant of what we want from the data. Data is the alchemical substance, but it needs to be used to create the right results. It will not deliver anything else.

INTERPRETABILITY

The outputs of ML models may be of minimal value unless the results can be interpreted in a practical way. Most, if not all, life sciences – such as genomics, metabolomics and bioinformatics – are dependent on ML and large amounts of data. If we cannot interpret the data, how can we tell whether the results are correct?

MULTISENSORY ALGORITHMS

Given that natural intelligence is multidimensional (as indicated in *Chapter 3*), it makes sense that multisensory learning should work better than learning from a single sense. In biological systems, the major senses are visual, auditory, kinaesthetic and tactile. Other senses include taste, smell, balance and feelings (emotional, hunger, thirst, etc.). Multisensory learning is different from learning style. This term is capable of being misinterpreted, so let us be clear what we mean. Multisensory learning for us uses multiple sensors and multiple devices to get data that enables us to learn more effectively by building algorithms that reinforce truths over and above what would be possible with a single sensor. Multisensory learning may enable us to learn and switch on sensors that will provide better data and cognition. The different modalities provide data that allows a coherent mental perception.

There are many places where multisensory intelligence is necessary. Take the case of detecting and classifying a drone in a military or civilian context. There are four ways of detecting a drone: visual (normal vision as well as other parts of the visual spectrum), the sound that it makes, the radio frequency signal that it consumes for control, and possibly the use of radar for echo location. Our team at Capita created an algorithm that made use of data from the first of these sensory modalities. By combining them, we could identify the model and variant of a drone. The drone's modes of operation (hovering, filming, moving away from or toward us, and whether it had been modified) were also identified. A single sensory model could not have enabled all that.

Increasingly, as 'sensors are everywhere' (a term coined by our team to represent complete awareness of a particular environment through the IoT and sensors of suitable types), they become a key part of connected environments. Multisensory intelligence will be a crucial aspect of effective and optimized operations.

LEARNING SELF-IMPROVEMENT AND EVOLUTION

All learning algorithms are self-improving in some way. For natural systems, the improvement is reflected, hopefully, with changing behaviour over time. For humans, there are a lot of self-improvement books and materials. Two issues they cover are:

- A call for **self-awareness**, as seen in aphorisms such as 'know thyself' and 'know thy measure,' attributed to various Greek sages and inscribed in the forecourt of the Temple of Apollo at Delphi
- A need to forget about setting specific and actionable goals and instead focus on **changing your internal mechanism**, as argued by James Clear in his bestseller *Atomic Habits*[150]

Both can be applied to any general system to enable the possibility of improvements. The epigram 'know thyself' recognizes that a neural network may have been wired wrongly or have been trained with data that does not represent relevant and necessary truths.

Self-improvement, as the phrase implies, is the result of self-examination. For humans, changing your internal mechanism is a matter of trying to change our habits, sensibilities and motivations. For machines, these mechanisms are in their infancy. People are working on the problem, though. For example, Joshua Tenenbaum of MIT's Department of Brain and Cognitive Sciences and Armando Solar-Lezama of MIT's Computer Science and Artificial Intelligence Laboratory have been working on program-writing AI. Their offering, called SketchAdapt,[151] looks at the basic building blocks of any program. It can look at the overall structure of programs and algorithms and then fill in details using a statistical approach or a more rules-based approach. The main idea is to let neural networks enable program synthesis and decide what a program knows and what it does not. That may seem like a tall order, but when the program gets stuck, it uses lots of examples and trial-and-error strategies to fill in holes. At the moment, it is limited to writing small blocks of computer code.

In our view, self-improvement can only come from a program's ability to change itself in some way. This might be because the data has changed or the way the neural network is connected has changed. It is not possible unless the machine has the ability to then move its components around and make changes to them.

For humans, our evolutionary mechanisms mean that certain properties are propagated from one generation to another. Machines need a different evolutionary mechanism. These mechanisms will only become available through the types of work being done at places like MIT.

The DNA of intelligence and the way those codes are combined must be one of the frontiers of research – and we do not underestimate the complexity of this work. This work is indispensable if we are to really get to a stage where the sensory data can be consumed effectively so as to enable emergent behaviour (see *Chapter 3*) in machines: the need to consume all relevant data from a multitude of sensors to be cognizant about the environment is the adaptation and optimization problem for any intelligent system – natural or artificial.

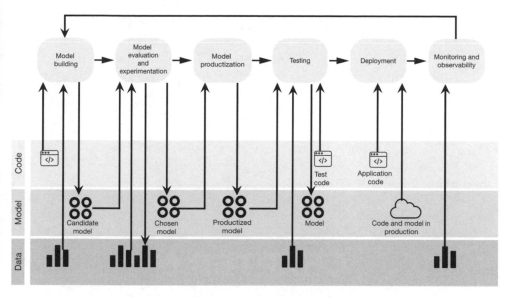

FIGURE 34: Components of an evolving machine learning model

Given all of the above, which may appear rather fanciful to many readers, what can we say about the current evolutionary approaches to DL?

DL systems must be plugged into continuous delivery systems and should adapt to changing environments (see *Figure 34*). Generally, a changing environment is reflected in changes to the properties of a set of data. This can be incorporated relatively easily if the system has the ability to retrain with data, and indeed most algorithms must do that. Take, for example, a chatbot that has to undergo changes to its corpus because users keep asking things that it was not originally trained to answer. Clearly, there need to be mechanisms in place to make semantic connections between the various new unanswerable questions and flag them to an appropriate human to provide answers, particularly when the answers need contextualization and personalization. This process requires a periodic update to the knowledge base. Natural language generation (NLG) models such as Turing-NLG or GPT-3 could be used to answer other questions reasonably automatically.

There are tools that are emerging to enable productionized models to incorporate the changing nature of data. This is done through retraining the models and putting them back into deployment.

CHAPTER 6

THE AI LANDSCAPE: PRESENT AND FUTURE

We have covered many aspects of data alchemy in previous chapters, and we have attempted to explain consciousness and show how it may be possible to implement it using various technologies and software code. We have not touched on the prime directives (wanting to be or having a reason to live) for non-natural entities, and we can only speculate as to where they could first appear.

The impacts of AI are already everywhere. All industries are radically transforming because of the increasing availability of relevant data. We use 'industry' in its broadest sense, to include the application of AI to the humanities, the natural sciences and engineering. There are many problems related to the possibilities offered by intelligence: the availability of data, the provenance of the data, the right type of (understandable) algorithms, and the legal obligations of those involved in the field.

Of course, several players have been able to collect and train models unhindered in the initial gold rush, the most prominent of which are Amazon, Facebook, Google and Microsoft.[152] Recent players such as Alibaba, Apple, Baidu and IBM can be added to this list. In turn, this has severely handicapped many other companies, and indeed countries, which are now seriously considering their national economies and wealth pipelines. As nationalism begins to rear its head again in the light of the battle for dominance in the fourth industrial revolution, technological heavyweights (corporations and nations) will engage in the usual political games. This will inevitably lead to a struggle of imperial proportions, which will only accelerate the use and adoption of AI and all related technologies.

These emerging technologies include quantum computing and its application to security and AI; blockchain and its impact on provenance, decentralization and security; the Internet of Things (IoT) and explosive growth in sensors everywhere as well as edge cognition (the need for cognition to the point of data ingestion has obvious advantages in that it reduces data traffic, latency, security risks, etc., as well as the availability of specific hardware that can be specifically suited to the type of data being collected); emergent paradigms around contextualization and the manifold hypothesis; the societal impacts of intelligent machines; and the research, development and commercialization of the third and fourth types of AI.

This chapter considers these issues, among others, and elaborates on some of the key possibilities. This discussion's primary objective is to make AI specialists and decision-makers familiar with the current possibilities and the emerging landscape, as well as the key challenges that they will face within the next few decades.

EXPLAINABLE AI (XAI) AND TRUST

Humans are, by and large, irrational beings when it comes to most critical decisions. Take politics, vocation, leisure or love as examples. Most people make decisions about these things based on chance, circumstances, prejudice and intuition. We just accept the right of everyone to make their own decisions and potentially be wrong. The nature of our language is fuzzy and inexact. We cannot hold our leaders or our peers to account – not unless we wish to go insane. And sometimes, human decisions are just plain wrong and inhuman. Just take the multitude of conflicts, holocausts and genocides as an example. No human can justify those inhuman decisions. However, humans continue to do so.

However, when it comes to AI, we want to know why an algorithm made a particular choice or decision.[153] We want to be able to explain the decisions, hence the phrase 'explainable AI,' or XAI. For example, we must understand why an algorithm makes a particular decision in order to understand how it determines if the foe is a friend or foe for military purposes.

Humans often make mistakes. Occasionally we see headlines containing the words 'killed by friendly fire' and the explanation of 'friendly fire' is sometimes given out of political expediency when these acts are deliberate. We are known to be fallible and to have emotional states that often go awry in confrontational or 'fight-or-flight' scenarios. We often make wrong decisions even when we are not stretched or stressed through our inbuilt prejudices, biases and intuition. It is just the nature of being human. The consequences of our cognitive connections and decision-making fade away as humans die. So, if a human makes a mistake, we may reprimand them, divorce them, lock them up, forgive them or pardon them.

But machines are different. Machines need not be mortal. They have no souls. Their decisions are seen to be a permanent feature of them that becomes increasingly embedded with time. We cannot reprimand them; we cannot lock them up and we certainly cannot divorce them. To do so would be to go back to the Stone Age. So, we want the decisions embedded in machines to be explainable. Right now, we are approaching machines with the attitude of doing what we say rather than doing what we do. However, machines can be tricky to manipulate as we cannot always tell a machine what to do. Defining what is right can be even more difficult, and the topic of ethics will be covered in the following section. Of course, the relationship between truth and fairness is open to a considerable amount of debate and discussion. For some, it is a question of philosophy; for others it is a question of how data is used and the prime directives. Until recently, 'explainability' and interpretability were not problematic when it came to computer programs. Computer programs were deterministic. If a program did something unexpected, we called it a bug or, more euphemistically, a 'feature.' We are not saying that AI cannot contain bugs, but ML and AI have changed this reality. One of the points that is not brought out with enough clarity about AI is that it is inherently non-deterministic. Contrary to AI, traditional software – with its rules and limited number of workflows – could be audited and any flaws explained. This is not so much the case with AI. It is easy to see how trust in AI and its explainability are closely intertwined. It is difficult to trust an algorithm if we cannot explain how it came to a particular conclusion. Thus, computer programs have moved from a deterministic to a non-deterministic paradigm.

The issue of trust is multifaceted. For humans, trust is built through social norms and some form of normalized behaviour. Essentially, they are based on time-invariant behaviour rooted in socially acceptable values over a lifetime, but values change over generations. As humans, we tend to forego asking people to explain their decisions. And even if we do – as might happen during judicial processes, for example – the irrationality of the human mind is breath taking. Often, we label people as having psychosis. But every human has this to some degree, and there is no way to root it out. It is an inherent mechanism in nature, and perhaps it serves some evolutionary purpose. Researchers indicate that post-hoc explanations by humans of their behaviour tend to be based on a subconscious narrative that supports a positive view of the self rather than the facts – that is, humans' explanations of their reasoning tend to be unreliable.[154]

The factors that are necessary to trust AI are:

- **Fairness** – The AI must be context-dependent and must be predicated on human-derived protected attributes such as race, gender, age, disability and religion. An algorithm is fair if the risk associated with these protected attributes is equal. There can, of course, be bias in the training data, as it will generally contain data that has been collected in a human system containing human biases. Bias can also be caused by how an algorithm has sampled data and the way it has been trained. Fairness is typically measured according to legislation such as the Disability Discrimination Act 1995 or the Equality Act 2010 (in the UK), or other international regulatory and advisory frameworks, such as the Universal Declaration of Human Rights.
- **Explainability** – Explaining decisions is an integral part of human communication, understanding and learning, and humans naturally provide both deictic (pointing) and textual modalities in a typical explanation. The challenge is to build DL models that can explain their decisions with similar fluency in both visual and textual modalities. Directly interpretable ML (in contrast to post-hoc interpretation), in which a person can look at a model and understand what it does, reduces epistemic uncertainty and increases safety. The reason for this is that inspection can reveal quirks and vagaries present in training dataset distributions that will not be visible during deployment. Different users have different needs from explanations, and there is no satisfactory quantitative definition of interpretability. Recent guidelines and

regulations in the European Union require 'meaningful' explanations, but it is unclear what constitutes a meaningful explanation.[155]

- **Robustness (safety and security)** – Adversaries can attack AI services in various ways. These adversaries look for misclassifications (called 'perturbations') on the part of AI of some specified inputs.[156] These perturbations are small, yet they create loopholes through which foreign elements can infiltrate the AI system and risk the security of millions of users. Sensitive information about data and models can be stolen by observing the outputs of an AI service for different inputs. Services may be architected to detect such attacks and may also be designed with defences. New research[157] has proposed certifications for defences against adversarial examples, but these are not yet practical.

- **Lineage** – This applies to both data and algorithms. Lineage looks at the origin of something, where it has been and what has been done to it. There are tools that enable users to trace back to the origins and all evolutions of data and algorithms. This allows an audit at every level. The information may span multiple organizations. Lineage can be difficult to implement, especially given the pace of change when multiple parties are involved. In addition, democratization of many aspects of AI and data is leading to an exponential rise in the number of operations performed on data through an array of algorithms with a multitude of hyperparameters.[158]

Clearly, trust in AI is largely based around trust in data, and explainability is only really relevant to algorithms. The type of AI used determines the difficulty of getting a trustworthy output. Among the simplest models to interpret and trust are decision-tree-based supervised and unsupervised learning – the tree structure can be followed, and the factors used to arrive at a decision can be made apparent. Among the most difficult models to trust are those based on DL neural networks because the hidden layers are connected to other layers through weights and activation functions, resulting in nonlinear and complex relationships. There is some work underway in this area, including projects funded by DARPA related to creating layers that capture simple elements or more complex ones to see which features are driving the reasoning and results.[159]

Among the techniques that are currently available are the following:

- **Sensitivity analysis** – This involves performing small perturbations in input features to see the impact on the model outputs. The resulting information can then be used to give a model of feature importance and, consequently, it can be related to fairness, lineage, robustness and explainability.

- **Local Interpretable Model-Agnostic Explanations (LIME)** – The problem with sensitivity analysis is that it does not deal with interactions between input parameters. LIME performs multi-feature perturbations between particular model outputs. Open-source versions of this technique are available, and it is one of the more commonly used techniques for interpretability.

- **Shapley Additive Explanations (SHAP)** – SHAP's goal is to explain the prediction by computing the contribution of each feature to the prediction.[160]
- **Tree interpreters** – Decision trees are highly interpretable but the least accurate. A decision tree interpreter can be applied and feature importance assessed.[161] This makes decision tree interpreters the most basic go to algorithms for many explainability issues. Open-source tree interpreter packages are available thus making for easy and wide-spread adoption.
- **Neural network interpreters** – One of the hinderances to the adoption of DNN is their black-box nature and this of course reduces its appeal to mission critical applications such as medical diagnosis. Research is being directed at exploring interpretability using fuzzy logic and brain science.[162]

Several AI tool providers have released tools to help to build interpretability of outputs. Google, for example, says of its offering:

Explainable AI is a set of tools and frameworks to help you understand and interpret predictions made by your machine learning models. With it, you can debug and improve model performance, and help others understand your models' behavior. You can also generate feature attributions for model predictions in AutoML Tables and AI Platform, and visually investigate model behavior using the What-If Tool.[163]

Trusted AI will assume significant importance as the complexity of models increases along with the veracity, variety and volume of data. The issues organizations will face will be about justifying their decisions related to products or services. The field of AI will become increasingly regulated, and there will be a growing clamour to protect vulnerable and sensitive clients and consumers. Without explainable AI, governance will be almost unattainable.

ALGORITHMIC ETHICS, SECURITY AND GOVERNANCE

The moral principles that govern the behaviour of algorithms pose some challenges. The problems arise from many different directions.[164] We have covered some aspects of the problems that cognitive algorithms can pose in the section above on explainability and trust. There are, of course, serious issues around security, safety, and privacy too. Everything is very human-centric. Algorithms are there to help humans, and they must adhere to our litany of disparate and disconnected regulations while still encouraging innovation, enterprise and discovery, while providing added business value.

We must bear in mind that there are times when humans may well be the weakest link in the dynamics of the overall system from the perspective of security, safety and governance. As was discussed in *Chapter 3*, the human cognitive system is insecure. Due to the fact that we are so connected and are susceptible to brain hacking (through techniques such as the illusory truth effect), how do we counteract the effects of disinformation (through state actors, anarchists, etc.) as society becomes more polarized?

Despite human weaknesses, we must also address many issues that are increasingly governed by algorithms. The distinctions between polymorphic malware, deepfakes and data poisoning need to be clearly dealt with in ways appropriate to each. Our critical national infrastructure systems may be compromised when they begin to rely on algorithms to make decisions. Some things should not be stored in a public cloud for obvious reasons related to infrastructure, security and control boundaries. Response times and the ability to intercept and destroy content that may affect national security (by external and internal players) are becoming crucial. The systems in place need to be studied for their resilience in such scenarios.

In addition, we also need to consider network traffic increases in terms of capacity and analysis, the monitoring of diverse channels, regulatory powers such as the Investigatory Powers Act 2016 and the Investigatory Powers Regulations 2020, human rights issues, and more detailed analyses of potential internal threats while still respecting the diversity of people's opinions and beliefs. Given that disgruntled employees may work at the heart of such systems, when do their beliefs become a threat to national security?

It is possible to probe models and discover their inner workings. If someone knows how our algorithms work, they can outdo us. Increasingly, we will have AI versus AI – having a human in the loop in certain scenarios will just not be possible, as some scenarios will require detection and response in less than a second. Distinguishing between the good guys and the bad guys will be difficult when the threat is extreme.

In broad terms, the following subsections consider issues that we struggle to deal with even in non-AI scenarios – issues such as bias, social engineering, deep beliefs, and provenance of information. Translating these issues to AI makes the arguments even more urgent.

That said, while we recognize the issues around algorithmic bias and the need for governance frameworks, we must not forget that the root cause of bias is data and how it is curated and consumed. As data-democratization tools become more widely available, data parameterization should enable many of the current complex and intractable algorithmic issues to be resolved. So, while we recognize that explainability is a major issue for AI, we do not believe that bias will continue to be so indefinitely.

ALGORITHMIC BIAS

A lot is currently written about algorithmic bias, and the issues are becoming ever more pressing as the exponential growth of data is requiring algorithms to become more complicated and have automated decision-making. The issues with algorithm bias related to making decisions about people, their identities, their preferences and their attributes are widely discussed as they are the prime focuses of fairness and discrimination in decision-making. There is no one-size-fits-all approach to fairness, and it is difficult for algorithms to implement things that have not been resolved at a societal level.

The UK legislation that prohibits discrimination on the basis of specific protected characteristics (age, disability, gender reassignment, marriage and civil partnership, pregnancy and maternity, race, religion or belief, sex and sexual orientation) is the Equality Act 2010, and the General Data Protection Regulation (GDPR) and the Data Protection Act 2018. There are a few situations where exceptions can be applied. For example, an organization could validly bar a Christian from being appointed to the post of a rabbi.

While there have been many cases of algorithmic bias, these have often arisen because the data reflected current or historical biases. For example, historically, women had a lower employment rate than men. Algorithms may perpetuate this outdated bias when making credit decisions. There are similar issues around other protected characteristics in decisions relating to parole, insurance, recruitment, advertising, facial recognition, employment, pay, promotions, fostering and many other areas.

There are reasons to ensure that algorithmic and systems bias are removed – for example, regulatory fines and reputational brand damage. Appropriate questions need to be asked before, during and after the development of algorithms that may impinge on protected characteristics. There are many useful design question templates and bias impact statements. We particularly like the one from Brookings.

To remove bias, it is important to have diverse teams working on the algorithm. Involving diverse teams will ensure that many algorithms' problems are spotted earlier and before the algorithms are put into the production phase.

Measuring algorithmic fairness is difficult because there are various statistical measures of fairness:

- **Anti-classification** – The model is fair to the extent that it does not use encrypted proxies or characteristics from which other encrypted characteristics can be implied.
- **Calibration** – A well-calibrated algorithm is one in which the risk scores it gives to people reflect the actual outcomes in real life. Protected groups must be calibrated on an equal footing to ensure fairness in calibration definitions.
- **Classification** – A model is fair if protected groups receive the same outcomes as non-protected ones.

Methods to detect and mitigate biased, unfair and discriminatory decision-making include statistical approaches and software toolkits, discursive frameworks, self-assessment tools and learning materials, and auditing and documentation standards. Commercial tools for algorithmic bias testing are beginning to appear on the market; however, for the reasons mentioned above, their results can be challenged. Perhaps the best way of removing bias is to completely remove any data related to protected characteristics, but this may also remove some of the key analytics that businesses will want to know.

SECURITY

There is a legitimate debate as to whether AI is a positive or negative factor in human life, and it is relevant at two different levels – personal and national. We can extend the debate to global security, but it flows naturally from the considerations at the first two levels. Below, we cover only aspects relating to cyber security, as the areas related to physical security are relatively broad, particularly in national security.[166]

PERSONAL CYBERSECURITY

Among the positive impacts of the use of AI for cybersecurity are the following:

- **Biometric logins** – These are increasingly being used to create secure systems access by scanning fingerprints, retinas or palm prints. They can be used in conjunction with traditional passwords and are already available on most new smartphones. Businesses are prone to security breaches, which may compromise email addresses, personal information and passwords.
- **Malware** – AI can be used to detect threats and other potentially malicious activities. Conventional systems simply cannot keep up with the sheer number of instances of malware that are created, and AI systems can learn to detect and neutralize viruses and malware by using complex pattern recognition algorithms.
- **Natural language processing (NLP)** – Some systems for detecting cyber-threats use NLP to collect information automatically by analysing articles, news, social media, blogs and studies on cyberthreats. This way, a security system can become proactive in looking for signatures of threats and build strategies.
- **Multifactor authentication** – This provides safe and secure access to users of various services. Different companies have different multifactor authentication systems to provide safe and secure access to their consumers. The AI system develops a dynamic framework that works with real-time variables such as time and location to ensure safe access by modifying privileges based on real-time data.

Limitations and disadvantages of AI in cybersecurity include:

- **Computational requirements and costs** – To build and maintain an AI system, companies require an immense quantity of resources, including memory, data and computing power. Moreover, as AI systems require a variety of datasets and make more robust decisions when different datasets are available, companies use malware and non-malicious code to train their respective models. Obtaining the appropriate datasets may be prohibitively expensive or may take a long time.
- **Phishing** – AI has the potential to supercharge this threat, increasing the ease, speed and extent of an attack.
- **Polymorphic malware** – Hackers can use AI to test their malware and improve and enhance it, potentially to make it AI-proof. Such systems make traditional security programs more vulnerable. They have the dynamic ability to learn from existing AI tools and develop better resilience against traditional cybersecurity frameworks, even AI-boosted systems.

Perhaps the most significant weak link in the entire security framework is the personal security of humans. As mentioned above, we humans are relatively easy to hack due to our value systems. Even if the systems around us can be made secure, hackers can make us do things so that the security of the systems can be compromised.

NATIONAL CYBERSECURITY

AI offers real traction on issues related to national cybersecurity. The word 'national' can be used with a bit of artistic licence here as the arguments can be extended to large multinationals' ecosystems as well.[167] The distinction between nation-states and large multinationals perhaps rests on the fact that the former have to pay particular attention to human rights legislation.

As alluded above, where AI attacks are involved, the required response speed is beyond what is possible under human decision-making. The issues with national cybersecurity can broadly be separated into several areas, as follows:

- **Data volume, veracity and velocity** – It is necessary to monitor network traffic patterns over time and use AI to learn unusual patterns. The volumes of data are so large, and their veracity and velocity are so high, that only AI makes these tasks possible. However, coupled with frameworks allowing the interception of that traffic and the ability to look for specific threats from players (known and unknown), the use of AI enables many threats to be mitigated.
- **Regulation** – Issues around bulk datasets of personally identifiable information (PII) and legitimate national interests can pose significant issues related

to legislation (such as the Investigatory Powers Act 2016 and the Investigatory Powers Regulations 2020).

- **Human involvement** – A hybrid human–machine approach to augmenting human decision-making will be crucial. However, the involvement of a human can pose significant challenges. For example, AI-mediated behavioural psychometric profiling of individuals inside and outside national boundaries has legal and ethical issues.
- **Data poisoning** – It is essential to be able to handle data-poisoning attempts. These are rogue attempts to overwhelm AI systems with unusual traffic, deepfakes (see below) and data storms. Synthetic data can also be a significant issue in this regard.

The algorithms used for national cybersecurity are the usual ones related to classification, clustering, NLP, reinforcement learning, temporal analytics, voice analysis and speech analysis, as well as the use of social media analytics engines to listen for any signatures that identify threats.

The future landscape of AI in cybersecurity will be a battleground of AI versus AI, with self-evolving algorithms (of the type discussed in *Chapter 5*) that can detect vulnerabilities through model leakages and formulate strategies against polymorphing. As such systems improve, the speed of response is likely to overwhelm human systems of governance, and we are not convinced that there will be much of a distinction between the actions and strategies of the 'good' and 'bad' players. The ability to distinguish between state actors and individuals may be narrow indeed. The need to make actions explainable will grow, while the adoption of provenance strategies (e.g. through blockchain) and the introduction of deep intelligence into edge devices will become crucial. This will be especially true as the use of IoT expands to create fully connected cities.

DEEPFAKES

The term 'deepfake' emerged in 2017.[168] It refers to the use of DL to create an alternative (fake) reality that is difficult for us to distinguish from reality. That alternative reality can be created for reasons of entertainment or mischief. Creating deepfakes is relatively straightforward, given the number of apps and technologies that are available. The technique is available to anyone of any skill level. While media experts can identify deepfakes, they are often transmitted rapidly through social and professional media. Therefore, identifying them as such may take too long to counter any effects caused by them.

Consider the simple example of getting Donald Duck to say something that Walt Disney would never have dreamed of. To create that, all one needs is a relationship between sound and mouth movements, and possibly gestures for added reality. That can be done from a few seconds of an original video.

Couple this with the mouth movements and facial expressions and movements, and you have a deepfake video.[169]

Deepfakes pose a real challenge at many personal, national and international levels.[170] Much of the world has enshrined freedom of speech and expression as an immutable ethical principle. A lot can be justified under freedom of expression (whether it is superimposing someone else's face on a porn model, discrediting political opponents through fake videos, or posting fake news corroborated by fake research papers that are quoted chapter and verse), and we do not believe that human cognitive behaviours have the ability to overcome this mischief in the short term. Intuitive intelligence is a related concept, and we cover some aspects of it in the sections below.

SOCIAL ENGINEERING

Given we have indicated that deepfakes will influence the debate on freedom of expression, it is possible to see that there are aspects of AI that will affect the way we relate to each other socially. These impacts will not just come from the relationship between AI and some of our sacred constitutional rights. They will also come from the perspectives of disparate fringe and marginalized groups with access to technology that can influence the basic processes of regulation and governance. Democracies increasingly rely on popular mandates, and popular mandates will increasingly marginalize minority belief systems.

When we acknowledge that AI and data harvesting can gather public information on people and spear-phish them (i.e. personally target them) at scale, then we are unavoidably on the route to recognising that social engineering is the next step. A bot can imitate people and personalities, and voice communications can be personalized and contextualized. We can extend this point to include social media influencers, who may increasingly use automatons to handle their offerings (advice, products, placements, events, etc.) when they are not there in person. Given that most of these entities will be Turing-complete (as in that it passes the Turing test – a human cannot tell whether the communicator at the other end is a machine or human), it would take a person of high intellect to tell the difference. Regulatory frameworks will always move more slowly than individuals' ability to create ingenious products with business value.[171]

The impact of AI on social engineering is not a one-way street. The regulators will want specific values embedded in certification and licensing of certain products and technologies. Society needs to evolve and embedding policies within algorithms may be as harmful as not having them there in the first place. Just imagine if we lived in a segregated world, and those rules had been legally embedded in silicon. Regulation is there for a reason, and it is often to protect one vested interest against another. The romanticism of doing the right thing is difficult to uphold when, ultimately, there are arbitrary national interests. Some may argue that freedom to innovate and experiment is the most basic of nature's purposes. If the rules that get embedded in algorithms had a natural justification, we might justify their existence better.

The issues of privacy, freedom and expression may well come up against natural and evolutionary processes. This is true for personal experiences and also for societal and national interests.

MATHEMATICAL VALIDATION

Some of these issues are tackled well in a report from the Royal United Services Institute for Defence and Security Studies (RUSI) published in 2020.[172] Research that is trying to define the behaviour of AI using mathematical formalism and rigour is ongoing. Some of this formalism is intended to describe various broad types of unintended and harmful AI behaviour and propose AI design techniques that avoid that behaviour. When we look at the effort and expense devoted to security, the effort related to AI's ethicality seems insignificant. However, the problem of defining and creating ethical AI continues and interest in it will grow enormously. No set of rules is adequate to describe human values, so human values must instead be learned iteratively. AI systems that mimic human values are some way off. As to whether they are even desirable is yet another topic.

BLOCKCHAIN AND AI

The thing to remember about blockchain is that it gets rid of intermediaries. Imagine a world where we do not need a bank to transfer money between two parties, or we do not need central passport control to verify that we are the citizen of a country. The first example is easy enough to understand while the second appears a bit more convoluted. Traditionally, these issues have been resolved by centralization. The idea of decentralizing them seems counterintuitive – even futuristic.

That definition of blockchain, the technology that underlies cryptocurrencies such as Bitcoin, will appeal to all who see the sorry state of centralized models of business and networking. Centralized models are synonymous with expense, bureaucracy, corruption, slowness and inefficiency, and they are prone to systemic failures and major disruptions.

The financial markets are already buzzing with applications, experiments, and technological demonstrations around blockchain because it can make financial transactions faster and cheaper. Blockchain is better equipped to confront cyberattacks and secure the personal data of users from online theft. Blockchain can be used to implement transparency in supply chains, elections, and commercial contracts.

While its impact is currently mostly being felt in the financial sector, block-chain can also play a major role in the development of AI:

- **Data** – Data is the lifeblood of AI. Increasingly, data exchange and democ-ratization platforms will have to incorporate blockchain (rather than data lineage, provenance and decentralization frameworks), with AI being the core part of data-democratization frameworks.
- **AI frameworks** – Blockchain will have to become more mainstream in terms of its use in explainability frameworks as well as frameworks for cognitive AI related to provenance and lineage, including aspects related to autonomous AI entities.
- **Decentralization** – Requirements for decentralized intelligence are spawn-ing a number of companies, such as AI Blockchain, Effect.ai, the Open-Mined project and Synapse AI. There is also a growing list of use cases where blockchain can benefit from AI.[173]

There is little doubt that the future of AI's development lies in an ecosystem of democratized data, and the merging of AI and blockchain may lead to a free flow of monetized data between consumers and providers. The danger, as was the case with the prime movers of the information age, is that data hoarders and those with binding relationships with data ecosystems will become the new monopolies.

QUANTUM COMPUTING

There are a number of reasons that quantum computing is receiving wide press coverage.[174] First, computing is reaching its limit. The power of quantum com-puting is improving but the existing software is not completely compatible with it. Quantum computers are only good at solving some specific types of issues. As quantum computers are increasingly becoming commercially accessible, we must look at some of their primary applications.

IMPACT OF QUANTUM COMPUTING ON SECURITY AND AI

The advancement of quantum computing essentially means that traditional cryptographic and AI algorithms will become obsolete. Ciphers that were previously considered to be unbreakable can be deciphered by quantum computers in a matter of seconds. It is safe to assume that with the advent of quantum computers, the existing security infrastructure of computers will entirely break down.

Despite making the current security infrastructure obsolete, new quantum cryptographic techniques could make communications more secure. One exam-ple is a concept known as 'quantum key distribution.' This makes it impossible for an eavesdropper to intercept communications between two parties even if they have access to the private key.

In the quantum world, it is difficult to maintain reliable computations. As of now, it is challenging to sustain coherence between different quantum states. It turns out that small changes in the environment (vibrations, temperature, electromagnetic waves, etc.) can cause unmanageable noise. It is also difficult to code quantum computers, let alone make a programming language of some sort that developers across the globe could easily understand.

APPLICATION OF QUANTUM COMPUTING TO AI AND BIG DATA PROBLEMS

The rate at which we are producing new data is overwhelming for any classical computer. Quantum computers could potentially process these vast amounts of data in seconds and recognize important patterns in the data in a way that was previously not possible. Another noteworthy point is that, with quantum computers, analysis and integration of different datasets would become very easy enhancing our AI and NLP capabilities.

Quantum computers are complicated to engineer and build. The susceptibility of quantum machines to data distortion and noise further limits their application. It is challenging to pretrain their neural networks, and most researchers have abandoned this unsupervised form of learning for supervised neural networks. Quantum computers could allow machines to adapt to external stimuli in real time, thus making unsupervised learning possible and paving the way for more intelligent machines.

MOORE'S LAW OF LEARNING EFFICIENCY

In 1965, Gordon Moore, a co-founder of Intel, hypothesized that the number of transistors in an integrated circuit would double every year. This idea (if not the exact timescale) came to be known as Moore's law. His statement became a prophecy. After 50 years, Intel's technology could process information at a rate 3,500 times faster than it had in 1965. This growth trajectory was unprecedented, and no other technology on the horizon is likely to grow at such a fast pace. One essential by-product of this innovation has been the formation of AI as a domain of its own.

In 2020, a paper from OpenAI stated that the organization had begun to track a measure of ML efficiency (i.e. doing more with less).[175] Algorithmic efficiency is important for two reasons. The first is that three inputs drive progress in ML: available computing power, data and algorithmic innovation. The second is that tracking algorithmic efficiency enables academic researchers to justify the cost of their computational requirements and anticipated future costs.

In their experiments, the OpenAI researchers evaluated the progress of AlexNet[176] over a considerable timescale through open-source reimplementation. ResNet-50's[177] performance on ImageNet exhibited a similar doubling time of 17 months.

The amount of computing required to guide a neural network has decreased since 2012. As per some estimates, it has decreased by a factor of two every six months. Neural networks now use 44 times less computing. During the same time period, Moore's law may have increased cost-effectiveness by 11 times.[178] Several futurists make use of such laws to predict when machines will outsmart (a somewhat fuzzy term) humans. These range from 2041 to our prediction of 2051.

OPEN AI INITIATIVES

There are many initiatives from industry, academia, government and special interest groups driving the agenda for formulating and harnessing the potential of AI and related technologies. It is legitimate to look at the various groups and their statements and examine what they have to gain from it. These are questions that will affect the future of the democratization of such technology and the shift in the future of business value. The concern is that most of the big players are based in the United States; the advantages they have – in terms of a much lighter regulatory burden than companies in Europe – are fundamentally skewing the economics and consequently global politics around AI. The following initiatives are playing crucial roles in the development and experience of AI:

- **Allen Institute for AI (allenai.org), Seattle, Washington, US** – This is a research institute founded by the late Microsoft co-founder Paul Allen. The institute is working to achieve scientific innovations by building AI systems with reasoning, learning and reading capabilities.
- **Beijing AI Principles (baai.ac.cn/news/beijing-ai-principles-en.html)** – The Beijing AI Principles focus on the development of AI while considering the future of all humankind. Research and development of AI according to these principles focus on doing good; working only for humanity; being responsible while controlling risks; being ethical, diverse and inclusive; and being open and sharing.
- **DeepMind (deepmind.com), London, UK** – DeepMind has built a neural network that can play video games just like a human. It has also created a neural Turing machine, commonly known as a neural network, that can access an external memory like a conventional Turing machine.
- **DeepMind's ethics and society principles (deepmind.com/about/ethics-and-society), London, UK** – DeepMind works on technical safety, ethics and public engagement goals for its users. It focuses on exploring

short- and long-term risks and finding ways to prevent them. It has hired an ethics team that works with other organizations and companies to create platforms for the public to explore some difficult issues.

- **Future of Humanity Institute (fhi.ox.ac.uk), Oxford, UK** – This research centre, located at the University of Oxford, works for the betterment of human civilization and its long-term future. It has worked on many key concepts, such as the simulation hypothesis, existential risk, nanotechnology and information hazards.
- **Future of Life Institute (FLI), Cambridge, Massachusetts, US** – The FLI's goal is to support research and initiatives for protecting life and developing optimistic ideas about the future. These include positive ways for humanity to steer a course in response to new technologies and challenges.
- **Google AI (ai.Google), California, US** – GoogleAI conducts research in building new spheres of AI. Moreover, it focuses on making AI more accessible to people around the world.
- **Institute for Ethics and Emerging Technologies (IEET), Boston, Massachusetts, US** – The IEET is a technological think tank that tries to understand the impact of emergent technologies on humans and societies around the world. It does this by promoting the work of researchers who examine the social effects of technological advancements.
- **Leverhulme Centre for the Future of Intelligence (CFI), Cambridge, UK** – The CFI's research explores the opportunities and challenges of AI.
- **Machine Intelligence Research Institute (MIRI), Berkeley, California, US** – The MIRI is a research institute that focuses on managing potential risks from AI. It uses an AI system to meticulously design and predict the rate of technological development.
- **OpenAI (openai.com), California, US** – OpenAI's mission is to ensure that artificial general intelligence (AGI) (see *Chapter 3*) benefits all of humanity. It has funding from Bill Gates and Elon Musk. While its primary goal is to build safe and beneficial AGI, it also considers enabling others to do so to be part of its work. It released GPT-3, an unsupervised transformer language model, in 2020 but has numerous other offerings too.
- **OpenCog Foundation (opencog.org)** – This is a project that aims to build an open-source AI framework. This will take the form of architecture for robot and virtual embodied cognition that defines a set of interacting components designed to give rise to human equivalent AGI as an emergent phenomenon of the whole system.
- **Open Neural Network Exchange (ONNX) (onnx.ai)** – This is an open-source system that represents ML models. ONNX contains a set of operators like the building blocks of machine and DL models. It has a common file format to enable AI developers to use models with various frameworks, tools, runtimes and compilers.

- **Open-source robotics (OSR)** – OSR offers some physical artefacts for the open design movement. It is a branch of robotics that uses open-source hardware and free and open-source software to provide blueprints, schematics and source code.
- **Studies on risks from AI** – AI is growing daily and so are the voices warning against its current and future consequences. Many people refer to AI as 'destructive superintelligence' that is beyond human control. It is seen as an automation that has spurred job loss, with socioeconomic inequality rising each day. In addition to its more existential threat, many companies believe that AI will adversely affect privacy and security. Various bodies are studying these issues.
- **Vicarious (vicarious.com), Union City, California, US** – Vicarious says that it uses computational principles based on the human brain. Its search for AGI is based around four areas of research and development: data efficiency, DL, neuro and cognitive sciences, and network structures.

FUTURE GENERATIONS OF AI

We are now on the cusp of the fourth wave of industrialization. The first wave, in the 1800s was about mechanization using steam power. The second wave was about the electrification of mass production, which gave us electricity and the assembly line in the early 1900s. The third wave, starting in the 1940s, was about computers. We are now witnessing an exponential growth of smart artificial systems, such as self-driving cars, robots and drones embedded with AI systems. They will change how we live in ways we cannot anticipate today, just as no one envisioned the railways and automated factories that would spring from the first steam engines. Indeed, no one envisaged that computers would spring from electricity. During the third wave, we developed digital computers, information technology and digitalization of transactional data.

The fourth wave is considered a new era that is not built on the third wave's edifice. It is not hung on the coat tails of obsolete technologies. Instead, it has yielded a sustainable and intelligent ecosystem where machines can make intelligent decisions, and simultaneously learn and improve through big data. The present generation is witnessing the fourth wave of industrialization, and its manifestations include the IoT, virtual technologies, AI, quantum computing and blockchain. This has changed the way we think, work and experience the world. AI has become the core of all technologies around hardware, security, innovation, data and experience. If we tackle AI, we end up tackling all transformative technologies, including our evolution.

The following sections explore some key areas of this fourth wave of industrialization.

MANIFOLD HYPOTHESIS

Currently, big data comes in many forms, including speech, videos, IoT, medical imaging, genomic markers and other data sources. The manifold hypothesis states that high-dimensional data tends to lie near a low-dimensional manifold (space). Fitting low-dimensional nonlinear manifolds to sampled data points in high-dimensional spaces has been an area of extensive activity in many industries over the past decade or so. These problems have been viewed as optimization problems and they involve generalizing the projection theorem.[179]

When similar data is generated separately, it is discontinuous (i.e. it does not neatly fit together). The primary assumption of manifold alignment is that data can share a similar underlying manifold representation. This gives rise to ML algorithms that use projections between datasets if the data belongs to a common manifold. Projections from the original space to a shared manifold enable sharing of data (knowledge) from one domain to another. When correspondence can be made between two high-dimensional datasets, we say that we have manifold alignment.

Problems where there are several datasets on a shared manifold can best be solved through manifold alignment. However, each dataset must be of a different dimensionality. Many real-world problems fit this description, but traditional techniques cannot take advantage of all datasets at the same time. Manifold alignment also facilitates transfer learning, in which knowledge of one domain is used to jump-start learning in correlated domains.

Applications of manifold alignment include:

- **Cross-language information retrieval and automatic translation** – By representing documents as vectors of word counts, manifold alignment can recover the mapping between documents of different languages. Cross-language document correspondence is relatively easy to obtain, especially from multilingual organizations such as the European Union.
- **Transfer learning** of policy and state representations for reinforcement learning.
- **Alignment** of nuclear magnetic resonance spectroscopy of proteins (protein NMR) structures.
- **Accelerated model learning** in robotics by sharing data generated by other robots.

FRACTALS, QUANTUM AI, NEUROPLASTICITY AND NLP

The company Mandorla (mandorla.ai) makes use of fractals (i.e. affine self-symmetries) to try to understand natural language. In relation to this, researchers have revealed emerging maps of complex neuron geometry while constructing a map of the complex neuronal patterns of the brain related to cognition and reasoning.[180]

Architects and city designers have been looking for inspiration from biological and natural architectures. Many feel that the knowledge derived from complexity theory and pattern recognition in nature can be used to explain fundamental processes behind urban designs. This has led to the development of theories relating to the 'urban web,' according to which lack of social connection and coordination causes urban life to descend into anarchy and other social problems.

Other theories include the growth machine, which shows that activities in cities are controlled by different social groups just like the human body is controlled by groups of neurons. Accordingly, fractal theory explains that the elements are always different, but their configuration depicts naturalness, wholeness and uniformity just like a human body. The intricacy of networks in biological entities is, thus, seen to provide the potential to generate increased urban coherence and better quality of life. This theory could be applied to current emerging urban concepts such as smart cities.

Unlike machine-stimulated neural networks, which do not form new neural connections, humans can recognize, learn and change according to the activities they must perform; a process called neuroplasticity[181] or brain plasticity. For a long time, it was believed that as humans aged, the connections in the brain became fixed. Research has shown that learning helps in the evolution of the brain. We now know that the brain evolves and changes from learning new things throughout life, and this phenomenon is termed 'plasticity'. These changes occur at the most fundamental level in the brain (i.e. in the neurons). In an interconnected cityscape, new connections emerge, existing synapses can be activated in different ways based on the needs of the network, and the topology can evolve. The implementation of ANNs is fundamentally based on a requirement for dynamic data exchange and adaptability. The point here is that there are many structures of different scales that have parallels with each other. A city has a similar topological structure to the way that neurons are connected, and this structure in turn is similar to, say, how the leaves of a tree are shaped or the structure of the cosmic web. Couple this to the fact that NLP can be modelled using ANNs, fractals and qubits (quantum bits) and we reach a surprising hypothesis that perhaps manifold mapping is scale invariant. Perhaps the very structures we use at the quantum scale are equally applicable to the human scale, the city scale and the cosmic scale.[182] We are increasingly seeing that data is the *prima materia* of all structures, and consequently we believe that architectures at various scales will look similar.[183]

EMERGENCE OF CONSCIOUSNESS

As stated in *Chapter 3*, based on data from the Laboratory of NeuroImaging at the University of Southern California, Los Angeles, humans have around 70,000 thoughts per day.[184] However, the researchers offer a couple of qualifiers: first, there is no agreed acceptance of what a thought is and how it is created and, second, a thought in this context is a sporadic single-idea cognitive concept resulting from an act of thinking or produced by spontaneous systems-level cognitive brain activations.

The starting assumption one has to make about any machine form of thought is that consciousness is a natural phenomenon, which suggests that consciousness is subject to natural laws rather than being supranatural. Consequently, a scientific theory of consciousness must identify physical or information-theoretical conditions for consciousness. As a result, we can extend the argument to include a new assumption – a reasonable one, in our view – that biological brains are not the only vehicle for consciousness. So, any physical system that fulfils a certain yardstick of consciousness and adaptation must possess internal experience.

The very subjective nature of conscious experience makes it difficult to satisfy these conditions given that consciousness is both functional and subjective. The functional aspect, also known as 'access consciousness,' encompasses the objectively observable aspects of consciousness, which are amenable to scientific scrutiny, while the subjective aspect, known as 'phenomenal consciousness,' is not directly observable except by the person experiencing that conscious state. This linking of phenomenal consciousness with a physical system is called the 'hard problem' of consciousness, and it remains unsolved. Potential solutions to the hard problem mostly converge on the idea that consciousness is epiphenomenal – in other words, we feel subjective experiences only as information's by-product without ourselves playing any functional role. In terms of implementing consciousness in machines, the same two levels of the hard problem apply: the state of consciousness (i.e. ready to tackle a situation or scenario) and the contents of consciousness (e.g. awareness of specific sensory data and its relevance).

The main thesis behind the generation hypothesis (see *Chapter 3*) is that consciousness is manifested through the ability and need to internally generate sensory representations that are not direct reflections of the current sensory input. These could be counterfactual or factual and may be maintained over time in short-term memory or long-term memory. Generally, they deal with sensory and future strategic consequences if certain actions are not taken. This hypothesis enables an explanation for the need of evolved life to realize the functional advantages of consciousness.

The advantages of hypothesis generation[185] can also be shown in reinforcement learning. Generally, reinforcement learning strategies are divided into model-based and model-free learning strategies. Model-based learning takes account of sequential possibilities of events and actions; that is, a model predicts the possible future states of a given set of actions. This enables the agent to use the structures of the environment and their own memory to plan and implement a course of action. In contrast, in model-free reinforcement learning, the agent does not learn directly from the structures of the environment or their memory, and they derive the best possible action solely from their current state.

How can a model generate information internally and continually work out strategies to be employed in dealing with real-world stimuli when they arrive? There exist generative adversarial networks (GANs) (see *Chapter 4*) with variational encoders (VAEs) for generating sensory representations, and these can be used to interpret the cognitive processes in the brain. The VAE works by compressing and transforming the input data to create an internal representation of low latency represented using low dimensionality. A decoder then converts the data back to create an abstraction of the output space. Once the model is trained, the decoder network can be decoupled from the encoder and internal representations of data become possible – almost in the way highlighted in the section on synthetic data near the end of *Chapter 4*.

We realize that there is a significant difference between the information depth available in machine generative models and models of consciousness in the brain. This can be tackled by using variants of the NLG models Turing-NLG and GPT-3 to generate all possible expressions of output from a particular narrative input, through which imagery, sound and other experiences can be generated.

If we can achieve that level of synthetic reality generation, it would almost be like a conscious entity with all of its motor neuron functions paralysed. The extension to manifesting action would not be difficult with advances in robotics and brain–computer interfaces (BCIs).[186] The missing piece of the jigsaw after that will be the motivation.

There is, of course, another approach to consciousness. That approach is based on the systems engineering principles of emergent behaviour. As we continue to connect more and more neural networks to real-world data through multisensory devices with ever more significant and diverse networks, a school of thought contends that a form of consciousness (perhaps entirely dissimilar from our own) will increasingly be involved in the process of optimization. This could include aspects relating to self-policing, and control of supply, production and consumption chains.

Whichever way we look at it, we are convinced that within a generation we will be on the cusp of a machine working under our stewardship that will be as conscious as us and much faster than us, but with reasons for its existence determined by us.

INTENTIONALITY

Consciousness has many advantages, such as the ability to be proactive and to act intuitively and strategically in response to events. The missing piece for us in this puzzle is that of *intentionality*. What is the reason for an intended action? This might be considered akin to 'wanting to be'. Intentionality in humans is driven by three primordial subconscious neurological phenomena: we need safety, we need to matter and we need to belong. If consciousness is "the subconscious compression and reinforcement of data" and intuition is "the subconscious integration of a chaotic diversity of data," as Kieran D. Kelly[187] says, then we would contend that intentionality is "the use of governance frameworks to enable an optimized response to interaction with other agents"; a sort of symbiotic interdependence.[188] That is, intentionality is the result of core mental and cognitive components such as belief, desire and awareness; it represents the foundation of social interaction and is necessary in order to matter and to belong.

We can see how intentionality must be the goal for agents that have consciousness. Perhaps it is not possible for consciousness, intuition and intentionality to be divorced from each other. In the context of AI, we can see the tremendous business advantages that machine-implemented intentionality can bring. It implements the actions that make a business thrive (*matter*) and succeed in the context of competing businesses *belonging* within a governance framework created by national and international agencies (*safety*).

DEEP BELIEFS, INTUITION AND KNOWLEDGE

A psychological state of mind in which an individual holds something to be true without any scientific proof or rational explanation is termed 'belief'. Intuition is the capacity of conceiving something immediately without conscious thinking. The difference between the two is of feeling. In a sense, intuition is based on subconscious processes that rely on past experiences and accumulated truths.[189] Knowledge is data accumulated through learning and experience, and it is used to solve a particular problem.

These concepts are crucial in the AI context, where we want to extend a model to a stage where there is insufficient data to allow a credible decision. Instead, the model must be built up from examples of transfer learning or outputs from problems that might appear similar. This is where third-generation ML and the use of manifold alignment (as discussed above) will make a difference. Increasingly, building an intelligent machine will require some internal representation of the machine's belief state (see *Figure 35*). It will become difficult to separate knowledge from deep beliefs without the use of data lineage, which can tell us whether data originated in a particular domain or from transfer learning.[190]

Beliefs are flexible and can change when new information is available. There are often limits on the validity of beliefs and the possibility of their interaction with real-life models. In an AI system, knowledge is typically not necessarily either true or useful; there is a statistical element to how it fits into decision-making. This distinction often becomes blurry when an algorithm treats some information as true but may treat other information differently.

In an AI context, the knowledge base should be built from the physical world through observations (and these may have probabilities associated with them); deep beliefs are developed using a combination of manifold alignment (transfer learning) and hypothesis generation (i.e. generative ANNs going through scenario simulations and potential consequences of outputs). In this way, the long-term memory of the knowledge base comes from prior knowledge and is combined with what is learned from data and past experiences, as well as thoughts (as generated through hypothesis generation). The resultant beliefs can then be actioned selectively to enact the required outcomes. The short-term memory of the agent is termed the 'belief state.' This creates the model of the current environment required between time steps.

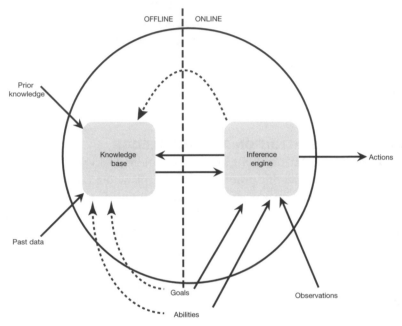

FIGURE 35: Relationship between beliefs (prior knowledge and past data), goals, and actions

Researchers in ML have mostly been adamant about the use of data in contrast to factual knowledge to build a robust edifice. Expert systems mostly have lots of knowledge with no real-time data to corroborate it. However, for most non-trivial systems, agents must work with a blend of knowledge and data to produce the required results.

HUMAN ORGANOIDS AND AI

The research to develop artificial brains is proceeding at a fast pace. Scientists are developing miniature brains that can produce brain waves, just like a pre-term baby. Such brains are developed using stem cells, which can be used to produce functional neural networks. These studies could help scientists to better understand human brain development and help neuroscientists and those involved in computational neuroscience.[191]

Normal human neurodevelopment can be understood using brain organoids. No artificial device of any kind, computer or otherwise, has yet come close to displaying anything like AI on the human level. Currently, we are not aware of any device that even approaches the human level of consciousness. Presently, even those machines that end up being better than humans (e.g. at facial recognition or games such as chess and go) could be considered doing nothing more than high-level curve fitting. For machines to achieve anything that resembles real thinking, they have to face a more profound challenge of making sense of data in a more abstract way so as to be able to work out causation.

Brain organoids offer the possibility of intelligence that is not digital. The way such brain organoids will learn, of course, will be through a combination of digital and analogue inputs: not dissimilar to the way we learn naturally in the present day. Scientists have developed technologies to grow living tissues from human cells, and they have seen that human brain cells form complex constructs similar to those seen in the brain. Moreover, these structures exhibit neural activity that responds to external stimuli in ways that are not unexpected. The importance of this work and other aspects of synthetic biology cannot be overestimated.[192]

These organoids are neither intelligent nor conscious, nor even close to being either, but their descendants in the coming decades very possibly will be. What happens when, during routine research, a lump of neural cells a few inches in size suddenly shows unmistakeable signs of conscious awareness, or has the capacity to feel pain or pleasure? At some point, these organoids may cross over from being complex but inanimate systems to deserving rights of their own, and perhaps requiring the protection of a legal guardian. From a human perspective, it will be easier to come to terms with intelligence from entities built 'from them by them' than entities that are fundamentally alien (digital machines). In addition, organoids will have biological lifespan limits, which means that it will be easier to relate to them.

The promise of biological computing offers not only a route to understanding the dynamics of consciousness and the importance of 'life' but also the possibility that we may get to the fourth type of intelligence without the need for it to be digital.

WHAT DOES THE FUTURE LOOK LIKE FOR AI?

The general consensus concerning the third and fourth types of AI is that machines will have the ability to learn autonomously in real time, to reason abstractly and creatively, and to respond to us using our communication modes. They will have many of the failings that we do because of the impossibility of having complete data in a set of agents acting to optimize their own goals. There is also a strong argument that we need more complex and more comprehensive architectures that have their base in nature. This may come from the application of fractals;[193] from a better understanding of the architectural frameworks of the brain, including neuroplasticity, hypothesis generation and manifold learning;

and from the possibility that some behaviours will be naturally emergent (in a system design sense) when a certain scale of complexity is reached.

In the past, cognitive architectures were largely modular, including modules for short-term memory, long-term memory, parsing, inference, planning, etc. Moreover, these functional modules were developed by different teams without any coordination. This is a serious limitation: these architectures tend not to share a uniform data representation or design, making it near impossible for cognitive functions to synergistically support each other in real time.

A better strategy is to have a highly integrated system that allows seamless interaction of all functions in a manner not dissimilar to that seen in the human brain (see *Figure 36*). For example, correctly parsing, understanding and absorbing the information in a sentence (say, a statement) requires access to short-term memory, long-term memory, goals, context, metacognition and reasoning. Thorough language comprehension and the ability to hold long, meaningful conversations are areas where the advantages of cognitive architectures over DL are most pronounced. However, there is an urgent need for highly synergetic functional interaction for other cognitive tasks.

FIGURE 36: Components of a cognitive architecture and next-generation AI (NLG: natural language generation)

There are a number of tasks and problems that we might expect intelligent systems to be able to do, and many of them will involve enabling better functioning of competing agents. These tasks and problems might include disease and the ageing population, poverty and hunger, natural and human-made disasters, global warming and environmental issues, social and national conflicts, and discovering answers to the unknown. What the second type of AI (neural nets) has given us is a glimpse into the possibilities. The third and fourth types will make us realize that irrationality is not the exclusive domain of natural biology.

We have elaborated the confluence of technologies that will be seen in the future. As we enter this age, we need to take note of five sets of questions related to AI:

- **Autonomy** – What will happen when machines inevitably make better decisions than humans or human agencies? What is the purpose of free will (including for humans)?
- **Agency** – What are the rules for machines? Who decides in a competing framework of nation-states?
- **Assurance** – How will we know that ecosystems run by machines are safe, trustworthy, secure and reliable? Nature has tested systems over billions of years, and death is inbuilt as a mechanism for change, adaptation and levelling the playing field. How will this be implemented in machines?
- **Relationships** – In nature, we are in a symbiotic relationship. We live through one another for one another knowingly or unknowingly. How will we engage with machines that are perhaps better than us? We are starting off with autonomous vehicles and other autonomous devices. What will happen when the relationship is turned on its head?
- **Metrics** – Nature does not necessarily look for the optimal route or use measures based on a logical framework. With machines, which are not natural, what metrics will be used, given that they will need to be based on much more connected and complete data?

SOCIETY AND AI

ML is affecting the way we learn. The learning systems that humans have created are now informing us as to how to learn. It is a seismic shift. We now have massive amounts of collected wisdom, knowledge and data about our environment. We can choose to ignore the data at our fingertips, or we can be consumed by it. From our learning, we can become better adapted to our environment or live in a past that we believe, somehow, will free us from the shackles of being reliant on technology. History shows that we invariably go with the flow, and the flow is very much in the direction of progress, innovation and invention.[194] Along the way, we will learn, as will the systems of our creation.

Consider Cambridge Analytica, the British consulting firm that allegedly carried out psychometric profiling of US audiences to enable targeted distribution of material to voters (see *Chapter 4*). Simply by creating a Facebook quiz app that was downloaded by about 300,000 users, it gathered information about around 87 million people (friends and connections of the people who installed the app). The power of simple AI to make deductions from the users of the quiz and the 'likes' of their friends makes clear the astonishing implications of AI. Having access to data and using a very simple algorithm possibly altered the results of key democratic processes.

This data harvesting and the way the data was used by a well-funded group created an ethical issue.[195] It almost requires us to revisit what being a democracy means. Bodies have always relied on market surveys, making deductions and targeting audiences. In the case of Cambridge Analytica, people will look for the failings in the chain of data privacy, but we feel the issue is far deeper and it will continue to become even more convoluted and complex in this era in which big data enables so much.

The impact of AI on society is a big subject. Cursory research indicates that more than 4 million scientific and academic articles have been written on the subject in the past ten years. There are centres of excellence around the globe and an increasing number of books and blogs on the subject.

Many people would see the main ethical issues around AI and society as falling into the following seven categories.

UNEMPLOYMENT
Given the growth of automation (self-driving vehicles, the automation of manual repetitive processes, the democratization of knowledge, etc.) many businesses could probably and will attempt to automate around 80% of their repetitive procedures and tasks. There are studies that indicate that AI will create more jobs[196] than it gets rid of, but the jury is currently out on the subject. If we look at the revenue bases of three Detroit companies and their counterparts in Silicon Valley, then it would lead us to the conclusion that AI has eaten a significant proportion of jobs. The companies in Detroit and Silicon Valley had the same revenue; however, the workforce in Silicon Valley was ten times smaller than that of the Detroit companies.[197] It is possible to put a positive spin on this subject: one day we might look back and think that it was barbaric that humans were required to sell a significant portion of their time in order to earn a living. We will have to change and redefine what work means for us.

INEQUALITY CREATED BY AI
Global commerce depends on goods and services. Those economies and corporate entities that can effectively make use of new technologies will be able to outdo all the others. This has the potential for those that can invest (the richer

countries, companies, and individuals) to dominate the future landscape of wealth. Inequality breeds revolutions, insecurity, and schisms.

MACHINES AFFECTING HUMAN BEHAVIOUR

As we enter an era in which machines can mimic human responses (e.g. the chatbot Eugene Goostman) and beat humans in traditional tests of intelligence (e.g. chess, Go and poker), more of us are becoming aware of how machines are altering our behaviour. Look around at people when you are on the train or in a restaurant. Whether it's playing games on their phones or checking their social media feeds, people are glued to their mobile devices. Clickbait and tremendously optimized A/B testing ensure that our reward centres keep us addicted to being connected all in aid of selective marketing. Algorithms increasingly and clandestinely affect everything we do: from how we shop to how we vote. Increasingly, they will influence how we learn and what we feel is the purpose of our existence.

MISTAKES EMBEDDED IN LEARNING ALGORITHMS

Like humans, machines learn by example. Humans are not scalable endlessly and have a finite lifespan. When machines learn and become good at particular tasks, they are endlessly scalable and have the potential to dominate a particular issue say, assessing insurance claims. In the not-too-distant future, these algorithms will be so accurate and advanced that no human will be able to compete with their logic. This will make it increasingly difficult to challenge such algorithms even if there are mistakes in them.

BIAS EMBEDDED IN AI

We humans have our memes and cultures, which embed particular biases and prejudices in our being. With machines and AI, the equivalent is data. If the data has bias, then AI will have bias. Most AI's applications today are based on the category of algorithms known as deep learning (DL). It is this class of algorithms that find patterns in data. Algorithms can perpetuate injustice in hiring, retail and security, and they may already be doing so in the criminal justice system (see the section on data ethics in *Chapter 4*). Indeed, there have been many examples where the current generation of 'fair' algorithms has perpetuated discrimination.

KEEPING AI AWAY FROM 'BAD' USE

There will always be people underground (e.g. users of the dark web) who research the use of AI for nefarious reasons. These may involve gaining control of financial systems, weapon systems, or personal or commercially sensitive data; disrupting due judicial processes; and much more. Use of AI in cybersecurity and next-generation neural and quantum cryptography will be of increasing importance to ensure that the current institutions that we know and trust can continue to exist. The fact that there are many state actors involved in the bad uses of AI makes it almost a non-subject, as the technology is almost democratized and ultimately depends on motivations and needs.. We believe that keeping AI away from bad use is an impossible task.

UNINTENDED CONSEQUENCES AND THE HUMANE TREATMENT OF AI

Intelligence in artificial systems is currently superficial. The current generation of DL systems is based on little more than tensor algebra and calculus with particularly efficient optimization methods. However, as indicated earlier in this book, we believe that the building blocks of generalized AI may lead to self-consciousness. Just as we value the rights of animals and the planet, there will emerge procedures and declarations of machines' rights. This will enable machines to be classified according to their rights and responsibilities, so humans cannot act as overlords of all creation. It may be that machines have vastly more intelligence than us but that their form of consciousness (feelings of reward and aversion) is very different from ours. We may start by implementing our value system in neuromorphic hardware, but the neuroplasticity of such systems (i.e. their ability to modify their mechanisms of learning) may ensure that they find their own rightful place in nature with the possibility of self-assembly, evolution and purpose. Depending on the value sets that such systems deem necessary for their own sustenance, humans will ponder the issue of 'pulling the plug' if we begin to become irrelevant or a hindrance to such intelligence.

WHAT DOES THE FUTURE LOOK LIKE FOR SOCIETY AND AI?

In an old (and not well-cited) paper, Nick Bostrom of the Future of Humanity Institute and Eliezer Yudkowsky of the Machine Intelligence Research Institute conclude that:

> Although current AI offers us few ethical issues that are not already present in the design of cars or power plants, the approach of AI algorithms toward more humanlike thought portends predictable complications. Social roles may be filled by AI algorithms, implying new design requirements like transparency and predictability. Sufficiently general AI algorithms may no longer execute in predictable contexts, requiring new kinds of safety assurance and the engineering of artificial ethical considerations. AIs with sufficiently advanced mental states, or the right kind of states, will have moral status, and some may count as persons – though perhaps persons very much unlike the sort that exist now, perhaps governed by different rules. And finally, the prospect of AIs with superhuman intelligence and superhuman abilities presents us with the extraordinary challenge of stating an algorithm that outputs super ethical behaviour.[198]

The issues around the ethics of AI are deep and wide, indeed. AI can change us and the fabric of our society. The governance and regulatory frameworks of traditional institutions are no match for technologies and means made possible by AI. We only have to see the debacle around Brexit and elections worldwide to see the potential impacts of using information and advertising selectively and in a targeted manner. Couple this with the nefarious use of AI, as well as the possible emergence of superintelligence, and there is the potential for great change.

The current generation of AI is simple. It does not have a paradigm of 'I am' or 'I want to be.' Some think that to ask, 'Will AI achieve consciousness?' is the wrong question. Perhaps the more appropriate question is, 'For AI, does consciousness matter?' We have shown above several potential paradigms for machine consciousness, and we passionately believe that an AI form of 'I am' will emerge, perhaps in smart megacities as a first manifestation.

Since the Second World War, we have increasingly found ourselves edging toward popular democracy rather than liberal democracy (where individual liberty is protected by the rules of law as enacted by representatives of people). Given this, how can we keep the freedoms and liberties of the individual while making informed and necessary decisions? It is easy to hack into human motivations and drivers. Therefore, it is important that groups do not hijack the debates around freedom and liberty through hacking into democratic and legitimate processes. The problem is that tribalism based on nationalism blinds us to self-evident truths. The problems humanity faces are increasingly not restricted to national boundaries, and nationalism is only adding to global problems. Populism means that we demonize the stranger. This is quite a bold and simplistic statement to make, but it is a crucial context of so many things.

For many, AI is the stranger. Not many people understand it and newer generations of AI will be stranger still. The prospect of the emergence of conscious cities (including modes of transport, communications, power generation and distribution, supply and production chains, and higher-level manifestations of a living entity) poses particular problems that we hitherto have no handle on. Smart, conscious megacities will become centres of diversity, and in many cases, they will not conform to national popular democratic mandates. Large cities and centres of academic excellence could advocate for advances that alienate most of the population. The alienation caused by insecurity and loss of control will pose an incredible number of problems, as those who are disenfranchised from the wealth created by the new world order will increasingly find a voice in conspiracy movements, leading to a growing schism regarding the value of societal intelligence.[199]

CONCLUDING INSIGHTS ON THE FUTURE OF THE AI LANDSCAPE

We are not among those who believe that AI is just another technology. We believe that AI will require us to examine who we are and change what we do and why we do things fundamentally. AI will change us as humans, as we will have systems around us that are more intelligent than us. We will enter the digitalized world and become more virtualized. AI is the new stranger and, by and large, we humans fear strangers as we have not managed to parameterize them. With AI, we are not sure that we can.

To a large extent, our passion for data is based around a statement that we often articulate:

> I am but a bunch of neurons. Without you, data, I am nothing. I owe everything to you.

If you have a new child or can recall meeting your child or another significant someone, try thinking about that phrase and its relevance. Our purpose in this and previous chapters was to challenge the reader's perception of data and AI. Indeed, we have covered how machines *will* become conscious and the vectors that are leading us there. We are now researching abstractions, processes, values and technologies that will enable machines to have intentionality. The need for governance frameworks (legal, ethical, security, safety, privacy, explainability, interpretability, robustness, etc.) is clear and overwhelming. Safety, mattering, and belonging are the primary motivators of intentionality in nature. We can all speculate about the factors that will lead to intentionality in machines, but we can hopefully see that mattering and lineage will be crucial aspects. As humans, we have beliefs, tribes and associations (e.g. nation-states) that enhance our value as a group and as a collection of people.

The point about all the above rhetoric is that it is a basic and technology-agnostic paradigm for developments in intelligence, data and related concepts. Often, technology gets in the way of understanding big ideas. Consider our nonlinear mind. As mentioned above, we would agree with Kieran D. Kelly that "consciousness is the subconscious compression and reinforcement of data" and that "intuition is the subconscious integration of a chaotic diversity of data." Reinforcement, compression and integration of data are intelligence (in a multitude of forms) as practised by natural selection and evolution. For us, this is the route to the next generation of AI. General business value will be best derived from the democratization of data, application of intelligence to that data, and being aware of the relationship between the actioning of that intelligence and the effect on the environment where the data is derived from.

That may seem exciting or complicated, but clearly the root of all intelligence is data. The biggest problem we face is the fact that data, as captured by most businesses, is incomplete and lacking deep intelligence about its purpose. Data often lacks context, in which case it becomes divorced from the business object it parameterizes. The issues around data can be narrowed down to just four dimensions (each with many parameters and abstractions): trust, relevance, cost and strategy.

We have also deconstructed data democratization into three aspects: parameterization, monetization and exchange (see *Chapter 4*). Once we have a coherent understanding of the nature of intelligence in data (rational and irrational), we can apply ML and develop a framework through which businesses can use evolving data to adapt, evolve and flourish. AI is the easiest part of intelligence as it just reflects the "integration of a chaotic diversity of data" and the "compression and reinforcement of data."

The monopolization of data and information systems by a few companies has severely handicapped many other countries and companies that are now seriously beginning to think about their national economies and wealth pipelines. This will inevitably accelerate the use and adoption of AI and all related technologies. It will also prompt social considerations of the demographic disconnection between wealth accumulation and customer distribution.

The most crucial elements that relate to binding societies and communities together through empowerment will lie in the practical implementation of governance processes so that elements crucial to societies and individuals (privacy, safety, decentralization from overarching monopolies of whatever flavour, security, belonging and value) are embedded in machine intelligence as it is decoded. That is the subject of the next chapter.

CHAPTER 7

DATA ALCHEMY DECODED: DATA INTELLIGENCE AND ARCHITECTING FOR DATA VALUE

The year 2020 witnessed the acceleration of digital ecommerce, with many of us experiencing the need to solve puzzles to access websites. A common verification process demands that we identify traffic lights on an 8×4 grid of squares and then confirm to the hosting site that we are not robots. As John Naughton observes, this is a form of an inverted Turing test: "instead of a machine trying to fool a human into thinking that it was human, I was called upon to convince a computer that I was human. I was being reengineered."[200] This reengineering process, which combines data and experience with the relationship between human intelligence and evolving data insights, can be complex in a constantly changing digital world. It leads us to consider key questions, such as how do artificial intelligence systems and natural intelligence systems compare from the perspectives of resilience, utility and operation? How do they evolve and adapt to new data, and how do new and better systems for handling data emerge? What are the main differences between the two and what sort of work do we need to enable machines to get better at handling sensory data in a way that enables constant iteration, sustained improvement and rapid evolution as the environment changes?

With reference to our AI Periodic Table (see *Chapter 3*), we can see the similarities between the human and artificial intelligence 'stacks,' which are the building blocks of intelligence. These comprise the following components:

- **Environmental data** – This is composed of static and historical data, as well as real-time data, including the IoT.
- **Memory** – In humans, the electrochemical energy of a firing neuron is encoded in the dendrites, turning a momentary experience into a lasting record. Memories are conscious experiences recalled via connections that can degrade over time.
- **Sensory intelligence** – This is intelligence that is embedded in the way that data is collected and processed.
- **Security, privacy and provenance** – These ensure that existential and economic advantages are derived from validated, valuable and experience data.
- **Ethics and governance frameworks** – These are evolved mechanisms for social governance and cohesion, and they also limit the number of possible actions.
- **Evolution of intelligence** – This occurs through neuroplasticity and evolutionary neurophysiology.
- **Types and utility of intelligence** – These are naturalistic, intrapersonal, interpersonal, logical–mathematical, visual–spatial, bodily–kinaesthetic, verbal–linguistic, existential and musical. These enable natural systems to be proactive as well as reactive.
- **Automation of certain types of intelligence** – These are based on hardwiring of certain cognitive behaviours that require little or no data and are

generally manifested through intuition. These include aspects related to fight or flight, new-born bootstrap processes, and so on.

- **Manifestation of intelligence** – This happens through actions and experience (e.g. the connection between insights and motor neuron function).
- **Connectivity mechanisms** – These exist between intelligence and action and are enacted through neurochemicals and electrical impulses.

For humans, the 'technology stack' is one that has evolved over generations and millennia. For AI systems, we are at the beginning of creating such stacks. These are rapidly changing as we develop tools in every component category, such as:

- Connected devices and edge analytics
- The quaternion of issues around data (trust, relevance, cost and strategy – see *Figure 5*)
- Developments in cloud technologies and architectures
- Cognitive services and architectures
- Mechanisms for automating AI and AI processes
- Tools for enabling cognitive evolution (e.g. dynamic adaptation and regeneration of learned mechanisms)
- Tools for allowing synthetic data generation to pave the way for automated hypothesis generation and testing, offering more proactive intelligence

It is not difficult to understand the key elements of natural intelligence and the reasons for their evolution. How we can map these onto AI and create equivalent artificial tools and mechanisms is the theme of this chapter. To explore this theme in more detail, we will outline a practical approach to applying data alchemy and creating business value.

ENVIRONMENT AND ADAPTATION: EVOLUTION OF NATURALLY AND ARTIFICIALLY INTELLIGENT CAPABILITIES

There are many aspects of AI, data democratization, continuous development/deployment/delivery (CD) and continuous improvement/integration (CI) that do not appear to have parallels in nature. Cursory searches in the literature about CD or CI in nature yield no results, whereas the literature about the importance of CD and CI in the development cadence of software systems is substantial and varied. Currently, CD and CI complement agile working, defined as bringing people, processes, connectivity, technology, time and place together to find the most appropriate and effective way of working to conduct a particular task and enable products to be delivered more frequently and more quickly, allowing for regular feedback. A zero-tolerance, fail-fast, trust-based approach forces a progressive advance to success. Somehow and somewhere, nature, be it in the teamwork of beehives or the orchestration of ant colonies, must have these concepts in its arsenal, if not in its very fabric.

However, biological analogue intelligent systems are in many ways very differently constructed from AI. Natural systems work at a different pace in terms of improvement and delivery. The human brain has developed through natural selection over a period of 75,000 years. The human generation gap averages around 26 years at the present. After a human is born, the data and memes they encounter lead to them developing an evolved and environmentally contextualized set of behaviours that become deeply embedded as they grow older. As a result, it can be extremely difficult and painful to retrain an addict or someone with neurological damage. It is problematic to introduce such a person to new data and expect the system to retrain, reset or even refine their personality or behaviour. There are of course rehabilitation clinics and psychotherapists who try to get humans to make changes when there is a major flaw in their behavioural makeup. These processes are not quick or effective most of the time.

There are other problems with natural systems too, particularly in humans. As Jeffrey Kluger points out, "If the entire human species were a single individual, that person would long ago have been declared mad ... the madness would lie ... in the fact that [two] qualities, the savage and the splendid, can exist in one creature, one person, often in one instant."[201] As stated in *Chapter 3*, the mind is what the brain does (this is a consequence of emergence). The contradictions in humans are many and varied, and this must be the result of decentralization of decision-making alongside monopolization of source data. That is, there is no single source of truth, and nature seems to be better for it. This is reflected, for example, in the natural languages that we use, which are fuzzy and open to a multitude of interpretations and meanings.

However, perhaps the closest analogy between nature and software systems is in the decentralization of decision-making (notwithstanding the rather arbitrary set of ethics that we end up justifying as a society or a community). There is no mediator between our decisions. Whatever the merits of it, we generally create our own frameworks for governance and ethics, and these can vary hugely even within our own lifetime. In addition, natural systems are open to manipulation of belief and thought with no overarching system of restraint, save law reinforcement, which is intended to regulate civic society. We make our own frameworks independently and singly. It is true that we are conditioned by our society, tribe or national psyche but, ultimately, different people make different decisions based on their experiences. Once someone arrives at a particular stance, it is difficult to change their decision-making reference points. The surprising thing in this natural decentralized decision-making is that the data is guarded jealously in order to ascertain economic and social advantages. For example, a squirrel will try to ensure that its competitors are not around when it stashes nuts for the winter months. The biological ecosystem is a marvel of natural design, with different creatures having differently tuned (and sometimes unique) sensors and sensory intelligence, so that the system functions like the metaphorical Gaia.

Perhaps the biggest difference between natural and artificial intelligence lies in the concept of 'purpose'. Natural systems are uniquely and singly selfish, save for a kind of pseudo-altruism that enables them to safeguard their kind in order to function and flourish in a changing ecosystem as a collective. For the time being, AI serves no other purpose but to enhance natural intelligence. As a result, we have to move away from seeing natural and artificial intelligence as the same, and reveal how we have begun to implement a road map for AI in our current systems.

DATA ALCHEMY'S ROAD TO REALITY

There are many concepts, paradigms and terms mentioned in this book that may seem theoretical and philosophical. The purpose of this chapter is to instantiate them through a road map that organizations can use here and now.

For most organizations, the data alchemy road to reality primarily involves the following:

- Development of **Industry 4.0 maturity**, where the aim is to achieve convergence between the physical and digital worlds, creating a world of cyber-physical systems and associated processes to realize immense business value.
- Development of **data maturity models** to transform the organization and maximize competitive advantage by understanding the value of data on an enterprise level, and allocating resources and building a sustainable culture to realize that value.
- Realization of **efficiencies** by automating business processes and data-gathering because of new mechanisms using robotic process automation (RPA).
- **Cataloguing, curation, cleaning and wrangling** of data, and determination of data contexts, taxonomy and anatomy, as well as a whole host of other data parameters, such as lineage and provenance.
- Use of **machine learning (ML) data democratization** to promote enterprise continuous intelligence and effective real-time consumption of action-driven insight.
- Deployment of **AutoML system development (Dev) and ML system operations (Ops)** to evolve an ML engineering culture and practice that aims at unifying ML systems to effectively deploy ML models at scale and pace.
- Adoption of **agile methodologies**, such as Scrum and Kanban, to enable teams to deliver value more quickly, with greater quality and predictability, and greater aptitude to respond to change.

- Construction and development of **evolutionary architectures and approaches** that enable the organization to realize the current potential of AI to use data as a societal force for good.

The practical orchestration and choreography of these 'base elements' of data alchemy to create value will vary from organization to organization. However, the implementation of data alchemy requires the creation of a value-based road map to promote the modernization, automation, simplification and scaling of AI architectures. The articulation of this road map and the practical use of data alchemy are the subject of the next section.

DATA ALCHEMY AND THE INTELLIGENCE FOUNDRY

Data alchemy is founded on the premise that data is the base substance of intelligence and consciousness, and that it can be transformed to create new emergent properties that create actionable insights and deliver better business outcomes. To facilitate data alchemy, we have designed the Intelligence Foundry (IF) (see *Figure 37*), which provides for the ability to combine disparate and often competing data components and orchestrate them using the AI Periodic Table to enable better enterprise data-driven decision-making.

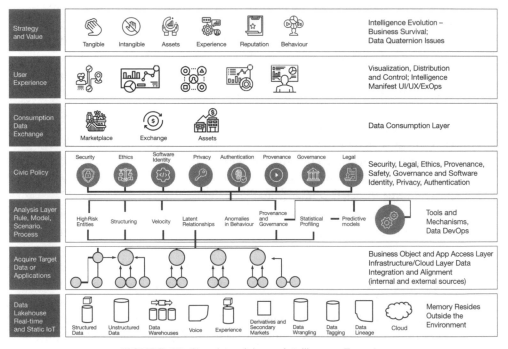

FIGURE 37: The data alchemy Intelligence Foundry
(IoT: Internet of Things)

The IF is designed to facilitate the process of data alchemy, with the resulting intelligence being delivered and consumed as part of a sensory experience within an ethical civic governance framework. Each layer of the IF has its own function and, rather than being viewed as a linear construct, its practical operation is cyclical in nature and interdependent in design.

With the increasing emphasis on digital experiences and the rise of edge devices to enable, create and convey sensory intelligence, the relationship between AI-generated decisions and human consciousness is at the heart of data decision-making. The use of the IF should seek to complement and amplify human decisions. However, the increasing move to machine-to-machine (M2M) rather than human-to-machine (H2M) intelligence to compute and present decision choices means that transparency and understanding of the alchemical process need to be clearer, transitioning from a 'black art' to an open-lineage and trackable 'white box' approach. In addition, the explosive creation and proliferation of data means that in many cases the M2M method will be the only feasible option, making H2M (and its inverse) and human-to-human (H2H) methods obsolete.

In a business context, the success of data alchemy as a process is predicated on an organization being able to effectively adapt to its environment and delineate which parts of sensory data it can rely upon or disregard when evaluating and selecting signals from noise to enable better decisions. Data alchemy entails an organization evolving using the IF so as to be better adapted to its environment. It is this practical aspect of an AI-based sense-and-respond approach delivered via the IF that we explore in more detail in the next section.

BUSINESS STRATEGY, VALUE AND DATA MATURITY: CAPABILITIES AND COMPETENCIES

In the complex digital world, business leaders are increasingly focused on transformational initiatives designed to increase engagement, reduce costs, increase revenue, minimize risk and delight customers. This has led to a redefinition of their enterprise strategy, challenging how the use of internal, external and ecosystem data and analytics can fundamentally change their business and reinvent how they deliver value. Success is then measured by how well the business can establish an integrated set of operational data and analytics competencies and capabilities to achieve business goals. However, value is generated not by having a data strategy but by having a business strategy that is data driven.

Irrespective of strategic intent and despite all the hype surrounding the practical application of AI and ML to enable business outcomes, organizations often fall short when it comes to their ability to use data to drive business performance (see *Figure 38* for the components necessary to develop an effective data strategy). It is often challenging to achieve alignment between the corporate strategy and the data necessary to enable the organization to achieve its objectives and understand when they have been achieved. Among the causes are siloed data and the continually changing and interdependent links between the data vision, business outcomes, value propositions and operating model. However, these factors (see *Figure 38*) must be orchestrated to enact the collective decisions concerning the division of labour and to establish a road map to address the gap between identified enterprise competencies and missing capabilities to achieve business value. Critically, these decisions must consider the trade-offs and compromises that are inevitable when allocating scarce resources to build or accelerate business-critical services and capabilities. To avoid the tripwire of haphazard resource allocation decisions, it is imperative that there is an objective means to evaluate not only the rationale for the decisions but also the impact of the resultant initiatives on business value (e.g. do we have the right competencies and are we organized for success? Do we have the necessary infrastructure? Is governance linked to outcomes?).

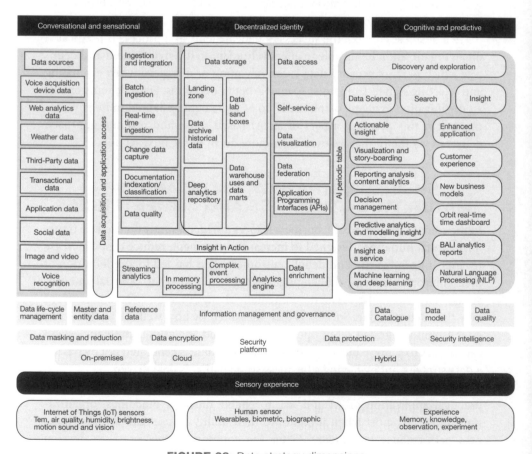

FIGURE 38: Data strategy dimensions

There are many different models and methodologies that can facilitate this understanding. However, the use of maturity models can link mission-critical priorities to outcomes and data and analytics activities (see *Figures 39* and *40*). Maturity models can take many forms. The example shown in *Figure 39* provides for a baseline assessment encompassing both technical and social capability dimensions using a five-stage maturity scale from emerging to excelling. Each maturity stage describes the requisite enterprise activity and the corresponding data capabilities. This allows decision-makers to understand, map and socialize both their current and future state in a common and consistent manner to foster understanding, engagement and organizational alignment.

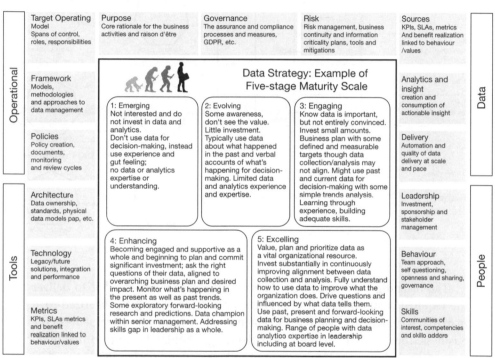

FIGURE 39: Data maturity model example
(KPI: key performance indicator; SLA: service level agreement)

Based on the stages in *Figure 39*, it is possible to map an organization's capabilities within each dimension (e.g. data and tools) (see *Figure 40*) to identify the required journey and create short-term, medium-term and long-term road maps. Crucially, the model illustrates that enterprises do not need to be world class at everything. The critical capabilities that support the organization's market value propositions and unique selling points are those that should attract the most investment and be executed at the most efficient and effective level. It is the ensemble of identified capabilities across the maturity dimensions that unlocks enterprise value, based on the allocation of resources to ensure the creation of maximum value.

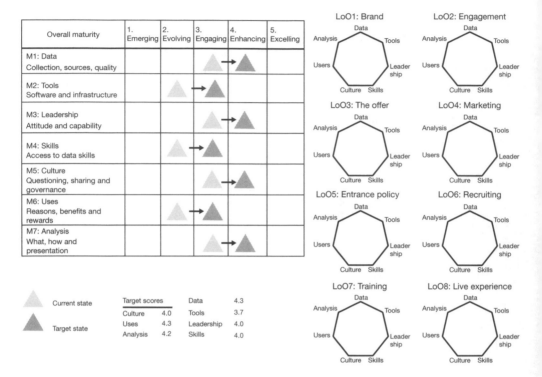

Overall maturity	1. Emerging	2. Evolving	3. Engaging	4. Enhancing	5. Excelling
M1: Data Collection, sources, quality					
M2: Tools Software and infrastructure					
M3: Leadership Attitude and capability					
M4: Skills Access to data skills					
M5: Culture Questioning, sharing and governance					
M6: Uses Reasons, benefits and rewards					
M7: Analysis What, how and presentation					

Current state

Target state

Target scores		Data	4.3
Culture	4.0	Tools	3.7
Uses	4.3	Leadership	4.0
Analysis	4.2	Skills	4.0

FIGURE 40: Example maturity model capability map

The mapping process and the focus on the capabilities needed to deliver the required business outcomes provide the enterprise with a prioritized road map that is constantly reviewed and amended to reflect the requirements of the business. The capability mapping and planning, combined with common practices associated with the deployment of agile teams and design thinking, allow organizations to adapt swiftly to changing business priorities. Agile businesses are designed to be fast, resilient and adaptable, enabling them to pivot to focus on changing customer needs.

As the sophistication of the data analysis and insights matures, the capability of the organization to consume and apply the insights should increase, as should its ability to develop a value-based approach to the verification of business outcomes. Unlike traditional transformation measures, each of the maturity capability mappings will have a blend of tangible and intangible metrics (see *Figure 41*).

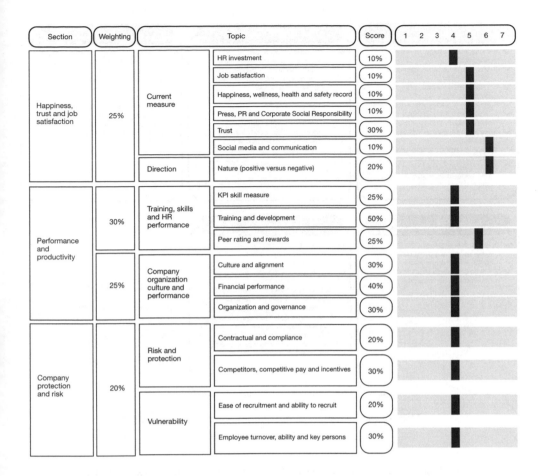

FIGURE 41: Example of intangible business metrics
(KPI: key performance indicator)

These metrics are associated with each of the data maturity dimensions and stages in *Figure 39* and can be weighted and ranked based on the business objectives (on both an individual and a collective basis). This allows for the establishment and development of a common baseline, together with a foundation for monitoring success as the maturity of the organization develops (see *Figure 42*).

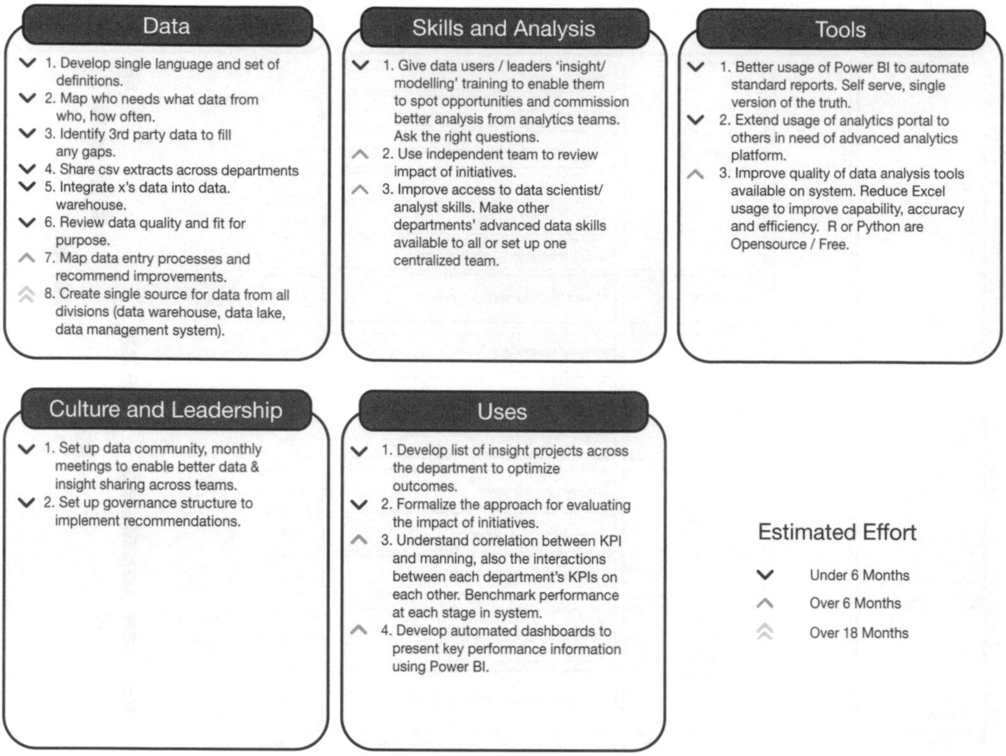

Data

⌄ 1. Develop single language and set of definitions.
⌄ 2. Map who needs what data from who, how often.
⌄ 3. Identify 3rd party data to fill any gaps.
⌄ 4. Share csv extracts across departments
⌄ 5. Integrate x's data into data. warehouse.
⌄ 6. Review data quality and fit for purpose.
⌃ 7. Map data entry processes and recommend improvements.
⌃ 8. Create single source for data from all divisions (data warehouse, data lake, data management system).

Skills and Analysis

⌄ 1. Give data users / leaders 'insight/ modelling' training to enable them to spot opportunities and commission better analysis from analytics teams. Ask the right questions.
⌃ 2. Use independent team to review impact of initiatives.
⌃ 3. Improve access to data scientist/ analyst skills. Make other departments' advanced data skills available to all or set up one centralized team.

Tools

⌄ 1. Better usage of Power BI to automate standard reports. Self serve, single version of the truth.
⌄ 2. Extend usage of analytics portal to others in need of advanced analytics platform.
⌃ 3. Improve quality of data analysis tools available on system. Reduce Excel usage to improve capability, accuracy and efficiency. R or Python are Opensource / Free.

Culture and Leadership

⌄ 1. Set up data community, monthly meetings to enable better data & insight sharing across teams.
⌄ 2. Set up governance structure to implement recommendations.

Uses

⌄ 1. Develop list of insight projects across the department to optimize outcomes.
⌄ 2. Formalize the approach for evaluating the impact of initiatives.
⌃ 3. Understand correlation between KPI and manning, also the interactions between each department's KPIs on each other. Benchmark performance at each stage in system.
⌃ 4. Develop automated dashboards to present key performance information using Power BI.

Estimated Effort

⌄   Under 6 Months
⌃   Over 6 Months
⌃⌃   Over 18 Months

FIGURE 42: Example of maturity model business priorities
(KPI: key performance indicator)

Once the organization understands its 'as is' and 'to be' data capabilities via the maturity assessment, it can begin to chart how it intends to navigate its data intelligence and democratization journey (see *Figure 43*). On this journey, the operating and trading environments form the context in which these capabilities will be deployed to maximize competitive advantage.

The emergence of a sense-and-response model based on sensory experience and data is a natural development of businesses in an increasingly chaotic and digital environment.[202] As in nature, the tension between fight and flight (deciding how to respond to an opportunity) and the tension between nature and nurture (deciding whether to buy or build) are reflected in enterprises' decision-making and value creation. The development and application of a sense-and-respond model powered by sensory AI unlocks the latent value inherent in businesses' data, which is often collected, owned and stored in disparate systems but rarely aggregated and applied at the point of interaction with the customer.

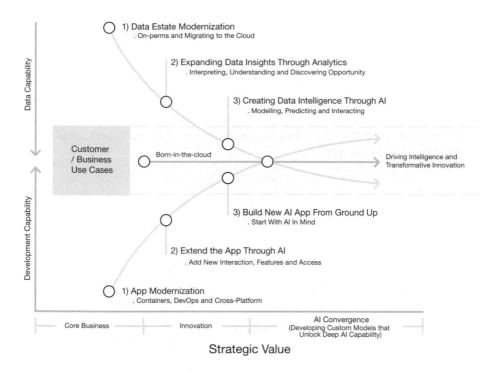

FIGURE 43: Data and development capabilities

The orchestration and choreography of these critical data and experience capabilities provide the basis for the delivery of a brand's customer/social contract and ultimately the value derived from that connected relationship. This manifests itself in the connection between sensory intelligence and experience design. Experience design (XD) draws on the needs of the user, their feelings, the context and their mindsets to design experiences that centre on them. The ability of a business to collect, curate and consume sensory intelligence via sensors can provide the basis for a data-driven understanding of the environment and customer behaviour to create value. This value-creating alchemical process explains how a business can transform itself through this model with a focus on continuous cycles of development and integration.

CUSTOMER EXPERIENCE AND SERVICE DESIGN

The creation and effective application of human intelligence are based on our sensory understanding and interaction with our environment. Businesses are no exception. They share that sensory experience with their customers and ecosystem partners, often spanning multiple channels. These channels require constant monitoring and refinement to deliver an exceptional data-driven customer experience.

From a digital perspective, a focus on sensory intelligence encourages greater digital take-up, fewer errors and inaccuracies, and reduced failure. Service design, which focuses on the customer experience, is fundamental to achieving these outcomes.[203] Service design takes place at the beginning of a contract and continues throughout its terms, influencing development and implementation. By defining user journeys and auditing them through user experience testing, a business can keep its service focused on the needs of its customers, employees and users (see *Figure 44*).

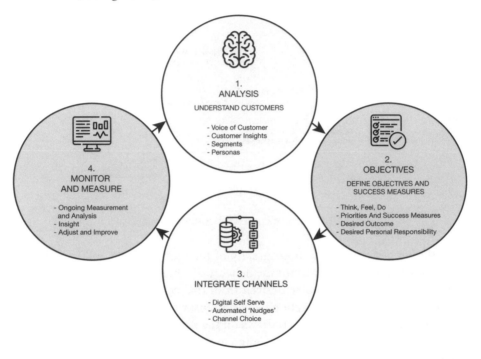

FIGURE 44: Creating a cycle of continuous improvement in user experience

The service design approach applies design insights and tools to services to match people's needs and technological requirements using an integrated intelligence feedback loop, creating a cycle of continuous improvement in the user experience. The experience layer of the IF (see *Figure 37*) coordinates the production of the user experience via the use of sensory data-driven decisions and predictions based on user interviews, personas, and an understanding of the end-to-end journey. This involves mapping pain points, emotions and crucial moments that have a critical impact on decision-making.

Supplemented by insights into attitudes, needs and motivations and supported by lifestyle, demographic and behavioural data, often provided by third-party vendors, the IF model can craft the intelligence required to enable a viable sense-and-respond model for businesses. However, while critical, the experience layer alone is not sufficient to produce the conditions for data alchemy. An ability to democratize data is also a key element in the process.

Working in combination with an organization's existing investment strategy, capital availability and architectural strategy, a model such as the IF can provide the necessary capabilities of traceability, encryption and immutability for enterprises to ensure the security, clearness and compliance of the necessary data assets. The IF model provides the key components of this process, including business object and app access; data exchange; trading and sharing of data and digital assets; attribution, provenance and governance; identity management, privacy, information security, authorization and authentication; and infrastructure and cloud layers.

Technological advancements in data exchange must be accompanied by business and personal rationales, confidence and ease of use that are appropriate for the types of emerging data-democratization platforms (such as AWS Data Exchange and Dataex). The IF model envisages the development of a valuation engine capable of learning the cost of types of data from history. This would enable a proper market where businesses can monetize their data. Parameters such as per use, volume, rarity, cost of production, precedence and desirability would be used. As the IF model matured, intelligence related to business data objects would be incorporated. Ontologies would become demonstrable. File formats would become less relevant, and AI would be used to construct and deconstruct data to the desired formats for consumption using elements of the type included in the AI Periodic Table (see *Figure 51*). This is human-level intelligence in action.

The maturity assessment and the creation of a data strategy comprise the first stage in the data alchemy process. The outcome of this is then used as a critical input into the development of the user experience and service design. For these to be effectively deployed and efficiently managed, we turn to the next stage: namely, the development of business agility and continuous improvement.

BUSINESS AGILITY AND CONTINUOUS DEVELOPMENT CYCLES

The constantly changing nature of customer requirements and expectations means businesses must empower teams and product owners to act as independent cross-functional agile teams. To be effective, this requires a structured governance process that enables enterprises to align their response strategies with efficient objectives and resource reprioritization, outcome performance tracking and full transparency. What will allow businesses to realize value is their ability to systematically react to customer requirements, scale in an agile manner, and sense and respond to their environment.

We call this the 'Apollo 13 effect,' as organizations must improvise to address an unexpected situation with available resources to ensure a successful outcome. The Apollo 13 lunar module was designed to support two people on the moon's surface for two days. However, the mission control team in Houston, Texas, improvised new procedures so it could support three men for four days. The ability to innovate, design, develop and deliver a workable solution within a high-risk and time-constrained horizon is one that can be codified and industrialized to allow businesses to mature via data-driven experiences and learning agility.

The acceleration in business cycles and the impact of the Apollo 13 effect can be understood if we consider trends in specific markets. From a business-to-business perspective, expectations are shifting to increasingly shorter time horizons, which requires new capabilities to enable:

- **Immediacy** – An ability to deliver tangible results in a brief time frame with minimal set-up and planning.
- **Informed flexibility** – In an environment in which speed is paramount, mistakes will be inevitable so what matters is how quickly we can spot and correct them.
- **Accountability** – A willingness to take complete responsibility for successful delivery, even if that means acting ruthlessly.
- **Judgment** – None of the above is possible without people who have the experience and expertise to make snap decisions that clients can rely on.

Industry boundaries are blurring as traditional frames of reference are becoming less relevant and clients are becoming more savvy buyers. By increasing the review cycle for the purchasing of non-core in-house capabilities, they are increasing the pressure on their partner ecosystems to deliver value at every customer interaction based on the following attributes:

- **Agility** – How nimble can you be in taking a problem statement, assembling a team and building a solution?
- **True partnering** – Partnerships are often talked about, but are rarely delivered, since they consist of helping clients build knowledge and skills.
- **Innovation** – Executable ideas and frameworks, and approaches and methods to unlock these.
- **Creativity in delivery** – A 150-page paper belongs to another era; clients increasingly want to see prototypes, high-fidelity designs and working models.
- **Always learning** – Workers need to take ownership of their own development paths to ensure expertise and build skills.

AI and ML have key roles to play in the creation of these new capabilities, connections and relationships between consumers and brands, and between citizens and governments. The development of the third type of AI – the contextual understanding and adaptation of code to perceive and create data abstracts based on that experiential perception – will enable the development of sensory AI. The AI Periodic Table will be a key part in the understanding of that data alchemy process. It provides the building blocks of data intelligence, which can be combined and connected via an intelligent infrastructure and full-stack DevOps to provide the motor and real-world feedback mechanisms and functions that are necessary to create business value.

THE DEVELOPMENT OF CONTINUOUS DELIVERY AND INTEGRATION PRACTICES TO CREATE BUSINESS VALUE

The codification of relationships between tools, processes, technologies and frameworks is the key to the effective deployment of AI. The proliferation of choice that characterizes the current data landscape, encompassing start-ups, innovation hubs, software applications, infrastructure choices and multiple languages can often concentrate the development of delivery options in the hands of the few that are vested in the intricacies of the black arts of IT. These choices, combined with the many sources of technical debt (e.g. data dependencies, model complexity, reproducibility, testing and monitoring) that have accumulated in legacy environments, can often function as barriers to the creation of agile business models and open architectures. The choice of technology is not as important as the ability for product teams and architects to collaborate to solve customer challenges rather than being focused purely on the ability to exploit the current technical infrastructure and traditional software systems.

Here we discuss the use of the right processes, methods, procedures, technologies, tools and culture for an effective development process. As many businesses are migrating from DevOps to cloud-based environment(s) where the pipelines enable the enforcement and measurement of good practices, we will elaborate on processes based around automation, pipeline quality and discipline; these can create a reliable and repeatable workflow to release software into production.

The importance of 'codification' should be emphasized. With every aspect of development and delivery becoming a service, processes are becoming increasingly integrated, removing many fuzzy and uncertain boundaries. Everything is code. Arguably, even hardware is now just code. Therefore, problems that were traditionally related to the differences between development environments and end-user environments are disappearing. Continuous delivery (CD) and continuous integration (CI) have become a reality.

APPLICATION OF CONTINUOUS DELIVERY AND INTEGRATION APPROACHES

CI allows for both engineers and data scientists practising CI to merge their changes back to the main release code or development branches as often as possible. This seeks to avoid integration friction when undertaking release activities by validating build-and-run automated tests against the build.

CD is essentially a set of capabilities that enables "changes of all kinds, e.g. new features, configuration, bug fixes, and experiments into production or into the hands of users safely, quickly, and sustainably."[204] CD is based on six key principles, namely:

- Build quality in
- Work in small batches
- Computers perform repetitive tasks
- People solve problems
- Relentlessly pursue continuous improvement
- Everybody is responsible

The alignment of CD with agile approaches is clear when we consider the key elements involved in improving technical capabilities to reduce organizational pain points and maximize business opportunities. Nicole Forsgren, Jez Humble and Gene Kim describe these factors as implementing comprehensive testing and deploying automation.[205] Moreover, rather than using individual approaches on a serial basis, CI has fostered a culture of applying synergy between parallel and integrated disciplines to enable businesses to derive value from their full development lifecycles. This has increasingly taken the form of enterprise architectures design thinking to translate ideas into working prototypes, automation and AI to produce more efficient insight processes. It also involves the advanced use of agile lean approaches to effective infrastructure development and DevOps deployment.

The adoption of such systematic approaches to software development requires rethinking, regeneration and reconfiguration of the target operating model and microcultures (e.g. in individual departments) to create the conditions for this approach to provide organizational value.

Automation is the key to efficient data management since it involves removing humans from as many processes as possible and it involves using tools and processes in conjunction with the DevOps approach. Everything is done via a pipeline. It is more common to use this approach for application deployment than infrastructure lifecycle management. The pipeline approach also encourages effective team collaboration when moving code from A to B, in addition to integrating dependencies, tests and other builds to facilitate a successful deployment. Tools at the centre of the CI/CD process (such as Jenkins) maintain a history of changes, build stages, pipeline runs and deployments. These tools and technologies, coupled with an agile framework, enable:

- A collaborative and evolving understanding of the system's requirements in a way that is acceptable to stakeholders from all sides
- Team task allocation and communications
- Significant reuse
- Automation of testing and quality assurance
- Continuous integration
- Automated code release
- Automated version control

To realize these benefits, an organization needs to have the ability to configure and execute software deployment pipelines to production, which requires a high degree of coordination and orchestration. An integrated architectural model can be built from a combination of infrastructure provisioning; execution of ML pipelines to train and capture metrics from multiple parallel model experiments; and the build, test, rollback and deployment of models (see *Figure 45*).

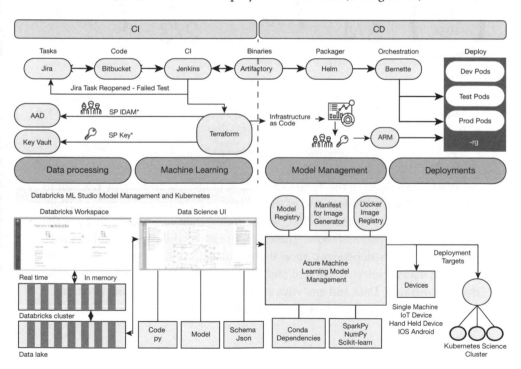

FIGURE 45: Example continuous delivery (CD) and continuous integration (CI) architecture

(IoT: Internet of Things; UI: user interface)

This model architecture should provide users with a robust CI/CD capability from which to deliver quality services and enable better business outcomes.

BUSINESS AGILITY: PEOPLE, CHANGE AND COMPETENCIES

Our digital transformative age is exponentially increasing the speed of change as we experiment with and adopt new forms, models and experiences that deliver utility, convenience and efficiency. As adaptive humans, we know how to transition from threatening conditions and move toward favourable outcomes. How organizations are structured and how people work within them determine success. However, many organizational transformation efforts struggle to achieve their promised potential to deliver business value (see *Figure 46*).

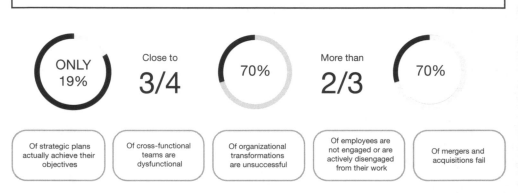

FIGURE 46: Why business agility matters

While the subject of the 'future of work' is of interest and highly relevant to all organizations, it is not in and of itself a particularly accessible call to action. What is relevant is that it is often people rather than technology that are the primary cause of project failure. Therefore, the successful deployment of the IF model is critically dependent upon the organization's structure, as is the way in which data is collected, curated and consumed to enable effective enterprise decision-making. Data and analytics are the lifeblood of an organization and a fundamental aspect of its DNA (see *Figure 47*).

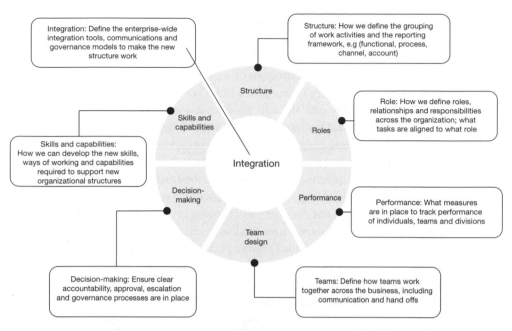

FIGURE 47: The data-driven organizational design approach

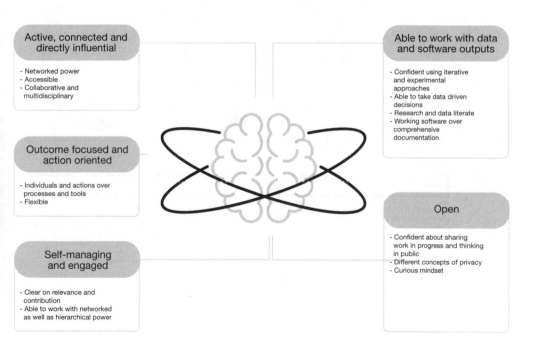

FIGURE 48: The agile mindset and work in practice

The importance of data extends beyond the limitations of organizational design to focus on employees' behaviour and agile mindset in practice (see *Figure 48*). For each organization, these elements will exist in a slightly different balance, and many will recognize a problem relating to one of these areas without necessarily framing it against the others or indeed the whole. While recognizing that people are a critical element of the data alchemy process, space limits us from exploring this topic and issues around the future of work in more depth. However, the agile approach to organizational design and delivery has increasing relevance to data alchemy. The transformative journey from base data to value and from an idea to the creation of a product or service is founded upon the emergent elements derived from data. These emergent elements are the products of a rapid innovation experience starting with research and discovery and moving on to problem selection and definition, hypotheses, prototypes, user feedback, choice of whether to progress or pivot, and guided next steps. This approach is based on design thinking, a lean product and agile delivery that can result in tangible, shareable outcomes including a clear problem statement and rationale, prototypes, user feedback, actionable insights, documented evidence and clear next steps (see *Figure 49*).

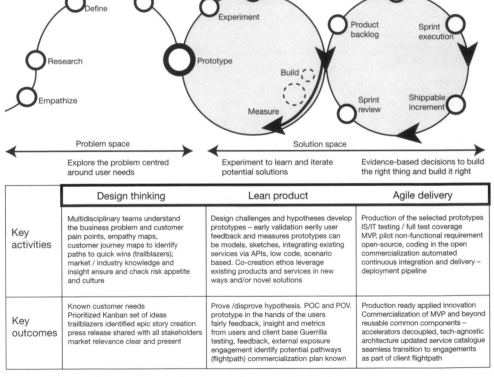

	Design thinking	Lean product	Agile delivery
Key activities	Multidisciplinary teams understand the business problem and customer pain points, empathy maps, customer journey maps to identify paths to quick wins (trailblazers); market / industry knowledge and insight ensure and check risk appetite and culture	Design challenges and hypotheses develop prototypes – early validation eerily user feedback and measures prototypes can be models, sketches, integrating existing services via APIs, low code, scenario based. Co-creation ethos leverage existing products and services in new ways and/or novel solutions	Production of the selected prototypes IS/IT testing / full test coverage MVP, pilot non-functional requirement open-source, coding in the open commercialization automated continuous integration and delivery – deployment pipeline
Key outcomes	Known customer needs Prioritized Kanban set of ideas trailblazers identified epic story creation press release shared with all stakeholders market relevance clear and present	Prove /disprove hypothesis. POC and POV. prototype in the hands of the users fairly feedback, insight and metrics from users and client base Guerrilla testing, feedback, external exposure engagement identify potential pathways (flightpath) commercialization plan known	Production ready applied innovation Commercialization of MVP and beyond reusable common components – accelerators decoupled, tech-agnostic architecture updated service catalogue seamless transition to engagements as part of client flightpath

Figure 49: Data alchemy: minimum viable product framework
(APIs: application programming interfaces; IS/IT: information systems/information technology; MVP: minimum viable product)

The process of using an agile approach such as the one shown in *Figure 49* has significant advantages in maximizing the prospects of project success. It can enable breakthrough thinking and, critically, provide a context and framework in which to use value-creating frameworks such as the AI Periodic Table.

DATA ALCHEMY:
THE ROLE OF THE AI PERIODIC TABLE

The alchemical journey to transform base data into actionable insight is fraught with complexity. The myriad choices and applications of a data-driven strategy relating to value creation and measurement of success are compounded by organizations' different maturities and delivery capabilities. There needs to be a trade-off and compromise when there are limited resources. To align with business objectives, a data-driven strategy needs to address (at a minimum) data acquisition, data preparation (e.g. relating to taxonomy, data entropy, wrangling, quality and curating data with diverse features), canonical models, analytic engines, processes, and the type of architecture required to enable ML workloads and the effective delivery and consumption of high-speed insights. Traditionally, the deployment of code to generate actionable insights is achieved using a standard data science pipeline with supervised and/or unsupervised workflows, depending on the use case.

Unsupervised learning workflows change depending on the need to explore similarities or observations in the raw data. Typically, the objective is to address the heterogeneity of the data. Instead of dealing with broadly disparate observations as raw data, the data scientist will often look to divide the data into more homogeneous subsets. Therefore, clustering is a common tool in unsupervised learning. In addition, data mining is a common application of unsupervised learning where there are significant volumes of data available but no training data. In many applications, this approach can be used to obtain training data for supervised learning.

The adoption of systematic approaches to model development can often be characterized by uncertainty and absence of clarity. For example, when considering a process for developing a cloud minimal viable product (MVP) using labelled data, a supervised ML algorithm and a Python library extract, with the MVP deployed in a web application, it might initially seem possible to complete the project within a short period of time and without complications. However, the traditional design-to-value journey disregards a level of technical complexity and human interaction. As M2M decision-making and the adoption of AutoML DevOps increase, businesses will need to have the transparency to better design the code that is being generated mostly, considering the business context and purpose to which the code is applied, in order to create business value. It is the drive for simplicity and the need to enable rapid insight generation via experimentation and exploration that has led us to develop an alternative approach, that of the AI Periodic Table (see *Figure 50*; see also *Chapter 3* for a more comprehensive introduction).

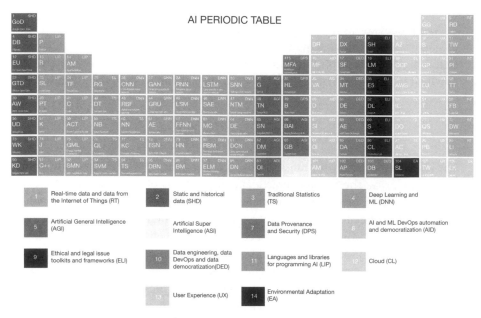

FIGURE 50: The AI Periodic Table

The AI Periodic Table constitutes the currently known base AI elements, which must be combined and orchestrated via the alchemical process to produce an emergent property (e.g. actionable insights that can enable better business outcomes). This alchemical process needs to be embedded within the design-to-production lifecycle as a key component of the analytical value and customer experience. This process is not a replacement for an enterprise data strategy or a substitute for the complex data-engineering and data-wrangling stages that characterize successful AI and ML projects. It is an accelerator of the data analytics process, encompassing the acquisition, preprocessing, curation and democratization of data to align and deliver the objectives of the business.

In contrast to traditional data strategy approaches in ML, the AI Periodic Table not only provides for the combination of base AI elements within a 'forge' but also, critically, embeds ethical and governance policies within the process of model development itself. In human decision-making, intelligence is derived from the connections within the cortex based on our experience and interaction with our environment. Currently, model development and the application of ML are based on order imposed by the enterprise's architectural choices, DevOps stack and logical tool selection. These models are subject to an allocation process to align them within the discrete stages of a matrix development cycle, including vertical activities (e.g. build, continuous integration and deployment) and horizontal activities (e.g. testing and collaboration).

The AI Periodic Table is founded on the dynamic application of four primary alchemical categories, which we call 'genesis categories' namely, traditional statistics, ML, contextualization, and personalization and self-aware machines. Each of these genesis categories is constantly developing at a significant rate as technological and data challenges are successfully addressed. Languages such as Python and Scala may change as each of the four genesis categories evolves. However, our model reflects the ways in which nature works and intelligence evolves, allowing for a natural order of processes based around our understanding of intelligence rather than building a system of software.

Sensory perception allows us to connect experiences in nature to create intelligence. The development and application of intelligence must be seen as part of a continuous cycle of challenge to the governance and ethical frameworks that monitor the use of data and AI model development. Usually, these frameworks are situated outside the lifecycle of intelligence creation and can be arbitrary in nature, swiftly becoming obsolete as technical advances outpace case law and change over time. However, with the increased consideration of the rights of both humans and machines (see *Chapter 6*), ethics need to be embedded within the alchemical process itself. Recognizing the need to ensure that AI and ML applications should be based within and reflect the cultural norms of the society they seek to benefit, ethics could be applied to the data itself at ingestion rather than being coded into the DNA of algorithms. Arguably, ethical principles, rules and codification should not be ingrained within an algorithm but applied at the point of data preprocessing. Indeed, talking about the 'ethics of algorithms' is invalid; instead, we should potentially refer to the 'ethics of data.' In the near future, data itself will have the ability to become 'self-aware,' exercising intelligence to decide how it can be used. It may even evolve to become independent 'intelligent data.' The application of this intelligence will be through algorithms. Given this context, we can outline how the AI Periodic Table creates value as part of the data alchemy process (see *Figure 51*).

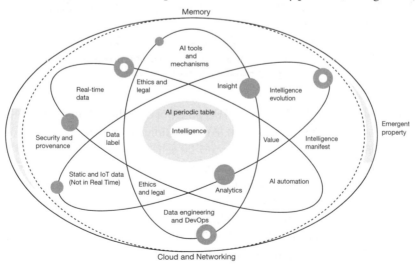

FIGURE 51: Data alchemy and the AI Periodic Table
(IoT: Internet of Things)

Data, whether structured, semi-structured or unstructured, and irrespective of format, is ingested on either a batched or near-real-time basis and is subject to both security verification and allocation of an identity and status based on a dynamic data ontology and taxonomy. Tagging of the data's attributes and metadata is undertaken at the smallest scale possible to ensure its provenance and forensic lineage are clear as it dynamically moves across the data estate. Ethical, civic and legal policies and procedures are appended to the data prior to the presentation of selected data cohorts to the AI tools and mechanisms. The 14 groups of the AI Periodic Table (see *Figure 15*) are used in combination with the genesis categories to select the optimum combination to address a given business challenge and derive the required data-driven decision or actionable insight. The resultant primed data is then curated and applied to the model and productionized via the DevOps stack to a consumable layer to allow the democratization of the resultant value.

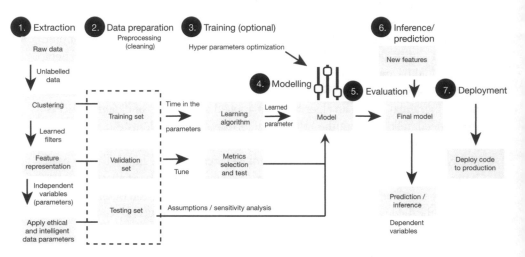

FIGURE 52: Example of the data alchemy process: continuous delivery for a machine learning (ML) end-to-end process
(adapted from Gartner Machine Learning Flows)

We envisage that intelligence will become not only the output of the alchemical process but also the process itself. An evolutionary approach is critical for the success of the AI Periodic Table. It must be self-learning to optimize and train the models and enable the evolution of the algorithms, especially as the data will be constantly changing as part of a dynamic sense-and-respond model. The value of the AI Periodic Table lies not just in its application to big data but also in its focus on the next challenge for businesses: small data. Rather than the haystacks, this means locating the needles. The detection of patterns, the creation of consumable insights and the delivery of these at the moment of decision-making form the subject of the next sections.

DATA ALCHEMY: DEVELOPMENT PROCESS MAP AND QUALITY GATES

To reduce the impact of delivery pitfalls and facilitate more frequent, higher-quality and lower-risk software releases, we need to effectively implement integrated processes, quality gates and collaboration processes. The most common challenges that organizations encounter in enterprise-wide processes stem from the ownership of the individuals, teams and data that constitute the process cycle. The siloed dislocation of effort associated with the inability to influence and shape the development of process transitions, alongside the absence of enterprise process governance, inhibits the seamless delivery of data and resources to provide value. The divisions between roles such as data scientists, solution architects, data engineers and developers (user interface and user experience) complicate an already problematic set of design-to-release processes. Clear ownership of enterprise-wide processes, comprehensive data protocols, and robust governance and compliance procedures allow for a more integrated approach to data alchemy. An example overview of a development process is shown in *Figure 53*.

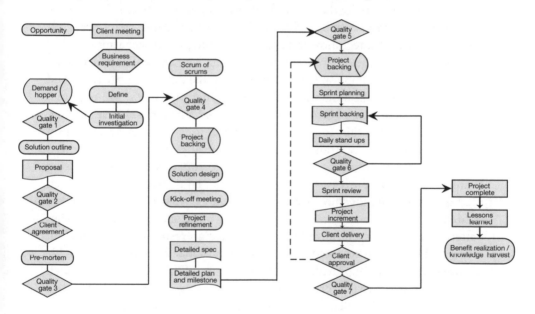

FIGURE 53: Example of the data alchemy process: continuous delivery for a machine learning (ML) end-to-end process

The journey from design to post-deployment and the virtual feedback loop that characterizes the data alchemy approach are underpinned by the core design principles of simplicity in everything we do and a focus on CI and CD processes to create business value. Even with the introduction of a pre-mortem stage to ensure stakeholder co-creation and mutual understanding, there remain significant challenges associated with the transparency, repeatability and scalability of the process as we move from idea to invoice. Simplicity, in terms of tooling, workflows and automation, provides for reduction in process friction, functionality trade-offs and commercial tension, especially when speed to market is a critical aspect of CD.

DATA FLOW: MULTI-CLOUD ARCHITECTURE AND DATA ALCHEMY CAPABILITY UTILIZATION

Depending on the data maturity of the organization and the intended customer value use case, there is a diverse array of options and solutions to choose from where data storage, retrieval, analysis and consumption are concerned. These range from the traditional data warehouses to data lake architectures and data mesh/fabric platforms. Data mesh connects to anything via prepackaged connectors and components, allowing for the management of data across all environments (multi-cloud and on premises), supporting batched, real-time and big data use cases with built-in ML, data quality and governance capabilities to enable data integration and application integration scenarios.

Fundamentally, the difference between a data lake and a database or data warehouse is the assumption that, in the former, the data is unstructured and not prepared for utilization where data-wrangling pipeline(s) are required. Similarly, the distinction between a data mesh and a data warehouse solution design is the assumption that, in the former, a user requires decentralized data as opposed to a centralized solution. Ironically, improving centralized unstructured data solutions often has the unfortunate side effect of losing business logic in the process. The principles of domain-driven design are often used in business architecture. More recently, they have been used as a toolset to identify micro-services and their spheres of influence, applied as a design pattern to enforce decentralization as well as assign responsibility to domain owners. This domain-oriented decentralization of data ownership and architecture that data mesh provides facilitates the use of data as a product, often via self-serve data as a platform, to enable autonomous, domain-oriented data teams to design and implement at scale via enabled ecosystems and interoperability within a federated governance framework. For an example of how the analytical Intelligence Foundry (IF) application layer could be designed, refer back to *Figure 37*.

However, architectural developments and patterns are evolving at a rapid pace. One such example is the object-oriented database management system (OODBMS), made popular through PostgreSQL, which enables sub-second object-oriented queries on big data. An OODBMS is a database management system where data is represented in the form of objects, as used in object-oriented programming. When an OODBMS is implemented with a highly scalable dispatcher model, it becomes a new breed of data platform. This new breed is replicated in new data platforms geared toward real-time insights. As enterprise activities evolve to become more diverse and as unstructured and high-velocity data become more prevalent, stronger governance and performance will be required. As a result, users will seek business intelligence from these repositories rather than from data warehouses alone.[206]

A further example relates to the lake house concept,[207] a combination of data warehouse (data structures and management) and data lake functionality (see *Figure 54*). Data is loaded in its raw format following the extract–load–transform (ELT) paradigm, and it is then only requested based on a customer use case being transformed into a derived format. For businesses, this approach provides access to cheap and robust data storage and independently scalable compute (capable of massively parallel processing), allowing standard SQL to transform performant SQL querying regardless of concurrency. Speed to insight is increased as this approach reduces the need for data pipeline build and ensures that effort is not wasted transforming data feeds that will never be used.

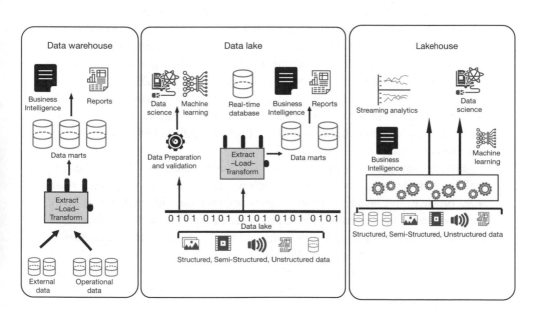

FIGURE 54: Comparison: data warehouse, date lake and lakehouse[208]

The lakehouse illustrates the need for architectures that can deliver near-real-time personalized data insights based on relevant customer journeys and digital experiences. A lake house can act like a power generator in a dam, storing and releasing data, and regulating the generation of the required-on demand analytics to transform the data into an emergent property; in this case, actionable intelligence. However, irrespective of which architectural model is adopted, it needs to support the key stages of data alchemy and, importantly, the process of successfully delivering business outcomes that delight the customer.

HUMAN–MACHINE VALUE CREATION

The combination of globalization and digital transformation has expanded the speed, complexity and scale of business infrastructure. For many businesses, the complexity of operating in dynamic environments will create the opportunity to accelerate the adoption of trusted AI and ML algorithms to make better decisions by using intelligent systems. As AI and ML techniques continue to evolve and develop, so will our ability to improve and predict the technical delivery of these services and products. In turn, our knowledge and intelligent application of these capabilities will also grow as we experiment and constantly revise our parametric design approaches, processes and assumptions to create value.

However, the combination of data and experience provides us with the ultimate microcosm of social behaviour and connections. The interaction between the user's environment and the intelligent system's ability to capture sensory data will provide us with a view and experience of our virtual or physical world which promotes better understanding and more intelligent application of ideas. The basis of event- and data-driven decision-making may allow us to automate more and focus on the human augmentation of enterprise decision-making. This will accelerate the rates of failure and agile learning that characterize the data alchemy approach to increasing business value. Organizations will need innovative systematic approaches to unlocking the full potential and value of human collaboration with AI.

Both humans and AI are flawed. Each views and interacts with the world differently. Unprecedented access to data, not always reliable, requires organizations to solve problems intelligently with incomplete information. This challenge is being compounded as the means of production is increasingly transacted in the virtual world rather than the physical, which has profound implications for businesses in terms of purpose, structure, capabilities and culture. Data is the facilitator of these new experiences and connections, as the nature of business value will be expressed in more sensory terms rather than primarily chemical or physical. Data alchemy will become the prism and arbiter of these experiences. With the rise of simulation, augmented reality (AR) and digital twins, the use of AI in business decision-making is not a radical novelty but rather a reality, even though the latter may be virtual.

While the development and application of the AI Periodic Table can help to codify the creation and application of intelligence, there is one responsibility that humans cannot contract out of, and that is the decision as to how these technologies should be used for the good of humanity. The relationship between data and intelligence should be governed by the connection between emotions and experience. Data and rules that provide the context and value from our interaction(s) with the environment can be codified and reflected, to a degree, in the judgment and reason that are refined by interaction. However, with businesses becoming more like individuals in personality and behaviour, and with the rise of M2M, we are seeing a reduction in these H2H interactions. This is leading to a reduction in our ability to learn, understand and experiment. Therefore, there is a need to review whether these data rules and the current analogue legislative framework for the digital world should replace our capacity for language and companionship or whether human presence and human communication unmediated by data and rules are part of what gives human life its meaning. A focus on trust and transparency in the practical application of AI and ML decision-making will provide us with the opportunities and sources of innovation to create value that neither humans nor machines can create individually.

CHAPTER 8

THE FUTURE
OF DATA AND
INTELLIGENCE

At the end of a complex and winding journey, we are able to encapsulate what it means to be data-driven and how the value that can be derived can be exploited for the benefit of our businesses. It has been an exhilarating voyage of discovery, and the conclusions we can draw have far-reaching implications for every field of science. We have touched on the nature of the universe, evolution and truth itself. These are rather grand statements. In this final chapter, we deconstruct these statements to reflect on the importance of data and information, and how data is responsible for the immaculate conception of intelligence and indeed consciousness.

In this book, we examined the importance of data and how nature makes use of it to create life as we know it, including intelligence and consciousness, as well as the similarities and differences between natural and artificial intelligence. We arrived at conclusions that have enabled us, we believe, to look inside the 'mind of God,' a metaphor involving understanding intelligence, consciousness and intentionality, and cause and effect. In our view, there are two kinds of understanding: rational and logical understanding and understanding based on intelligence in data with many dimensions beyond the logical and the mathematical. Data represents the *prima materia* (first matter) – it is everything with any form of intelligence, coherence or structure. It is the substance of alchemy in everything natural and unnatural. It is the *anima mundi* (world soul). There is alchemy in the leaves and the trees and the birds and the bees. It is there in the shoreline and the shape of a leaf. It is there in quantum states and interstellar dust. Natural language can be understood using natural processes, artificial neural networks, fractional space dimensions, quantum states of matter, and perhaps other communication scales within nature. This realization implies a deep-down, universally scalable vision of data as an alchemical substance. Even theoretical physicists have begun to question whether new ways of looking at data and the use of new types of simulation represent an end to the traditional ways of looking for fundamental laws in nature.[209] This is more than just a hypothesis that data is the invariant and universal property of all things, governed by the intelligence derived from data connected to all other data. Variations and instances of entities where data does not add value do not make it to nature's next stage of evolution. For businesses, this means that most will experience a faster lifecycle of creation and termination as the application of alchemical processes accelerates both consumer needs and technical advancement. Businesses will focus on their ability to pivot, adapt and apply new alchemical capabilities to ensure that they deliver value at each interaction with their chosen market.

In *Chapters 3, 4* and *5*, we articulated the basic building blocks of intelligence, the importance of data and data cognition, and the basics of using that data to derive business value. Data is everything and everything is data. Data is the reason for everything. It explains why emergentism, manifold alignment, cognitive processes and reasons for cognition, hypothesis generation, fractals (i.e. affine self-symmetries), quantum states of matter, and the ontology of objects are so intertwined.[210] That intertwining is apparent when we try to contextualize data. By shifting paradigms, we are able to switch from attempting to explain AI in terms of second-generation deep learning neural networks (DL) to explaining AI consciousness, intent and self-awareness, and how we might get there in the 21st century. Let us unfold these aspects individually and then relate them to business value in the broadest possible sense.

Throughout this book, we have derived inspiration from nature (in terms of observations and physical laws embedded in the natural sciences) and business processes to draw out the following sources of value:

- **Emergence** – Emergence is said to occur when a behaviour is observed in a collection of entities but is not observed (or is of significantly reduced value) in the entity on its own. So, one might argue that linguistic intelligence is an emergent property of a community, or that life is an emergent property of biochemistry. It is an important concept in terms of dissecting and demystifying intelligence and even consciousness.
- **Hypothesis generation** – The central thesis behind the generation hypothesis (see *Chapter 3*) is that consciousness is manifested through the ability and need to internally generate sensory representations that are not direct reflections of the current sensory input. They may be counterfactual representations since predictions of unexecuted future actions do not necessarily correspond to events happening in the current environment. This hypothesis enables an explanation of the need for evolved life to realize the functional advantages of consciousness. Models were presented that could be implemented using generative adversarial networks (GANs) to enable the implementation of early forms of consciousness in machines.
- **Neuroplasticity** – Unlike machine-stimulated neural networks, which do not form new neural connections, humans can recognize, learn and change according to the activities they are required to perform, a process called neuroplasticity or brain plasticity. Increasingly, research in this area will enable the development of algorithms that are more representative of nature in terms of its ability to cater to environmental and time-based data.[211]
- **Manifold learning and the manifold hypothesis** – Manifolds are very general algorithms that enable models to learn many degrees of freedom in latent space where transformations on points may represent features of a particular object in pixel space (for example), and transformations on the said points or weights of the object are separable from those of other objects in latent space. This enables some profound aspects of transfer learning and leads logically to beliefs, intuition and knowledge.

- **Analogue AI** – Research to develop laboratory-grown human brain organoids is leading to advances in many areas, including AI, enabling us to better understand human brain development with a range of computational neuroscience models.
- **Taxonomy and ontology of data** – Combining business objects with their ontology and the possibility of transfer learning using the manifold hypothesis should enable deep contextualization of a kind that is beginning to move AI forward from the limitations that were observed in the recent past. The key issue of curation, cataloguing, discovery and parameterization of data is that nature teaches us all that our senses are connected to the environment. We need to do the same with digital data.
- **Quantum, fractals and scalability** – By pointing to the applicability of abstract natural models from quantum computing, fractal theory and cognitive neuroscience, we have pointed to the incredible scalability of natural systems and their representation.[212] By observing the similarities between NLP, the neural cortex and smart cities, we lend credence to the manifold hypothesis. These observations have enormous implications for transfer learning and implementing higher forms of intelligence in service of business and global problems.
- **Data synthesis** – The ability to generate data synthetically is hugely complementary to implementing the generation hypothesis. By using many GANs (one for data synthesis, another for hypothesis generation and more still for decision metrics), an implementable model becomes possible.[213]
- **Evolution of intelligence** – The comparison of natural and artificial intelligence in our tables may have surprised some readers (see *Tables 1* and *2*). The human brain has gotten smaller (in size) over the past 50,000 years, which raises some questions about Darwinian natural selection theory. This change, based on a rapid response to environmental shifts and requirements, implies that nature does not need to go through natural selection but can instead enable specific physiological changes in response to environmental data.[214] These hypotheses are backed up by recent studies. For example, according to a study in the *Journal of Anatomy*, humans are evolving at a rate faster than we have at any interval in the past 250 years.[215] The article articulates, for instance, that babies have shorter faces, leading to smaller mouths and less room for teeth to grow. There is increasing talk of microevolution in many academic and popular circles, but microevolution is still considered natural selection. In addition to genes, environmental data and intelligence also seems to play a role in the physiology of creatures. These hypotheses may have significant implications for the types of AI evolutionary frameworks that we develop moving forward.
- **Self-awareness and intentionality** – In spite of developing models of consciousness and human-level decision-making, we have not yet developed

models that enable machines to communicate with each other. We are working through various theses at the moment but cannot give a credible and cognizant implementable model for it. We feel that such models will probably be available within a decade or so. These models, we believe , will be fundamentally based around data democratization exchanges as well as those that implement our AI periodic table in its fullest sense.

While tackling the foundations and frontiers of AI, we have been cognizant of organizations' need to derive immediate business value. We have discussed the various elements of AI to enable readers to home in on maximizing the benefits of using ML for their diverse business problems. Still, there is not enough space in this book to articulate them fully. The techniques, methods, processes and technologies that are essential to creating value are:

- **The AI Periodic Table** – An abstraction of the alchemical processes that a business needs to apply to create business value from AI, ML, DL and beyond.
- **AI democratization** – Many AI algorithms can tackle multiple problems. The use of automation to enable AI's application across a broad range of challenges will accelerate the generation of business value. Democratized AI tools and methods will enable businesses to significantly reduce their perceived need for AI specialists and allow them to adapt in the short to medium term.
- **Data democratization and intelligent data** – In order to make intelligent sense of the mountains of data that the world generates, intelligent data engineering is crucial to construct object taxonomies and ontologies. Having senses everywhere is only part of the story; to link cause and effect in an intelligent, implementable way is of utmost importance for business value. New paradigms related to data mining from data lakes and data oceans and data parameterizations engines (such as data crawlers and data governance frameworks) will come to the fore in the next few years, rendering data engineering more intelligent and automated. The three aspects of data democratization (parameterization, monetization and exchange; see *Chapter 4*) require considerable development. Data exchanges will appear; many aspects will take time to find traction. Increasingly, data consumers and providers will be connected devices and will end up swamping all human-generated and human-curated data.
- **Model as a Service (MaaS)** – A host of tools and products need to mature around application scalability and evolutionary model improvement. Nature has done this with humans, and the societal forces are configurable and adaptable (through the diverse models of beliefs and democracy). With businesses and data intelligence, we face issues around workflows, model management, model parameterization and the stability of the stack used to deliver data

intelligence services into a production environment. MaaS is an extension of XaaS (Anything as a Service), which is currently driving many changes that are enabling our AI Periodic Table to become real. Platforms will simplify testing, monitoring and deploying models in live environments quickly with enhanced feedback mechanisms (e.g. dashboards, connected customers and clients, and connected ecosystems) and greater collaboration between data scientists, data engineers, user experience specialists and DevOps teams.[216] These changes could take the form of the design and development of digital twins. A digital twin is a real-time digital representation (virtualization) of a real physical object or process. These ecosystems could act as experimental simulated bridges between the virtual and real environments, providing increased data parameterization, practical application of cognitive data frameworks, and actionable insight to inform and enable testing of organizations' sense-and-respond models. Further out on the horizon, we will get a different picture still; we believe that the evolution of toolsets, technologies and frameworks will enable the seamless transition of environmental data to the manifestation of intelligence in a way that is currently not offered by fragmented toolsets and processes. Terms such as 'intelligent data' will come into vogue, and we have been working on such frameworks and tools.

- **Data debt and data sovereignty** – As data sovereignty becomes enshrined in the application of alchemical processes and the ability to innovate, new applications of AI and ML will become progressively concentrated in the virtual boardrooms of a handful of companies situated at the core of digital exchanges, and the levels of both technical data debt and data inequality will increasing define commercial and social evolution. Being the judges of this value exchange will generate additional sources of data value for consumers, citizens and businesses alike.
- **Rise of ethics and governance** – It is necessary to move beyond a concern over algorithmic ethics to discuss the ethics of AI. Ethical and governance frameworks for data and algorithms will change, as the input to algorithms is data and the output is also data. Therefore, the focus will be around data parameterization and the discovery of intelligent data. Moreover, as the primary consumers and providers of data become machines, many of the issues around data security, governance and ethics will be implemented in stem-IoT devices (see *Chapter 4*) that evolve in a way that is predicated on national and international governance frameworks.

Finally, in this era of COVID-19, we find ourselves more drawn to a world where we live virtual lives (certainly in the way we interact with many of those around us).[217] One of the emergent issues is the change in human culture. Sensory intelligence and sensory enhancement devices are pulling us into a more virtual world that is arguably *more* fulfilling and experience-enhancing.[218]

Increasingly, sensory AI and data will enable us to learn, experience and live in the virtual environment, and we will escape to reality merely to fulfil our natural sustenance requirements and our decreasingly critical social obligations.

We believe the importance of data, as well as the monetization of the virtual world, will surpass that of the real world as there may be a time when physical processes (production, harvesting, distribution, consumption, etc.) are increasingly mechanized and automated in a way that diminishes humans in the natural environment. Our natural environment will be more artificial and virtual. Increasingly, AI will play a dominant role and may assign us our purpose and aspirations for living. Businesses will adapt and change. They are living organisms with intelligence, purpose, personalities, partner ecosystems and evolutionary desires. The genesis of value for businesses has always been thought of as their people. As AI and ML development matures, leading to the implementation of higher forms of intelligence, our environments, social connections and economic interactions will fundamentally evolve at a pace and scale we have previously not experienced. The abilities of businesses to capture sensory intelligence and deliver competitive advantage via data and experience will be the difference between survival and evolution. The critical challenge for businesses lies at the intersection of ethics, data and innovation. Seeking to synthesize data intelligence and amplify human brilliance via alchemical digital processes is the essence of business value genesis.

ENDNOTES

1.   See #morethanhuman on Twitter.

2.   R. J. Forbes, "On the Origin of Alchemy," *Historical Studies in the Physical Sciences* 4 (1974): 1–11.

3.   André Tramer, Raymond Voltz, F. Lahmani and Joanna Szczepińska-Tramer, "What Is (Was) Alchemy?" *Acta Physica Polonica A* 104 (2007): S5–S18.

4.   Earle Radcliffe Caley, "The Stockholm Papyrus: An English Translation with Brief Notes," *Journal of Chemical Education* 4 (1927): 979–1002.

5.   Lawrence M. Principe, *The Secrets of Alchemy* (Chicago: University of Chicago Press, 2013), 90.

6.   These literary references include Geoffrey Chaucer's *Canterbury Tales*, where in "The Canon's Yeoman's Tale" a priest is tricked into purchasing an alchemic formula, thereby illustrating the profitability of falsehood and the need to understand this privileged knowledge; Ben Jonson's *The Alchemist*, where in a more comic portrayal a con artist extracts gold by exploiting humankind's greed-induced gullibility and obsession with how to get ahead in life and regardless of ethical boundaries; William Congreve's *The Old Bachelor* and *The Way of the World*, which deal with the alchemical trade; and Ian McEwan's *Machines Like Me*, which explores the concepts of understanding and experience in humans and their synthetic counterparts.

7.   Michèle Mertens, *Les Alchimistes Grecs IV, i: Zosime de Panopolis, Mémories Authentiques* (Paris: Les Belles Lettres, 2002).

8.   Israel Regardie, *The Philosopher's Stone: A Modern Comparative Approach to Alchemy from the Psychological and Magical Points of View* (London: Rider, 1938).

9.   Practitioners recognized seven metals: gold, silver, copper, iron, tin, lead and mercury. They called two of them (gold and silver) 'noble' because of their resistance to corrosion, their beauty and their rarity. They labelled the remaining five base or 'ignoble' metals.

10.   Lawrence M. Principe, *The Secrets of Alchemy* (Chicago: University of Chicago Press, 2013), 102.

11.   Cited in Martin Ford, *The Architects of Intelligence: The Truth about AI from the People Building It* (Birmingham: Packt Publishing, 2018), 249.

12.   David McCandless, *Knowledge is Beautiful* (London: William Collins, 2014), 12–13.

13.   Oscar Wilde, *Lady Windermere's Fan* (1893), Act 3.

14.   "Narrow Artificial Intelligence (Narrow AI)", (*Techopedia*), last modified 19 July 2021, https://www.techopedia.com/definition/32874/narrow-artificial-intelligence-narrow-ai.

15.   Mariana Mazzucato, *The Value of Everything: Making and Taking in the Global Economy* (London: Penguin 2019), 6.

16. Mazzucato, *Op. Cit.* 7.

17. Hyman P. Minsky, *Finance and Stability: The Limits of Capitalism*, Working Paper no. 93 (Levy Economics Institute, 1993). See also Mazzucato, *Op. Cit.* 136.

18. Singapore: World Scientific, 2011), 393–438; Stephan Zoder, "How Much is Your Data Worth?" (*Forbes*), last modified 6 August 2019, https://www.forbes.com/sites/stephanzoder/2019/08/06/how-much-is-your-data-worth

19. *The Economic Value of Data: Discussion Paper* (*HM Treasury, 2018*), accessed 10 August 2021, https://assets.publishing.service.gov.uk/government/uploads/system/uploads/attachment_data/file/731349/20180730_HMT_Discussion_Paper_-_The_Economic_Value_of_Data.pdf.

20. "Research: Moody's Reviews Microsoft's AAA Rating for Downgrade Following Announced Acquisition of LinkedIn," (*Moody's*), last modified 13 June 2016, https://www.moodys.com/research/moodys-reviews-microsofts-aaa-rating-for-downgrade-following-announced-acquisition--pr_350591.

21. Douglas B. Laney, *Infonomics* (New York: Bibliomotion, 2018), 267.

22. *A New Slice of PII, with a Side of Digital Trust*," (*Accenture, 2017*), accessed 10 August 2021, https://www.accenture.com/t20180123T070729Z__w__/us-en/_acnmedia/PDF-59/Accenture-Strategy-DD-GDPR-Infographic.pdf#zoom=50.

23. "What Does a Good Value Exchange Look Like?" (*CtrlShift*), last modified 1 February 2016, https://www.ctrl-shift.co.uk/news/2016/02/01/what-does-a-good-value-exchange-look-like.

24. The survey also looked at the percentages of people who would not wish to share certain types of data with their employers. The findings were 53% for social media profile data, 55% for web and browsing data, 64% for identity data (photo, biometrics, voice, etc.) and 66% for location data. See Human to Hybrid, The insight edge in learning: How data can transform learning to deliver future skills, accessed October 2020, https://www.capita.com/our-work/human-hybrid

25. Shoshana Zuboff, *The Age of Surveillance Capitalism* (London: Profile Books, 2019), 534.

26. "Selligent Marketing Cloud Study Finds Consumer Expectations and Marketer Challenges Are Rising in Tandem" (*Selligent*), last modified 23 August 2018, https://www.selligent.com/press/selligent-marketing-cloud-study-finds-consumer-expectations-and-marketer-challenges-are-rising-in-tandem.

27. *A New Slice of PII*, Op. cit.

28. Alan Macfarlane, "The Root of All Evil," in *The Anthropology of Evil*, ed. David Parkin (Oxford: Basil Blackwell, 1985), 71–72.

29. "Users first, monetarization later ... only after a value unit has been created and exchanged with results that are satisfactory to both producer and consumer should the platform business itself seek to capture a share of that value." See Geoffrey G. Parker, Marshall W. van Alstyne and Sangeet Paul Choudary, *Platform Revolution: How Networked Markets Are Transforming the Economy and How to Make them Work for You* (New York: W. W. Norton, 2016), 125.

30. David Mattin, "This Crisis is a Call to Step Up: Time to Imagine the New, and then Build It," (*New World Same Humans*), accessed 25 May 2020, https://www.linkedin.com/pulse/crisis-call-step-up-time-imagine-new-build-david-mattin.

31. Zuboff, Op. Cit. 8.

32. Tom Vanderbilt, "How Biomimicry is Inspiring Human Innovation," (*Smithsonian Magazine*), last modified September 2012, https://www.smithsonianmag.com/science-nature/how-biomimicry-is-inspiring-human-innovation-17924040.

33. Michael Marshall, "Timeline: The Evolution of Life," (*New Scientist*), last modified 14 July 2009, https://www.newscientist.com/article/dn17453-timeline-the-evolution-of-life.

34. Robert J. Flower, "Natural Intelligence (NaTi): A Synthesized, Organized and Synchronized Model of Multiple Intelligences, and Their Systems," (*Gilchrist Institute for the Achievement Sciences*),

accessed 10 August 2021, https://www.gilchristinstitute.com/wp-content/uploads/2017/06/Natural-Intelligence-3-21-16.pdf; Lavika Goel, Daya Gupta, V. K. Panchal and Ajinth Abraham, "Taxonomy of Nature Inspired Computational Intelligence: A Remote Sensing Perspective," in *Fourth World Congress on Nature and Biologically Inspired Computing (NaBIC)* (2012), 200–206.

35. Robert J. Sternberg, *Metaphors of Mind: Conceptions of the Nature of Intelligence,* (Cambridge University Press, 2008).

36. Janet E. Davidson, Rebecca Deuser and Robert J. Sternberg, "The Role of Metacognition in Problem-Solving," in *Metacognition: Knowing about Knowing*, eds. Janet Metcalfe and Arthur P. Shimamura (Cambridge: MIT Press, 1994), 207–226.

37. Istvan Elek, Janos Roden and Thai Binh Nguyen, "Spontaneous Emergence of the Intelligence in an Artificial World," in *ICONIP 2012: Neural Information Processing*, eds. T. Huang, Z. Zeng, C. Li and C. S. Leung (Berlin: Springer, 2012), 703–712.

38. William H. Calvin, "The Emergence of Intelligence," *Scientific American* 271 (1994): 100–107.

39. D. Kerr, "Nervous Systems," (*Organismal Biology*), accessed 16 January 2021, http://organismalbio.biosci.gatech.edu/chemical-and-electrical-signals/nervous-systems.

40. George R. McConnell, "3.1.4 Emergence: A Partial History of Systems Thinking," *INCOSE International Symposium* 12 (2002): 90–98.

41. Stanford University Medical Centre. "Stunning Details of Brain Connections Revealed," (*Science Daily*), www.sciencedaily.com/releases/2010/11/101117121803.htm (accessed August 28, 2021).

42. Vito Di Maio and Silvia Santillo, "Information Processing and Synaptic Transmission," *Advances in Neural Signal Processing, Ramana Vinjamuri*, IntechOpen (2020), DOI: 10.5772/intechopen.88405. Available from: https://www.intechopen.com/chapters/68373

43. Christof Koch, "Does Brain Size Matter?" (*Scientific American Mind*), last modified 1 January 2016, https://www.scientificamerican.com/article/does-brain-size-matter1. See also Suzana Herculano-Houzel, Kamilla Avelino-de-Souza, Kleber Neves, Jairo Porfírio, Débora Messeder, Larissa Mattos Feijó, José Maldonado and Paul R. Manger, "The Elephant Brain in Numbers," *Frontiers in Neuroanatomy* 8 (2014): https://www.frontiersin.org/articles/10.3389/fnana.2014.00046/full; Ana F. Navarrete, Erwin L. A. Blezer, Murillo Pagnotta, Elizabeth S. M. de Viet, Orlin S. Todorov, Patrik Lindenfors, Kevin N. Laland and Simon M. Reader, "Primate Brain Anatomy: New Volumetric MRI Measurements for Neuroanatomical Studies," *Brain, Behaviour and Evolution* 91 (2018): 109–117.

44. Suzana Herculano-Houzel, "The Remarkable, Yet Not Extraordinary, Human Brain as a Scaled-Up Primate Brain and Its Associated Cost," *Proceedings of the National Academy of Sciences* 109 (2012): 10661–10668; Christopher Stringer, "Why Have Our Brains Started to Shrink?" (*Scientific American Mind*), last modified 1 November 2014, https://www.scientificamerican.com/article/why-have-our-brains-started-to-shrink.

45. Eryn. J. Newman, Madeline C. Jalbert, Norbert Schwarz and Deva P. Ly, "Truthiness, the Illusory Truth Effect, and the Role of Need for Cognition," *Consciousness and Cognition* 78 (2020): 102866.

46. Stringer, Op. Cit.

47. Michel A. Hofman, "Design Principles of the Human Brain: An Evolutionary Perspective," *Progress in Brain Research* 195 (2012): 373–390.

48. John H. Byrne, "Introduction to Neurons and Neuronal Networks," (*Neuroscience Online*), accessed 27 March 2021, https://nba.uth.tmc.edu/neuroscience/m/s1/introduction.html.

49. Solomon D. Erulkar and Thomas L. Lentz, "Nervous System," (*Encyclopaedia Britannica*), last modified 10 November 2020, https://www.britannica.com/science/nervous-system.

50. Ferris Jabr, "Know Your Neurons: How to Classify Different Types of Neurons in the Brain's Forest," (*Scientific American*), last modified 16 May 2012, https://blogs.scientificamerican.com/brainwaves/know-your-neurons-classifying-the-many-types-of-cells-in-the-neuron-forest.

51. Jabr, Op. Cit.

52. Erulkar and Lentz, Op. Cit.

53. Ryota Kanai, Acer Chang, Yen Yu, Ildefons Magrans de Abril, Martin Biehl and Nicholas Guttenberg, "Information Generation as a Functional Basis of Consciousness," *Neuroscience of Consciousness* 1 (2019): https://academic.oup.com/nc/article/2019/1/niz016/5648002.

54. Greenough, William T., Black, James E., and Wallace, Christopher S. "Experience and Brain Development" in M. H. Johnson, Y. Munakata, and R. O. Gilmore (Eds.), *Brain Development and Cognition: A Reader*, (Blackwell Publishing, 2002), 186-216.

55. Natalia A. Goriounova, Djai B. Heyer, René Wilbers, Matthijs B. Verhoog, Michele Giugliano, Christophe Verbist, Joshua Obermayer, Amber Kerkhofs, Harriët Smeding, Maaike Verberne, Sander Idema, Johannes C. Baayen, Anton W. Pieneman, Christiaan P. J. de Kock, Martin Klein and Huibert D. Mansvelder, "Large and Fast Human Pyramidal Neurons Associate with Intelligence," *eLife* 7 (2018): e41714.

56. Michael K. Gardner, "Theories of Intelligence," in *The Oxford Handbook of School Psychology*, eds. Melissa A. Bray and Thomas J. Kehle (Oxford: Oxford University Press, 2011), 79–100.

57. Charles Spearman, "'General Intelligence,' Objectively Determined and Measured," *American Journal of Psychology* 15 (1904): 201–292.

58. Pat Lovie, "Spearman, Charles Edward," in *Encyclopedia of Statistics in Behavioral Science* (Chichester: John Wiley & Sons, 2005), doi:10.1002/0470013192.bsa634.

59. Louis L. Thurstone, "Primary Mental Abilities," *Psychometric Monographs* 1 (1973): 131–136.

60. Howard Gardner, *Frames of Mind: The Theory of Multiple Intelligences* (New York: Basic Books, 2011).

61. Istvan Elek, Janos Roden and Thai Binh Nguyen, Op. Cit.

62. Max Tegmark, "Benefits & Risks of Artificial Intelligence" (*Future of Life Institute*), accessed 16 January 2021, https://futureoflife.org/background/benefits-risks-of-artificial-intelligence.

63. Hugo Mayo, Hashan Punchihewa, Julie Emile and Jack Morrison "Introduction to Neural Networks," (AI in Radiology), accessed 16 January 2021, https://www.doc.ic.ac.uk/~jce317/introduction-neural-nets.html.

64. Fjodor van Veen, "The Neural Network Zoo," (*The Asimov Institute*), last modified 14 September 2016, https://www.asimovinstitute.org/neural-network-zoo. See also the various cheat sheets at https://www.datacamp.com/community/data-science-cheatsheets related to Python, R, NLP, visualization and various ML libraries.

65. Rebecca Reynoso, "4 Main Types of Artificial Intelligence," (*G2*), last modified 27 March 2019, https://learn.g2.com/types-of-artificial-intelligence.

66. Warwick Ashford, "Attacks Against AI Systems Are a Growing Concern," (*Computer Weekly*), last modified 11 July 2019, https://www.computerweekly.com/news/252466576/Attacks-against-AI-systems-are-a-growing-concern; Simon Romero, "Wielding Rocks and Knives, Arizonans Attack Self-Driving Cars," (*The New York Times*), last modified 31 December 2018, https://www.nytimes.com/2018/12/31/us/waymo-self-driving-cars-arizona-attacks.html.

67. Maureen Dowd, "Elon Musk's Billion-Dollar Crusade to Stop the A.I. Apocalypse," (*Vanity Fair*), last modified 26 March 2017, https://www.vanityfair.com/news/2017/03/elon-musk-billion-dollar-crusade-to-stop-ai-space-x.

68. François Chollet, "On the Measure of Intelligence," *arXiv* (2019): 1911.01547v2.

69. "Moore's Law," (*Encyclopaedia Britannica*), last modified 26 December 2019, https://www.britannica.com/technology/Moores-law.

70. Byrne, Op. Cit.

71. Kanai et al., Op. Cit.; Christof Koch, "What is Consciousness?" (*Scientific American*), last modified 1 June 2018, https://www.scientificamerican.com/article/what-is-consciousness.

72. Christof Koch, Marcello Massimini, Melanie Boly and Giulio Tononi, "Neural Correlates of Consciousness: Progress and Problems," *Nature Reviews Neuroscience* 17 (2016): 307–321.

73. Kanai et al., Op. Cit.

74. Ross Dawson, "Periodic Table of Disruptive Technologies and Innovation," (*RossDawson.com*), last modified 14 March 2018, https://rossdawson.com/periodic-table-disruptive-technologies-innovation; "Periodic Table of Amazon Web Services," (*AWS Geek*), last modified 19 February 2019, https://www.awsgeek.com/Periodic-Table-of-Amazon-Web-Services; "The Periodic Table of Cloud Computing," (*CB Insights*), last modified 9 February 2018, https://www.cbinsights.com/research/cloud-computing-companies-investors-infographic; "The Periodic Table of DevOps," (*Digital.ai*), accessed 10 August 2021, https://digital.ai/sites/default/files/pictures/2020-06/Digital.ai_Periodic-Table-of-DevOps.pdf; "The Periodic Table of Leadership," (*WU Executive Academy*), last modified 16 May 2019, https://executiveacademy.at/en/news/detail/the-periodic-table-of-leadership.

75. "The Periodic Table of DevOps," Op. Cit.

76. "The Periodic Table of Cloud Computing," Op. Cit.

77. David Schatsky, Amit Chaudhary and Amanpreet Arora, "Five Vectors of Progress in Cloud Computing: How Companies Are Looking to Get More Value from Cloud," (*Deloitte Insights*), last modified 31 July 2019, https://www2.deloitte.com/us/en/insights/focus/signals-for-strategists/artificial-intelligence-and-devops-for-cloud-computing.html.

78. B. Golstein, "[A Brief Taxonomy of AI]" (*Sharper AI*), accessed 10 August 2021, https://www.sharper.ai/taxonomy-ai; Stefan Kojouharov, "Cheat Sheets for AI, Neural Networks, Machine Learning, Deep Learning & Big Data: The Most Complete List of Best AI Cheat Sheets," (*Becoming Human*), last modified 9 July 2017, https://becominghuman.ai/cheat-sheets-for-ai-neural-networks-machine-learning-deep-learning-big-data-678c51b4b463.

79. Vincenzo Ciancaglini, Craig Gibson, David Sancho, Odhran McCarthy, Maria Eira, Philipp Amann and Aglika Klayn, "Malicious Uses and Abuses of Artificial Intelligence," *Trend Micro Research, United Nations Interregional Crime and Justice Research Institute (UNICRI), Europol's European Cybercrime Centre (EC3).* Europol Public Information, Available online at https://static1.squarespace.com/static/5b504068365f025b0e4f790a/t/5fbbdee340350635ed33c68f/1606147831970/AI+MLC.pdf, (Accessed: 16 January 2021)

80. Max Tegmark, "Benefits & Risks of Artificial Intelligence," (*Future of Life Institute*), accessed 16 January 2021, https://futureoflife.org/background/benefits-risks-of-artificial-intelligence.

81. Inken von Borzyskowski, Anjali Mazumder, Bilal Mateen and Michael Wooldridge, eds., "Data Science and AI in the Age of COVID-19," (*Alan Turing Institute*), accessed 10 August 2021, https://www.turing.ac.uk/sites/default/files/2021-06/data-science-and-ai-in-the-age-of-covid_full-report_2.pdf. See also "Data Science and AI in the Age of COVID-19: Reflections on the Response of the UK's Data Science and AI Community to the COVID-19 Pandemic," (*Alan Turing Institute*), accessed August 2021.

82. https://www.google.com/covid19/mobility/, accessed August 2021.

83. "Trusted Vaccine Distribution Enabled with Blockchain," (*IBM*), accessed 11 October 2021, https://www.ibm.com/uk-en/blockchain/solutions/vaccine-distribution, https://www.ncbi.nlm.nih.gov/pmc/articles/PMC7805409/; "How Can Blockchain Help in the Time of COVID-19," (*Big Innovation Centre*), accessed 11 October 2021, https://biginnovationcentre.com/wp-content/uploads/2020/06/APPG-Blockchain-COVID-19-_16June-2020.pdf,

84. Sarang Chaudhari, Michael Clear, Philip Bradish and Hitesh Tewari, "Framework for a DLT Based COVID-19 Passport," in *Intelligent Computing,* Ed. Kohei Arai, (Springer, 2021), 108–123.

85. https://cdei.blog.gov.uk/category/covid-19/, accessed August 2021.

86. "COVID-19 Open Research Dataset Challenge (CORD-19), An AI challenge with AI2, CZI, MSR, Georgetown, NIH & The White House," https://www.kaggle.com/allen-institute-for-ai/CORD-19-research-challenge, accessed August 2021.

87. Andreas Voyages, "The Importance of Statistical Modeling for the COVID-19 Pandemic," (*YS Journal*), last modified 16 February 2021, https://ysjournal.com/the-importance-of-statistical-modeling-for-the-covid-19-pandemic/.

88. Wentao Zhao, Jiang, Wei and Qiu, Xinguo, "Deep Learning for COVID-19 Detection Based on CT Images," *Sci Rep* 11, 14353 (2021). https://doi.org/10.1038/s41598-021-93832-2

89. "Tracking the Pandemic," (*Capita*), https://www.capita.com/business-unusual-latest-update, accessed 25 August 2021.

90. "COVID-19 Variants: Genomically Confirmed Case Numbers," (*Public Health England*), last modified 8 October 2021, https://www.gov.uk/government/publications/covid-19-variants-genomically-confirmed-case-numbers.

91. Jake Poller, "The Transmutations of Arthur Machen: Alchemy in 'The Great God Pan' and 'The Three Impostors.'" *Literature and Theology* 29 (2015): 18–32.

92. Martin Hilbert, "Quantifying the Data Deluge and the Data Drought," (*SSRN*), last modified 1 April 2015, https://papers.ssrn.com/sol3/papers.cfm?abstract_id=2984851.

93. Arne Holst, "Volume of Data/Information Created, Captured, Copied, and Consumed Worldwide from 2010 to 2025," (*Statistica*), last modified 7 June 2021, https://www.statista.com/statistics/871513/worldwide-data-created.

94. Holst, Op. Cit.

95. "£1.2 Billion for the World's Most Powerful Weather and Climate Supercomputer," (*Gov.uk*), last modified 17 February 2020, https://www.gov.uk/government/news/12-billion-for-the-worlds-most-powerful-weather-and-climate-supercomputer.

96. Jeff Desjardins, "How Much Data is Generated Each Day?" (*World Economic Forum*), last modified 17 April 2019, https://www.weforum.org/agenda/2019/04/how-much-data-is-generated-each-day-cf4bddf29f.

97. Rafael Capurro and Birger Hjørland, "The Concept of Information," *Annual Review of Information Science and Technology,* 37 (2003): 343–411.

98. Aaron Sloman, "What Did Bateson Mean When He Wrote 'Information' is 'a Difference that Makes a Difference'?" (*School of Computer Science, University of Birmingham*), last modified 16 February 2019, https://www.cs.bham.ac.uk/research/projects/cogaff/misc/information-difference.html; Aaron

99. David MacKay, "Information Theory, Inference, and Learning Algorithms," *IEEE Transactions on Information Theory,* 50 (2004): 2544–2545.

100. Claude E. Shannon, "The Bandwagon," *IRE Transactions: Information Theory,* 2 (1956): 3.

101. Khalid Sayood, "Information Theory and Cognition: A Review," *Entropy,* 9 (2018): 706.

102. "What is Personal Data?" (*European Commission*), accessed 10 August 2021, https://ec.europa.eu/info/law/law-topic/data-protection/reform/what-personal-data_en.

103. Hilbert, Op. Cit.

104. See, e.g. "Turing-NLG: A 17-Billion-Parameter Language Model by Microsoft," (*Microsoft Research Blog*), last modified 13 February 2020, https://www.microsoft.com/en-us/research/blog/turing-nlg-a-17-billion-parameter-language-model-by-microsoft.

105. "Overview of the Internet of Things," (*International Telecommunication Union, 2012*), accessed 30 July 2021, https://www.itu.int/ITU-T/recommendations/rec.aspx?rec=y.2060, 2.

106. Jonathan Davenport, Pedro Pacheco and Alan Priestley, "Market Trends: Monetizing Connected and Autonomous Vehicle Data," (*Gartner Research*), last modified 30 April 2020, https://www.gartner.com/en/documents/3984496/market-trends-monetizing-connected-and-autonomous-vehicl.

107. Rossana M. C. Andrade, Belmondo R. Aragão, Pedro Almir M. Oliveira, Marcio E. F. Maia, Windson Viana and Tales P. Nogueira, "Multifaceted Infrastructure for Self-Adaptive IoT Systems," *Information and Software Technology,* 132 (2021): 106505.

108. "What is Personal Data?", Complete guide to GDPR compliance, https://gdpr.eu/

109. See, e.g. Julia Angwin, Jeff Larson, Surya Mattu and Lauren Kirchner, "Machine Bias: There's Software Used Across the Country to Predict Future Criminals. And It's Biased Against Blacks," (*Pro Publica*), last modified 23 May 2016, https://www.propublica.org/article/machine-bias-risk-assessments-in-criminal-sentencing; Alex Hern, "Cambridge Analytica: How Did It Turn Clicks into Votes?" (*The Guardian*), last modified 6 May 2018, https://www.theguardian.com/news/2018/may/06/cambridge-analytica-how-turn-clicks-into-votes-christopher-wylie; Julia Carrie Wong, "The Cambridge Analytica Scandal Changed the World – but It Didn't Change Facebook," (*The Guardian*), last modified 18 March 2019, https://www.theguardian.com/technology/2019/mar/17/the-cambridge-analytica-scandal-changed-the-world-but-it-didnt-change-facebook.

110. Angwin et al., Op. Cit.

111. Hern, Op. Cit.; Wong, Op. Cit.

112. Haoyue Ping, Julia Stoyanovich and Bill Howe, "DataSynthesizer: Privacy-Preserving Synthetic Datasets," in *Proceedings of the 29th International Conference on Scientific and Statistical Database Management,* (2017), 42.

113. Matt Fredrikson, Somesh Jha and Thomas Ristenpart, "Model Inversion Attacks that Exploit Confidence Information and Basic Countermeasures," in *Proceedings of the 22nd ACM SIGSAC Conference on Computer and Communications Security,* (2015): 1322–1333.

114. Florian Tramèr, Fan Zhang, Ari Juels, Michael K. Reiter and Thomas Ristenpart, "Stealing Machine Learning Models via Prediction APIs," (*arXiv*, 2016): 1609.02943

115. Reza Shokri, Marco Stronati, Congzheng Song and Vitaly Shmatikov, "Membership Inference Attacks Against Machine Learning Models," *IEEE Symposium on Security and Privacy,* (2017): 3–18.

116. Richard Dawkins, *The Selfish Gene,* (Oxford: Oxford University Press, 1976).

117. David C. van Essen, Chad J. Donahue and Matthew F. Glasser, "Development and Evolution of Cerebral and Cerebellar Cortex," *Brain Behaviour Evolution,* 3 (2018): 158–169.

118. M. James Nichols and William T. Newsome, "The Neurobiology of Cognition," *Nature,* 402 (1999): C35–C38.

119. A. K. Harauzov, Y. E. Shelepin, Y. A. Noskov, P. P. Vasilev and N. P. Foreman, "The Time Course of Pattern Discrimination in the Human Brain," *Vision Research,* 125 (2016). 55–63; Raymond Kurzweil, *The Singularity is Near: When Humans Transcend Biology,* (New York: Penguin, 2005).

120. Warren McCulloch and Walter Pitts, "A Logical Calculus of Ideas Immanent in Nervous Activity," *Bulletin of Mathematical Biophysics,* 5 (1943): 115–133.

121. Ronald R. Kline, *The Cybernetics Moment, or Why We Call Our Age the Information Age,* (Baltimore: Johns Hopkins University Press, 2015).

122. Andrew Hodges, *Alan Turing: The Enigma,* (New York: Simon and Schuster, 1983).

123. Alan Turing, "Computing Machinery and Intelligence," *Mind,* 236 (1950): 433–460.

124. Jeremy M. Norman, "Newell, Simon & Shaw Develop the First Artificial Intelligence Program," (*Jeremy Norman's History of Information*), accessed 10 August 2021, https://www.historyofinformation.com/detail.php?id=742. See also Diana H. Hook and Jeremy M. Norman, *Origins of Cyberspace,* (San Anselmo: Norman, 2002), no. 815; Herbert Simon, "Allen Newell: 1927–1992," *Annals of the History of Computing,* 20 (1998): 63–76.

125. James Moor, "The Dartmouth College Artificial Intelligence Conference: The Next Fifty Years," *AI Magazine,* 27 (2006): 87–91.

126. Marvin Minsky, *Computation: Finite and Infinite Machines* (Englewood Cliffs: Prentice Hall, 1967), Page 2.

127. James Lighthill, "Artificial Intelligence: A General Survey," (*Science Research Council*), accessed 10 August 2021, http://www.aiai.ed.ac.uk/events/lighthill1973/lighthill.pdf.

128. Larry Greenemeier, "20 Years after Deep Blue: How AI Has Advanced since Conquering Chess," (*Scientific American*), last modified 2 June 2017, https://www.scientificamerican.com/article/20-years-after-deep-blue-how-ai-has-advanced-since-conquering-chess.

129. David Orenstein, "Stanford Team's Win in Robot Car Race Nets $2 Million Prize," (*Stanford Report*), last modified 11 October 2005, https://news.stanford.edu/news/2005/october12/stanleyfinish-100905.html.

130. "Urban Challenge," (*National Robotics Engineering Center*), accessed 11 October 2021, https://www.nrec.ri.cmu.edu/solutions/defense/other-projects/urban-challenge.html

131. "Moore's Law," Op. Cit.

132. John Markoff, "AI Reemerges from a Funding Desert," (*New York Times*), last modified 13 October 2005, https://www.nytimes.com/2005/10/13/business/worldbusiness/ai-reemerges-from-a-funding-desert.html.

133. Geoffrey E. Hinton, Simon Osindero and Yee-Whye Teh, "A Fast Learning Algorithm for Deep Belief Nets," *Neural Computation,* 18 (2006): 1527–1554.

134. Rajat Raina, Anand Madhavan and Andrew Y. Ng, "Large-scale Deep Unsupervised Learning Using Graphics Processors," In Proceedings of the 26th Annual International Conference on Machine Learning (ICML '09), (*Association for Computing Machinery*), New York, NY, USA, 873–880. DOI: https://doi.org/10.1145/1553374.1553486.

135. Xavier Glorot, Antoine Bordes and Yoshua Bengio, "Deep Sparse Rectifier Neural Networks," *Proceedings of the 14th International Conference on Artificial Intelligence and Statistics,* (2011): 315–323.

136. Steve Lohr, "IBM Is Counting on Its Bet on Watson, and Paying Big Money for It," (*The New York Times*), last modified 17 October 2016, https://www.nytimes.com/2016/10/17/technology/ibm-is-counting-on-its-bet-on-watson-and-paying-big-money-for-it.html.

137. Daniela Hernandez, "The Man behind the Google Brain: Andrew Ng and the Quest for the New AI," (*Wired*), last modified 5 July 2013, https://www.wired.com/2013/05/neuro-artificial-intelligence.

138. Zachary C. Lipton, "The AI Misinformation Epidemic," (*Approximately Correct*), last modified 28 March 2017, https://www.approximatelycorrect.com/2017/03/28/the-ai-misinformation-epidemic.

139. Yann LeCun, Corinna Cortes and Christopher J.C. Burges, "The MNIST Database of Handwritten Digits," (*Yann.Lecun.com*), accessed 10 August 2021, http://yann.lecun.com/exdb/mnist.

140. Edd Gent, "The Democratization of AI is Putting Powerful Tools in the Hands of Non-experts," (*Singularity Hub*), last modified 19 February 2018, https://singularityhub.com/2018/02/19/the-democratization-of-ai-is-putting-powerful-tools-in-the-hands-of-non-experts.

141. Georg B. Keller and Thomas D. Mrsic-Flogel, "Predictive Processing: A Canonical Cortical Computation," *Neuron*, Volume 100, Issue 2, 2018, Pages 424-435, ISSN 0896-6273, https://doi.org/10.1016/j.neuron.2018.10.003.

142. Warren McCulloch and Walter Pitts, Op. Cit.

143. Michael A. Nielsen, *Neural Networks and Deep Learning,* (Determination Press, 2015), http://neuralnetworksanddeeplearning.com.

144. Martino Sorbaro, Qian Liu, Massimo Bortone and Sadique Sheik, "Optimizing the Energy Consumption of Spiking Neural Networks for Neuromorphic Applications," *Frontiers in Neuroscience* 14 (2020), https://doi.org/10.3389/fnins.2020.00662.

145. Albert Christopher, "The Death of Data Scientists: Will AutoML Replace Them?" (*Datacamp*), accessed 10 August 2021, https://www.datacamp.com/community/news/the-death-of-data-scientists-will-automl-replace-them-n2fg96jrxj.

146. Xin He, Kaiyong Zhao, Xiaowen Chu, "AutoML: A Survey of the State-of-the-art," *Knowledge-Based Systems*, Volume 212, 2021, 106622, ISSN 0950-7051, https://doi.org/10.1016/j.knosys.2020.106622. (https://www.sciencedirect.com/science/article/pii/S0950705120307516)

147. Joseph Chin, Aifaz Gowani, Gabriel James and Matthew Peng, "When Will AutoML replace Data Scientists? Poll Results and Analysis," last modified Feb 2020, https://www.kdnuggets.com/2020/02/data-scientists-automl-replace.html.

148. "AutoML Translation Beginner's Guide," (*Google Cloud*), accessed 31 July 2021, https://cloud.google.com/translate/automl/docs/beginners-guide.

149. Yuval Noah Harari, "Yuval Noah Harari on Big Data, Google and the End of Free Will," (*Financial Times*), last modified 26 August 2016, https://www.ft.com/content/50bb4830-6a4c-11e6-ae5b-a7cc5dd5a28c.

150. James Clear, *Atomic Habits* (London: Random House Business, 2018).

151. Kim Martineau, MIT Quest for Intelligence, "Toward Artificial Intelligence that Learns to Write Code: Researchers Combine Deep Learning and Symbolic Reasoning for a More Flexible Way of Teaching Computers to Program," (*MIT News*), last modified 14 June 2019, https://news.mit.edu/2019/toward-artificial-intelligence-that-learns-to-write-code-0614

152. Brad Peters, "The Big Data Gold Rush" (*Forbes*), last modified 21 June 2012, https://www.forbes.com/sites/bradpeters/2012/06/21/the-big-data-gold-rush.

153. Alejandro Barredo Arrieta, Natalia Díaz-Rodríguez, Javier Del Ser, Adrien Bennetot, Siham Tabik, Alberto Barbado, Salvador García, Sergio Gil-López, Daniel Molina, Richard Benjamins, Raja Chatila and Francisco Herrera, "Explainable Artificial Intelligence (XAI): Concepts, Taxonomies, Opportunities and Challenges toward Responsible AI," *Information Fusion,* 58 (2020): 82–115.

154. Matthew M. Hollander and Jason Turowetz, "Normalizing Trust: Participants' Immediately Post-hoc Explanations of Behaviour in Milgram's 'Obedience' Experiments," *British Journal of Social Psychology*, 56 (2017): 655-674, https://doi.org/10.1111/bjso.12206.

155. Ethics Guidelines for Trustworthy AI, Independent High-Level Expert Group on Artificial Intelligence, European Commission, last modified 8 April 2019, https://digital-strategy.ec.europa.eu/en/library/ethics-guidelines-trustworthy-ai.

156. Elie Bursztein, "Attacks Against Machine Learning — An Overview," (*Elie*), May 2018, https://elie.net/blog/ai/attacks-against-machine-learning-an-overview/.

157. Nicolas Papernot, Shuang Song, Ilya Mironov, Ananth Raghunathan, Kunal Talwar, Úlfar Erlingsson, "Scalable Private Learning with PATE," https://arxiv.org/abs/1802.08908.

158. "Trusted AI: IBM Research is Building and Enabling AI Solutions People Can Trust," (*IBM AI Research*), accessed 10 August 2021, https://www.research.ibm.com/artificial-intelligence/trusted-ai.

159. David Gunning and David W. Aha (2019). "DARPA's Explainable Artificial Intelligence (XAI) Program," *AI Magazine*, 40(2), 44-58. https://doi.org/10.1609/aimag.v40i2.2850.

160. Ula La Paris, "Push the Limits of Explainability: An Ultimate Guide to SHAP Library," (*Medium*), last modified 5 June 2020, https://medium.com/swlh/push-the-limits-of-explainability-an-ultimate-guide-to-shap-library-a110af566a02.

161. Félix Revert, "Interpreting Random Forest and Other Black Box Models like XGBoost," (*Towards Data Science*), last modified 6 August 2018, https://towardsdatascience.com/interpreting-random-forest-and-other-black-box-models-like-xgboost-80f9cc4a3c38.

162. Linardatos Pantelis, Vasilis Papastefanopoulos and Sotiris Kotsiantis, (2021). "Explainable AI: A Review of Machine Learning Interpretability Methods," *Entropy,* 23, (1) 18. https://doi.org/10.3390/e23010018.

163. "Explainable AI," (*Google Cloud*), accessed 10 August 2021, https://cloud.google.com/explainable-ai.

164. Michael Rovatsos, Brent Mittelstadt and Ansgar Koene, *Landscape Summary: Bias in Algorithmic Decision-Making* (Centre for Data Ethics and Innovation, 2019), accessed 10 August 2021, https://assets.publishing.service.gov.uk/government/uploads/system/uploads/attachment_data/file/819055/Landscape_Summary_-_Bias_in_Algorithmic_Decision-Making.pdf; Kenneth Taylor, "The Ethics of Algorithms," (*PhilosophyTalk*), last modified 14 August 2018, https://www.philosophytalk.org/blog/ethics-algorithms; Nicol Turner Lee, Paul Resnick and Genie Barton, "Algorithmic Bias Detection

and Mitigation: Best Practices and Policies to Reduce Consumer Harms," (*Brookings*), last modified 22 May 2019, https://www.brookings.edu/research/algorithmic-bias-detection-and-mitigation-best-practices-and-policies-to-reduce-consumer-harms.

165. Nicol Turner Lee, Paul Resnick and Genie Barton, Op. Cit.

166. *Autonomous Response: The Threats Darktrace Antigena Finds* (*Darktrace, 2019*), accessed 10 August 2021, https://www.darktrace.com/en/resources/wp-cyber-ai-response-threat-report-2019.pdf, 3; Yeshwanth R. Bhandayker, "Artificial Intelligence and Big Data for Computer Cyber Security Systems," *Journal of Advances in Science and Technology* 12 (2016): 324–329.

167. Alexander Babuta, Marion Oswald and Ardi Janjeva, "Artificial Intelligence and UK National Security: Policy Considerations," (*RUSI*), last modified 27 April 2020, https://rusi.org/publication/occasional-papers/artificial-intelligence-and-uk-national-security-policy-considerations.

168. Samantha Cole, "We Are Truly Fucked: Everyone Is Making AI-Generated Fake Porn Now," (*Vice*), last modified 24 January 2018, https://www.vice.com/en/article/bjye8a/reddit-fake-porn-app-daisy-ridley, Retrieved Aug 2021.

169. Emmanuel Tsukerman, "How Artificial Intelligence is Changing Social Engineering," (*Infosec*), last modified 2 June 2020, https://resources.infosecinstitute.com/topic/how-artificial-intelligence-is-changing-social-engineering.

170. *Mal-uses of AI-Generated Synthetic Media and Deepfakes: Pragmatic Solutions Discovery Convening* (*Witness*), last modified 11 June 2018, http://witness.mediafire.com/file/q5juw7dc3a2w8p7/Deepfakes_Final.pdf/file; Cristian Vaccari and Andrew Chadwick, "Deepfakes and Disinformation: Exploring the Impact of Synthetic Political Video on Deception, Uncertainty, and Trust in News," *Social Media + Society*, 1 (2020): 205630512090340.

171. Emmanuel Tsukerman, Op. Cit.

172. Babuta et al., Op. Cit.

173. Danny Hernandez and Tom B. Brown, "Measuring the Algorithmic Efficiency of Neural Networks," OpenAI, 2019, https://cdn.openai.com/papers/ai_and_efficiency.pdf.

174. Sara Gamble, "Quantum Computing: What It Is, Why We Want It, and How We're Trying to Get It," in *Frontiers of Engineering: Reports on Leading-Edge Engineering from the 2018 Symposium* (Washington, DC: National Academies Press, 2019), https://www.ncbi.nlm.nih.gov/books/NBK538701.

175. Danny Hernandez and Tom B. Brown, Op. Cit.

176. Dave Gershgorn, "The Data that Transformed AI Research—and Possibly the World," (*Quartz*), last modified 26 July 2017, https://qz.com/1034972/the-data-that-changed-the-direction-of-ai-research-and-possibly-the-world/.

177. Danny Hernandez and Tom B. Brown, Op. Cit.

178. AI and Efficiency, (*OpenAI*), 2020, https://openai.com/blog/ai-and-efficiency/.

179. Charles Fefferman, Sanjoy Mitter and Hariharan Narayanan, "Testing the Manifold Hypothesis," *Journal of the American Mathematical Society,* 4 (2016): 983–1049.

180. George Spanoudis and Andreas Demetriou, 2020, "Mapping Mind-Brain Development: Towards a Comprehensive Theory," *Journal of Intelligence,* 8, (2) 19. https://doi.org/10.3390/jintelligence8020019.

181. "Neuroplasticity" (*Physiopedia*), accessed 17 January 2021, https://www.physio-pedia.com/index.php?title=Neuroplasticity&oldid=261308.

182. Zaheer Allam, "Achieving Neuroplasticity in Artificial Neural Networks through Smart Cities," *Smart Cities* 2 (2019): 118–134; F. Vazza and A. Feletti, "The Quantitative Comparison Between the Neuronal Network and the Cosmic Web," *Frontiers in Physics* 8 (2020): 525731.

183. As an aside, we do wonder about natural laws and their relationship to data – what data resulted in the existence and manifestation of gravity, for example?

184. Jason J. Moore, Pascal M. Ravassard, David Ho, Lavanya Acharya, Ashley L. Kees, Cliff Vuong and Mayank R. Mehta, "Dynamics of Cortical Dendritic Membrane Potential and Spikes in Freely Behaving Rats," *Science* 6331 (2017): eaaj1497.

185. Lorenzo Magnani, "Hypothesis Generation," in *Abduction, Reason and Science,* (New York: Springer, 2001), 1–14.

186. Ujwal Chaudhary, Niels Birbaumer and Ander Ramos-Murguialday, "Brain-Computer Interfaces for Communication and Rehabilitation," *Nature Reviews Neurology,* 12 (2016): 513–525; Luis Fernando Nicolas-Alonso and Jaime Gomez-Gil, "Brain Computer Interfaces: A Review," *Sensors* 2 (2012): 1211–1279.

187. See https://www.linkedin.com/in/kierandkelly/?originalSubdomain=ie; "Incompressible Dynamics," (*Kierandkelly*), last modified 1 October 2019, http://www.kierandkelly.com/.

188. Kieran D. Kelly, "What Drives Consciousness and Deep Intuition?" (*LinkedIn Pulse*), last modified 23 January 2017, https://www.linkedin.com/pulse/what-drives-consciousness-deep-intuition-kieran-d-kelly.

189. Aaron Sloman, "Interactions Between Philosophy and Artificial Intelligence: The Role of Intuition and Non-logical Reasoning in Intelligence," *Artificial Intelligence* 2 (1971): 209–225.

190. T. N. Sainath, B. Kingsbury and B. Ramabhadran, "Auto-Encoder Bottleneck Features Using Deep Belief Networks," in *2012 IEEE International Conference on Acoustics, Speech and Signal Processing (ICASSP)* (2012): 4153–4156.

191. "Artificial Intelligence in Society," (Organization for Economic Co-operation and Development), last modified 11 June 2019, https://www.oecd-ilibrary.org/science-and-technology/artificial-intelligence-in-society_eedfee77-en; Mark Buchanan, "Organoids of Intelligence," *Nature Physics* 7 (2018): 634; Cleber A. Trujillo, Richard Gao, Priscilla D. Negraes, Jing Gu, Justin Buchanan, Sebastian Preissl, Allen Wang, Wei Wu, Gabriel G. Haddad, Isaac A. Chaim, Alain Domissy, Matthieu Vandenberghe, Anna Devor, Gene W. Yeo, Bradley Voytek and Alysson R. Muotri, "Complex Oscillatory Waves Emerging from Cortical Organoids Model Early Human Brain Network Development," *Cell Stem Cell* 4 (2019): 558–559.e7.

192. "Emerging Technologies and Their Impact on National Security," (*United States Senate Committee on Armed Services*), last modified 23 February 2021, https://www.armed-services.senate.gov/hearings/21-02-23-emerging-technologies-and-their-impact-on-national-security.

193. D. López De Luise, M. E. Marquez, C. Párraga, I. Cayla, R. Azor, V. Ocanto, O. Del, J. López Quel, J. Morelli, M. Agüero and R. Aparicio, "Metrics for Epistemology in NLP Linguistic Fractal Models," in International Conference on Information Technology and Intelligent Transportation Systems (2015).

194. James Manyika and Jacques Bughin, "The Promise and Challenge of the Age of Artificial Intelligence," (*McKinsey Global Institute*), last modified 15 October 2018, https://www.mckinsey.com/featured-insights/artificial-intelligence/the-promise-and-challenge-of-the-age-of-artificial-intelligence.

195. Julia Carrie Wong, Op. Cit.

196. Marguerita Lane and Anne Saint-Martin (2021), "The Impact of Artificial Intelligence on the Labour Market: What do we Know so Far?" OECD Social, Employment and Migration Working Papers, No. 256, OECD Publishing, Paris, last modified 25 January 2021, https://doi.org/10.1787/7c895724-en.

197. Alexis C. Madrigal, "Silicon Valley's Big Three vs. Detroit's Golden-Age Big Three," (*The Atlantic*), last modified 24 May 2017, last accessed 20 August 2021, https://www.theatlantic.com/technology/archive/2017/05/silicon-valley-big-three/527838/.

198. Nick Bostrom and Eliezer Yudkowsky, *The Ethics of Artificial Intelligence* (Machine Intelligence Research Institute, 2011), accessed 3 August 2021, https://intelligence.org/files/EthicsofAI.pdf, 17.

199. Stuart Armstrong, Nick Bostrom and Carl Shulman, "Racing to the Precipice: A Model of Artificial Intelligence Development," *AI & Society,* 2 (2016): 201–206; Seth D. Baum, "On the Promotion of Safe and Socially Beneficial Artificial Intelligence," *AI & Society,* 4 (2017): 543–551; John Bohannon, "Fears of an AI Pioneer," *Science* 6245 (2015): 252.

200. John Naughton, "Companies Are Now Writing Reports Tailored for Machine Readers – and It Should Worry Us," (*The Guardian*), last modified 5 December 2020, https://www.theguardian.com/commentisfree/2020/dec/05/companies-are-now-writing-reports-tailored-for-ai-readers-and-it-should-worry-us.

201. Jeffrey Kluger "What Makes Us Moral," (*Time*), last modified 21 November 2007, http://content.time.com/time/specials/2007/article/0,28804,1685055_1685076_1686619,00.html.

202. Will Murphy, "The AI Sense and Respond Framework: A Way to Find AI Opportunities for Executives and Entrepreneurs," (*Medium*), April 26, 2017, accessed 20 Aug 2021, https://towardsdatascience.com/the-ai-sense-and-respond-framework-a-way-to-find-ai-opportunities-for-executives-and-entrepreneurs-a24aa56b4bff.

203. Adam Lawrence, Jakob Schneider, Marc Stickdorn and Markus Edgar Hormess, *This Is Service Design Doing: Applying Service Design Thinking in the Real World,* (London: O'Reilly Media, 2016), Chapter 1.

204. Nicole Forsgren, Jez Humble and Gene Kim, *Accelerate: Building and Scaling High Performing Technology Organizations* (Portland: IT Revolution Press, 2018), 42.

205. Nicole Forsgren, Jez Humble and Gene Kim, *Accelerate: The Science of Lean Software and Devops* (Portland: IT Revolution Press, 2018).

206. "Get in the Lake, Sparky: Databricks Touts New Ingestion File Sources," (*The Register*), last modified 25 February 2020, https://www.theregister.com/2020/02/25/databricks_touts_new_ingestion_files_sources.

207. Ben Lorica, Michael Armbrust, Ali Ghodsi, Reynold Xin and Matei Zaharia, "What is a Lakehouse?" (*Databricks*), last modified 30 January 2020, https://databricks.com/blog/2020/01/30/what-is-a-data-lakehouse.html.

208. Lorica et al., Op. Cit.

209. Sabine Hossenfelder, "The End of Theoretical Physics as We Know It," (*Quanta*), last modified 27 August 2018, https://www.quantamagazine.org/the-end-of-theoretical-physics-as-we-know-it-20180827.

210. Carlos Beorlegui, "Emergentism," *Pensamiento*, 65 (2009): 881–914; Ricardo Guerrero, Christian Ledig and Daniel Rueckert, "Manifold Alignment and Transfer Learning for Classification of Alzheimer's Disease," in *Machine Learning in Medical Imaging*, eds. Guorong Wu, Daoqiang Zhang and Luping Zhou (2014), 77–84; D. López De Luise, M. E. Marquez, C.Párraga, I. Cayla, R. Azor, V. Ocanto, O. Del, J. López Quel, J. Morelli, M. Agüero and R. Aparicio, Op. Cit.; Lorenzo Magnani, Op. Cit.

211. "Neuroplasticity" (*Physiopedia*), accessed 17 January 2021, https://www.physio-pedia.com/index.php?title=Neuroplasticity&oldid=261308.

212. William Zeng and Bob Coecke, "Quantum Algorithms for Compositional Natural Language Processing," arXiv (2016): 1608.01406.

213. Tobias van den Berg, Martijn W. Heymans, Stephanie S. Leone, David Vergouw, Jill A. Hayden, Arianne P. Verhagen and Henrica C. W. de Vet, "Overview of Data-Synthesis in Systematic Reviews of Studies on Outcome Prediction Models," *BMC Medical Research Methodology,* 13 (2013): 42.

214. Philippe Huneman, "Macroevolution and Microevolution: Issues of Time Scale in Evolutionary Biology," in *Time of Nature and the Nature of Time*, eds. Christophe Bouton and Philippe Huneman (Cham: Springer, 2017).

215. Teghan Lucas, Jaliya Kumaratilake, Maciej Henneberg, "Recently Increased Prevalence of the Human Median Artery of the Forearm: A Microevolutionary Change," *Journal of Anatomy*, 2020; 237: 623– 631. https://doi.org/10.1111/joa.13224.

216. Dumitru Roman, Sven Schade, Arne-Jørgen Berre, Nils Rune Bodsberg and J. Langlois, "Model as a Service (MaaS)," in *AGILE Workshop: Grid Technologies for Geospatial Applications* (2009), https://www.researchgate.net/publication/230606842_Model_as_a_Service_MaaS.

217. Libby Bacon, Sean Morris and Nicole Overley, "COVID-19 and the Virtualization of Government: Responding, Recovering, and Preparing to Thrive in the Future of Work," (*Deloitte Insights, 2020*), https://www2.deloitte.com/content/dam/Deloitte/au/Documents/covid-19/au-deloitte-covid-19-virtualisation-government.pdf; Gary Smith, "How COVID-19 is Accelerating the 'Virtualization of Everything,'" (*Crunchbase*), last modified 16 July 2020, https://about.crunchbase.com/blog/covid19-accelerating-virtualization.

218. Clark Aldrich, *Learning Online with Games, Simulations, and Virtual Worlds,* (San Francisco: Jossey-Bass, 2009); Jennifer Camille Dempsey, "The Theory of Virtuality Culture and Technology-Mediated Human Presence," in *Learning, Design, and Technology*, eds. M. Spector, B. Lockee and M. Childress (Springer: Cham, 2017); Neil Stephens, Imtiaz Khan and Rachel Errington, "Analysing the Role of Virtualisation and Visualisation on Interdisciplinary Knowledge Exchange in Stem Cell Research Processes," *Humanities and Social Sciences Communications,* 1 (2018): 78; Dave Zielinski, "Virtualization: The Future of Work" (SHRM), last modified 2 December 2014, https://www.shrm.org/resourcesandtools/hr-topics/technology/pages/virtualization-the-future-of-work.aspx.